I PRAYED FOR DEATH

Instead He sent me Angels...

TERRESA ANDERSON

Outskirts Press, Inc.
Denver, Colorado

Outskirts Press, Inc.
http://www.outskirtspress.com

ISBN: 978-1-4327-4659-9

Outskirts Press and the "OP" logo are trademarks belonging to Outskirts Press, Inc.

PRINTED IN THE UNITED STATES OF AMERICA

For Terry

Table of Contents

Instead...

Years ago in sorrow
I sat in ill-repose
With a plan to end it all
Would it be a lethal dose

I was lost and all alone
With the torture in my head
A vision of my future
Left me wanting death

I couldn't see the light
With the darkness closing in
The love and peace I craved
Were lost within the din

So I took a leap of faith
And swallowed all those pills
And prayed to God to take me
But that was not His will

Instead he sent me angels
To guide me back to health
Through this long and arduous journey
That has brought me so much wealth

A wealth of friends and knowledge
And blessings from above
I'm thankful for this chance
To be an instrument of love

Introduction

When I recently told a friend that I wanted to write about my journey from mental *illness* to mental *health,* she asked, "Why?" The answer was simple: To help someone. To help someone who was suffering through the darkness of mental illness as I had for so many years. To offer hope when all seems hopeless. To offer light when you think you don't deserve it. And to share the love, compassion and understanding that I myself received in what was truly *my* darkest hour. Because of a caring doctor and my wonderful therapist Lyle, I'm not only alive... I'm *thriving!*

In one of my journal entries, near the end of therapy, I wrote, "This journey has been long and difficult, but well worth every single moment I've gone through." I remember Lyle saying that we were going to "grow" a new Terresa, and in a way we have, but it's more than that. Together, we've taken the shattered empty shell of the person I was and put her back together with the glue of self-love. Through self-discovery, and the building of a strong and stable core, the "shell" has become a vessel; filled to the brim with everything that I am.

Lyle used to ask me if I thought my life was sacred, and the answer was always no. I've had a change of heart since then. Not only is my life sacred, but I want to spend the rest of it helping others to tap into their *own* sacredness. Their *own* inner light. Their *own* connection to something bigger. The possibilities are endless and everyday is a new opportunity to *be* an instrument of God's love and grace; to bring light into this world and into the lives of others. My heart truly *is* overflowing with the joy of being loved. So, to answer Lyle's question, "Is my life sacred?" *Yes!* ... How can it be anything less?

When I look through my journals, I'm once again reminded that miracles *do* happen. I'm living proof! It's difficult to recall how down and lost I felt on the day I overdosed. I just know that at the time, I wanted more than anything to *not* exist; to stop hurting. I remember *begging* God to end the mental anguish, the torture that held my mind hostage. My thoughts raced wildly, non-stop, and without order. I could no longer see the logic in living. The opening poem mentions, "The torture in my head." For someone who's never experienced the depression or the mixed episodes of bipolar disorder, that phrase might not mean anything.

In Kay Jamison's book, *An Unquiet Mind*, she refers to the *mixed* episodes of bipolar disorder, as "Black Agitated Manias." I couldn't agree more with that description. It's *not* a place you want to be. Depression, mixed with the energy of Mania, can be a lethal combination. At the time of my attempted suicide, I was not yet diagnosed with anything other than mild depression. I would soon find out that not only did I suffer from untreated bipolar disorder, but I also had the nasty complication of a *borderline personality*. (This would prove to be *much* more difficult to treat than the bipolar.) The suicide rate is high for either one of these disorders, but for someone with *both*... I know in my heart, that without the medication for the bipolar and the counseling for the borderline, I would *not* be here today.

There were many times in my life, before my eventual diagnosis and recovery, when I reached out for help and it *seemed* that no one reached back. It wasn't that people didn't care; they just didn't know how truly troubled I was. It's my hope that by sharing my story in all of its ug-liness *and* beauty, that my words will reach those who need to hear them; to let them know that they are *not* alone. And that not only is recovery possible, but so is a full and joyous life! It's my wish to be *the one who reached back*!

Prologue

I am invisible. Nobody sees me. Nobody hears me. I am alone in a family of nine. Don't make waves. Keep the peace. Don't draw attention. Stay out of the way.

I long for someone to hear me, to notice me, to love me. But nobody does. I'm not worthy. I don't matter. I begin to feel angry, but I certainly can't show it. Not in *my* family. Anger is unacceptable. It's not okay. So what do I do with it? This anger! It won't go away! I *must* be bad! What a horrible person I am to feel such anger, such **rage**! It's building inside to the point of eruption, but what can I *do* if I'm not allowed to express it?

My anger has reached its boiling point, but I have to keep it hidden. For some reason, that I can't explain, I'm drawn to a blade. I run the razor-sharp edge across my skin. Lightly at first. Then deeper and deeper… until I draw blood. An overwhelming sense of relief floods my entire being and a calmness fills my soul. The tension is gone. I don't know it yet, but this is just the beginning. The cutting will get worse, *much* worse, before it gets better... and three decades will pass before it stops.

28 years later...
12-15-05

The voice in my head is back. It' screams, "You're worthless, hopeless, an imposter! You don't deserve to live!" It's telling me I'll *never* be normal. *Ever.* My thoughts are racing and jumbled. They won't slow down! They don't make sense. The noise won't stop! There really is no hope. I can feel myself sinking further and further into a vast, black, bottomless well. Totally immersed in darkness. My only ray of hope? That death will come soon and I can cease to exist.

What's the point of mortal life
Tell me what's the use
And must I go on living
In a soul beyond the noose
I want to get away from me
It's what I really wish
But if life continues after death
Then Hell will still exist
So going on is not a choice
Simple, cut and dried
I'm stuck with me forever more
Even when I die

PROLOGUE

12-17-05

It's getting worse. The racket in my head won't stop! It's 2am. My bed felt hard, like concrete, so I got up. Been pacing for hours. Feel like a caged animal. Needing to burst out of my skin. Such an awful sensation. My soft baggy pajamas feel restricting and scratchy and heavy! How can that be? I keep hearing music, but the radio's off. I can't sit still. *Need* to keep moving! If I could, I'd jump out of my skin. It doesn't feel right. Wanting to physically explode. So much turbulence inside. But why?

12-18-05

Tons of energy! Lots to do. Sorting through things I don't want people to see after my death. Preparing the gift and card for my niece's 16th birthday, which isn't until May, but I won't be here. Need a haircut, but what does it matter? I'll be gone soon.

12-23-05

Feeling wired. Agitated. Drove way too fast. Almost hit another car. Twice. Everything is so loud and everyone is so *god-damned slow*! I was in the store, but I couldn't stay. The lights were too bright and there was so much noise and so much chaos! Hundreds of voices talking at once! It was driving me crazy! I asked my daughter if the commotion was bothering her too, but she didn't know what I was talking about. Why doesn't anyone else hear what I hear? How can they *not* hear? My co-workers keep telling me I'm like a chipmunk on speed. I've never even done speed. But speaking of speed, I have been speeding. I can't sit still. It's killing me to sit still long enough to scribble these words.

12-26-2005

Trouble slowing down. Ran my shopping cart into the woman in front of me. She was going too slowly and I *told* her so. What's wrong with me? "Lost it" at work. Usually I'm nice, but lately everyone's in my way. Punched the frig in the break room. Knuckles are blue and swollen.

Nothing compared to some of the stuff I've done to my body. No need to go there.

12-29-2005

Wrote my suicide letter today:

To the people I love,

> I'm so sorry for hurting you. Please forgive me. My mind won't stop racing. I can't shut it off. I don't know how to be normal. I feel so hopeless. I just want the pain to stop.

To my darling daughter,

> You are the light of my life. I hope you know that my love for you will go on forever, even when my physical body is gone. You are a wonderful human being with so much to offer. I'm so proud of you!
>
> I love you

To my husband,

> Thank you for putting up with me all these years. You deserve so much better than me. Please find someone perfect for you. I love you and I want you to have the best.

To my dear twin,

> You have been my best friend my entire life. I love you so much. Thank you for loving me.

PROLOGUE

And to all my other loved ones,

Please forgive me and know that you are loved.

Peace be with you.

1-1-2006

I can't stand another minute in this body, in this mind. Why can't I shut it off? The chatter. It keeps getting louder. It won't stop. I'm so tired. So tired of trying to be normal. So tired of trying to fit in. So tired of *trying*. Even the cutting isn't helping anymore. Truly hopeless.

1-4-2006

Is today the day? I just can't do it anymore. God forgive me… but if dying is the only way to stop the pain, the turmoil, the internal and incessant dialogue, then my choice is made. I only pray that my family can forgive me and somehow understand that it was *me* I couldn't live with, not them. They've been wonderful and I believe that, in the long run, they'll be better off without me. It seems I hurt everyone who loves me. I don't mean to, but I do. And whether I'm alive or dead, I'll still hurt them. I don't want to hurt anyone. I just can't live with *me* anymore.

The Diagnosis

My eyes open and I'm in the hospital. How'd I get here? I note that my family is present. It appears they're upset, maybe even crying. *Why* am I still here? I'm supposed to be *dead!* Then darkness descends and I am folded into nothingness. *Blessed nothingness.*

It's morning and I'm having a hard time focusing, both mentally and visually. My attempted suicide has landed me in the Critical Care Unit and my Doctor is sitting next to my bed. He's telling me that I'm "bipolar" and I'm thinking bi-*what?* What the heck is bipolar? He patiently explains that it's a condition that causes extreme highs (mania) which are inevitably followed by extreme lows (depression). And sometimes they can occur at the same time (mixed episodes). He was honest enough to tell me, that by recently agreeing to increase my dose of Prozac per *my* request, he inadvertently sent me into a mania that quickly turned into a mixed episode. (Anti-depressants, when used alone, can be *deadly* for a person with bipolar disorder.) In hindsight, we would both see that I'd exhibited the signs and symptoms of mania *and* depression for many years prior to my hospitalization. But, because my natural personality tends to be bubbly and energetic, it was easy to think that my manias were just an extension of that personality. It never occurred to me, or anyone else, that my "highs" were actually a part of a mental disease!

My boss came to visit me while I was in the CCU. He was very kind and told me not to worry about my job. He said that he just wants me to get better, and he'll help me however he can. I told him about the bipolar diagnosis and he confessed that his own daughter struggles with manic-depression. (Another term for bipolar disorder.) He warned me that it's not as simple as taking a pill. I'll need counseling, along with medication, and maybe even treatment as an in-patient for awhile. An in-patient? Is he crazy?

I have absolutely no memory of my time in the ER. I was later told that the ER Doctor called in an Internist by the name of Dr. Bond, who specializes in drug overdoses. Dr. Bond told my husband, that with the pills I took, I should have been dead! It was Dr. Bond who oversaw my care in the ER and admitted me to the CCU. While I was being transferred to the unit, my husband stepped out of the ER and at that same moment, Dr. Stoune, my regular physician, walked by. He saw Bill and asked him what was going on. Bill told him that I had tried to kill myself and that I'd written a suicide letter. Although my husband refused to read the note, Dr Stoune did read it and from what I'd written, along with my known history, he was able to make the diagnosis. Dr. Stoune took over my care from that moment on. I am so grateful that his path crossed Bill's that day. I could have so easily slipped through the cracks. Again.

1

January 2006 thru March 15th, 2006

My husband is so angry with me! I am such a screw-up! He can hardly stand to look at me. I'm truly heartbroken at his reaction. I want so desperately for him to take me in his arms and tell me that everything's going to be alright; that he loves me and he'll help me in any way he can, but all I get from him is a palpable hostility. I hate myself more than ever! I am such a loser! I couldn't even succeed at killing myself! What a failure!

I feel horrible for hurting my daughter. Her tears broke my heart. Why the hell am I still here, still suffering? Right before I took the pills, I told God that I was ready to *come home*. As an afterthought, I asked Him to get me the help I needed if for some reason He couldn't take me home just yet. Well I'm still here, so now what?

The medication is starting to work. I'm feeling calm, stable even. Dr. Stoune prescribed an antipsychotic called Seroquel. Bill always did say I was "psychotic." Neither one of us realized that there was some *truth* in his teasing, or perhaps he knew something I didn't?

I went back to work today. I work in a hospital with 500 employees, so I was nervous about facing my co-workers and not knowing "who knows." I had an appointment with Dr. Stoune this morning before my shift. At my appointment, my pulse was racing and my oxygen level was low. When I asked Dr. Stoune about it, he said it was *fear* that was causing the abnormal readings. He then told me something that made me feel better. He said that I'd done a very *courageous* thing by attempting to end my life! (Wow, I didn't expect that!) Apparently, in the process of trying to end my *own* life, I ended up touching a lot of other lives. It seems that my desperate "cry for help" caused people to stop and think: If this could happen to always-cheerful Terresa, then it could happen to *anyone*. It could happen to *them*!

Work's going ok. I'm still deeply embarrassed. I was going to say *ashamed,* but that's not really what I'm feeling. Maybe Dr. Stoune's comment about *courage* was meant to help me with that issue.

Dr. Rice stopped by my desk this afternoon to ask me how I was doing. He told me that he'd been on his way to visit me in the CCU when he heard I had been discharged. I was touched by his concern. It reminded me of something that Dr. Stoune had said to me. He told me that if I *ever* need help, I have a whole network of people right here in the hospital who would be glad to help. I just need to ASK! And God bless that man; he even gave me his personal phone numbers! (To his cell *and* his home.)

I went to my first counseling session with a woman named Bea. She said that she was old enough to be my mother and after I told her about being the eldest of seven, born in five short years, she said that she would try to re-parent me in weekly sessions. I told her about how I'd always felt "lost in the crowd" growing up; like I was just part of the *herd;* like I didn't matter. She promised to provide a safe place for me to talk *without* judgment.

It's been 2 weeks since the suicide attempt. I'm relieved to have a diagnosis. (Especially since it explains so much!) The medication is working well. I'm feeling really good; *not* high, just good. I've apologized to my family and I've promised them that I will never do "*it*" again. For the first time in my life I feel "normal." I'm filled with hope for the future *and* for the present. I'm looking forward to making up for the hurt that I have caused my family. Bill's been reading everything he can about bipolar disorder. He has also been trying to caution me about the long road ahead. Apparently, even with medication, I will still have highs and lows.

I was a total mess yesterday. I went to my second appointment with the counselor and she let me down big time. First, she got there late and kept me waiting. *Then*, right off the bat, she verbally attacked me! She tried to put me on a guilt trip for the pain that I have caused my family. (As if I wasn't already feeling guilty enough?) She went on to ask me how *I* thought the bipolar originated. Isn't that *her* job?

When I mentioned some of my feelings about my marriage, she directed me to break up the relationship! (A union of 23 years!) I thought therapy was about healing *me* so *I* could make *sound* decisions about my life and the people in it! The breaking point for me, in this second visit, was when she suggested I check in with her next *month.* Last week she talked of re-parenting me over the course of many weekly sessions and then today she tells me she'll see me next *month?* What happened to the weekly visits to heal me emotionally? I felt abandoned and disillusioned. I quickly began a downward spiral. By the time I got home, I had mentally crashed! The hope I had felt earlier in the day was gone. The suicidal thoughts were back and I couldn't stop crying. Bill was concerned. He urged me to call Dr. Stoune. When I finally did, Dr. Stoune, who was vacationing 2,000 miles away, answered my call and calmed me down. He increased the dose of my medication and instructed me to call him back the next day. I think that man actually cares!

I called Dr. Stoune as promised. He seemed relieved to hear that I was feeling better. He asked me to call him again tomorrow. God bless that man!

I feel so much better today! Bill deserves a healthy wife and, with the right medication and by keeping the lines of communication open, I hope I can give him that. I was still pretty down yesterday. In fact, I was very afraid of what the future might hold for me. I was playing the "what if?" game. What if I never find a medication that works? What if I go off the deep end again and lose my job (or worse?) What if I can *never* have a normal life? I was filled with fear; enough to let my family help me. I gave Bill a copy of Dr. Stoune's phone numbers. (Just in case a time comes when I'm too depressed to make the call.)

Lots of energy at work today! I felt productive and happy. I've started talking to my co-workers about what happened that last day at work before the OD. The few people I've confided in told me that *everyone* knows, but they were instructed to keep quiet. That's a little unsettling! In thinking back over the events leading up to my suicide attempt, I can see that I'd been escalating to the point of no return. I remember sitting at my desk, rambling incoherently, when Dr. Carlson walked by. He thought I was talking to him, and maybe I was, but I wasn't making any sense! When he gave up trying to figure out what I was saying, I felt somehow rejected; persecuted even! A few minutes later, a pushy patient walked back into the restricted area and *demanded* to know when I was going to help him. I don't remember too much after that, although I *do* recall sitting in my car with a very large quantity of pills. In the months prior, I'd researched several drugs and had decided that this particular tranquilizer would be my best bet. Years earlier, I'd tried to overdose with another drug, but my stomach rejected and *ejected* the entire lot! No one ever found out.

We've been very short-handed at work and it's stressing me out a bit. Bill and I went out with friends last night. The guys drank way too much as usual and I was embarrassed by Bill's loudness and inappropriate comments. He's so preoccupied with sex! Maybe I'm a prude, but I think sex should be *sacred* or at least private! Bill even announced, to everyone at our table, that Mac's wife gave her husband a "knob-job" before meeting at the bar because she can't have sex for three weeks due to some female surgery. God that's private! I was so irritated that Bill took something that should be special and made it cheap and shallow. I swear he wants every encounter to be nasty and porn-like! Why can't it be *love*-making? At least once in awhile. I've told him, again and again, that being groped, grabbed and fucked, does NOT make me feel loved! Not at *all!* He claims that's his way of *showing* love. Bullshit! I have *begged* him to show me affection in non-sexual ways, both in and out of the bedroom. Showing me a little tenderness could go a long way in the romance department.

Damn-it! I need to feel valued for more than my body parts!

One of the girls we were out with last night just called. She said she was worried about me because she noticed a big shift in my mood last night. I had started out cheerful and outgoing, but as Bill got louder and cruder with each drink, I became more and more withdrawn. I was embarrassed by his behavior. I also felt hurt that he never *heard* me, even though we were sitting right next to each other! (I had tried several times to get his attention, but he was too busy being the life of the party!) When I tried to visit with the other members of our group, no one even acknowledged my presence! No matter how loud I spoke up, no one could hear me! The drunker everyone got, the *louder* they got. They all talked at once and *nobody* listened. I felt lost in the crowd. *Again.*

I spent the day with Bill's Aunt Sue and his cousin Sarah. They didn't know about the suicide attempt and it felt wrong *not* to tell them. I tried *all* day to get my courage up. Finally, near the end of our visit, I confessed. They were both visibly upset and I wondered if I shouldn't have told them? I haven't told any of *my* family and I *don't* plan to. Bill did tell his mom and I felt really bad for him, because she blamed *him*; saying he was just like his father! *How* could a mother say that to her son? Even if she thought it was true, she didn't have to *say* it! He needed her support; *not* her criticism!

I talked to Sue again, later in the evening, and she started to cry. I promised her that I was fine and I reassured her that the medicine would keep me well. She ended up telling Don because she was too upset to hide it. Uncle Don was furious, but not at *me*. He was angry at Bill's mom for *not* telling them! I was so afraid that Don would hate me (because his own brother killed himself years ago) but that wasn't the case at all. Maybe my disorder will allow some healing to take place in their family, allowing them to realize that their loved one was *not* to blame for his actions… A *sane* person does not commit, or attempt, suicide. No one, in their *right mind*, kills themselves.

A few days ago, a coworker gave me the number to a therapist who helped her. His name is Lyle. She told me that I would really like him. I left a message for him to call me. My husband wanted me to okay it with Dr. Stoune, so I left a message telling him that I had switched therapists. Dr. Stoune called me later and told me he was glad I had called because a friend of his, Dr. Williams, had called him earlier to express concern about me not connecting very well with the first therapist. Wow! People I *don't* even *know* are trying to help me! (Both my husband *and* Dr. Stoune are friends of Dr. Williams, but *I* don't know him personally.)

Lots of energy! I got so much done today! I'm enjoying all of the people in my life. My outlook has never been better! I feel hopeful and loving and excited for the future. My boss granted me a set-schedule which should help immensely in keeping me stable. I feel like I've really got a handle on this whole bipolar thing! I have an appt with Lyle tomorrow and I'm looking forward to meeting him. Even with the manic-depressive stuff under control, I know that I have some other issues that need to be addressed. Hopefully Lyle can help me with those.

Lyle really knows his stuff! I'm meeting with him again in three days. I have a really good feeling about him. Until my OD, everyone thought

I was always happy. Lyle told me that I've been hiding behind a "mask" for so long that I don't even know who I am. Maybe he's right.

I AM SO FUCKING PISSED RIGHT NOW!!! I am sick and tired of my family expecting *me* to drop *everything* in order to run to see what they want; like the god-damned world revolves around them! Both Rachel and Bill were upstairs while I was downstairs trying to get some chores done. I was also trying to figure out *what* to wear to the Super Bowl party that we had to go to later that day. The very minute I undressed, to try on an outfit that *Bill* wants me to wear, they both start yelling for me to hurry and come upstairs to look at something. I kept yelling "just a minute" as I scrambled to put some clothes on, but they couldn't hear me over their blaring music! I heard Bill say something about "missing it" and I assumed he was talking about me. (Because I was taking too long.) When I finally got upstairs, they both acted like it was no big deal whether I'd shown up or not! I busted my butt for *that* reception? I tried to be calm as I asked about the "missing it" comment. Rachel said that it was just about Steve "missing a spot" when he had painted earlier. *Why* couldn't one of them have just come downstairs to get me? They could have told me, at that time, that there was no hurry. Instead, they just stayed upstairs and hollered! When I told them that I'd been busy and that I had tried to get there as fast as I could, they acted like it was no big deal. So *why* were they hollering like I was missing something earth-shattering? I was *pissed!* I felt like it was *them* against *me*! Again. No matter how hard I try, I will never figure out what it is that I'm supposed to do! (In their eyes.) It seems like I'm always the one who's *wrong*.

After I came back downstairs, I punched myself repeatedly. I've been trying to stick with *hitting* myself, rather than *cutting*, because it's too stressful to keep the injuries and scars hidden from everyone. Bill would be disgusted with me if he knew about the self-injury. I'm writing now just to let off more steam! I *want* to cry, but I *WON'T!* Why didn't I just ignore their yells? I am so damn tired of trying to please everyone; *especially* when they don't give a damn about me!

Once I was calmed down, I went back upstairs and asked Bill *why* he didn't come look for me when he first started yelling? He said that he *did*, and he heard me say "just a minute." I told him that I never heard him acknowledge me, and he said that's because he *didn't!* When I asked him *why*, he shrugged his shoulders and said that he didn't know that he *needed* to. How fucking hard can it be to show a little courtesy? To your wife no less! I'm furious, frustrated and ***pissed off!*** Am I *always* in the wrong? How can something so trivial cause me so much pain? Just minutes ago, I was going along, having a nice day, minding my own business, and *now* I'm trying to hold back tears! Bill and Rachel are the *normal* people. I'm just the "cross they have to bear." It's hard to understand why they were so upset with me for trying to kill myself. I'd think they'd be glad to have the *crazy* person gone. I'm a curse to myself and I'm a curse to them! I feel like nobody will ever love me. How can they? Rachel and Bill are so bright and so *with it!* They can see the *whole* picture at a glance, while I struggle just to see bits and pieces of it! I feel so dumb when I'm around them. They say they love me, but I can't feel it.

Lyle instructed me to record three individual memories from specific times in my life: *Childhood. Early adulthood. Recent adulthood.*

The following are the "snapshots in time" that first came to mind:

As a child of about six, I remember my mom lovingly comforting one of my friends. I stood there watching, my heart crying out silently. I wanted her to hold *me* like that! I so desperately wanted to be the object of her affection, but I was just "one of the herd."

I suffered two years of postpartum depression. (Induced, in part, by a severe lack of sleep.) I remember quite clearly the day that my mother-in-law offered to come to my house to watch the baby, so I could take a much needed nap. About the time I fell asleep, Bill fired up the chainsaw right outside our bedroom window! Could he really be that insensitive?

Recently, I was extremely touched that Dr Stoune would answer my call while he was on vacation! His willingness to do so, made me feel loved and cared for.

Lots of energy! Only slept 4 hours last night. Feeling very happy, almost giddy. Thinking I may have been too loud at work today. Laughed a lot! Is it me or is it mania? How can I know for sure?

I decided to do the "memory" assignment again:

Childhood memory: When I was 6 or 7, I accidentally stepped on some broken glass during a family camping trip. I cut my foot pretty bad, and I should have had stitches, but my dad just wrapped my foot up with gauze. I had to stay in the camper by myself while the rest of the family sat around the campfire singing songs and roasting marshmallows. I felt left out.

Adult memory: My parents were so late to Rachel's first birthday party that she was cranky and ready for bed by the time they finally arrived! I was upset and my dad basically told me to get over it.

Recent memory: Bill went out of his way to pick out a very special and thoughtful Christmas gift for me.

Very tearful today. No energy. Didn't want to talk to anyone. Boss asked if I was okay. He said he was worried about me. I assured him that I wouldn't do anything "stupid." He said that's not what he meant. He's just concerned. When I got home, Bill told me that he'd read my journal entry from Super Bowl Sunday. (I had left it out and had previously told him that I didn't care if he read it.) We talked for hours. He wants me to be well *now*. He thought the medicine would *fix* me. We're both confused and don't know whether or not we should stay together.

I cried myself to sleep last night. I've made such a mess of things! I wish I'd never been born! The things that go on inside my head can't be seen or felt by anyone but me, so there's no way for anyone else to know how much I hurt; how hard I struggle.

Session with Lyle went well. My new assignment is to be *aware* of my emotions. Am I feeling sad, angry, happy or afraid? That's a tough one though, because sometimes I can't *feel* anything. We talked about my marriage. Lyle doesn't advocate divorce. He said that the main thing right now is for me to work on *me*. I also need to understand that I'm *not* responsible for other people's happiness *or* their anger.

Lyle and I went through some of the forms I had filled out. Lyle chuckled a bit when he read that I think *everyone else* is moving too slowly! I laughed when I realized, for the first time, that maybe it's *me* who is moving too fast!

Had a nice family day with Bill and Rachel. Before going to sleep, I hugged Bill and asked him if we were going to be ok. I felt disappointed when he said, "I hope so." That wasn't exactly the reassuring answer that I had wanted. "I hope so" leaves a lot of room for "maybe not."

My new assignment, in addition to being *aware* of my feelings, is to step back and problem solve. If someone says something disrespectful, then I need to ask, "What did you mean by that?" A lot of misunderstandings occur when we *assume* something rather than just asking. Such a simple concept.

I talked to Lyle about trying to be aware of *what* emotion I'm feeling at any given moment. A lot of the time I don't *feel* anything. He said that even though I think I'm *not* feeling anything, deep down I really am. At those times, it's probably sadness or anger. (Or a combination of the two.) For me, it feels *safest* to be *numb*. To feel anger or sadness is too intense, too difficult, too *scary*!

After work last night, I stayed a few extra minutes to visit with a friend. I knew Bill would worry so I called home, but the line was busy. Before I left work, I tried again and this time I got through. Rachel said, "Dad wants to talk to you." My first thought was, "Oh great, he's probably pissed at me for not coming straight home." When he got on the phone, he was very short with me. He told me that Jay had called and wanted us to set up a meeting at the school with some of the other parents, to discuss some concerns. Bill figured I'd be home by eight and had told Jay that I'd call him then. Bill was really irritated with me for not being home to make the call promptly at 8pm. First of all, why the hell is it *my* responsibility to call Jay back? And second, I don't have enough facts from Rachel, about the "problem teacher," to even *want* to set up a meeting just yet! Also, I'm sick of having to check in at home every time I'm going to be a few minutes late! I feel like a frickin little kid who's always in trouble! Bill insisted that I call Jay immediately! I could tell he was not at all happy with me, *especially* when I told him that I didn't want to call Jay. He's not used to me saying no, but I won't let him boss me around anymore! It's always about what *he* wants! And *he* wants what he wants *now!* Without *any* regard to my feelings! (Or anyone else's for that matter.)

Being *aware* of my emotions is exhausting! I'm surprised at how quickly I bounce from anger to sadness and back to anger again. I don't know which is worse, sad or mad. And the *reasons* for my anger are so stupid sometimes. Today it was because the cord to the curling iron kept tangling! I got so mad that I started throwing things! And then I was furious because I'd wasted so much time trying to look decent! (Not good, just decent.) I'm *always* disappointed when I see my reflection. Who am I trying to kid? I'm a frumpy, unattractive, middle-aged woman!

I'm really missing the highs I used to have. I liked bouncing off the walls and being goofy and having fun. I miss the boundless energy. I don't know who the hell I am anymore.

I've changed my mind about letting Bill read my journal. (I can't be totally honest if I know someone's going to read it.) Lyle thinks I'll be able to open up more if I know that I'm the *only* one who'll read my innermost thoughts and feelings.

At my session today, I told Lyle that "being aware of my emotions" is too damn draining! I don't know how much longer I can keep doing this, or *if* I can keep doing this! I'm more fucked up than I realized. Can I make it through the amount of therapy it will take to heal me? Is healing even possible? I'm having serious doubts. The road ahead looks too long, and too steep, to stay on it for long.

Work was okay today. My session with Lyle went well. We talked about how I always feel the *need* to please everyone and we wondered aloud about the origins of that specific behavior. Lyle went through the DSM-IV CRITERIA for *Borderline Personality Disorder*. I had 9 out of 9! Guess it's official. I'm a *loon*!

Talked with Lyle about *trust*. I try to trust, but I always get hurt. Even Dr. Stoune, who I think I really do trust, had a negative effect on me at work the other day. He walked into the lab and I was so happy to see him, but he was angry because a test result he wanted wasn't done yet. Even though he wasn't angry at *me*, I took it personally. I tried not to, but since I'm associated with the lab, *I* felt attacked. I know, intellectually, that *I* am *not* the lab. I'm an individual doing a damn good job. But, because we are understaffed, I can't always get everything done as fast as I'd like.

I feel like my whole identity is tied up with work. It's the one place where I *know* that I'm extremely competent, so when I'm forced to do a half-assed job, because of staffing problems, I can't help but take it personally. I'm being set up for failure and it doesn't help that I get most, if not all, of my self-worth from doing my job well. Anywhere else, I'm not worth the space I take up. If I can't feel valued at work, then there really is no hope for me.

Lyle asked, "What makes Terresa happy?" I've been thinking about that question all day. As a child, I remember that the happiest time of day for me was getting home from school and going outside to be *alone*. Since my siblings watched TV after school, I knew that, at least for a little while, I could count on being by myself. I craved solitude! There were times when I even hid behind our backyard fence so that I could get away from everyone. I *hated* being one of seven! And, as the eldest of seven children born in five short years, I was either invisible *or* I was forced to take on responsibilities too advanced for someone so young.

"What makes Terresa happy?" I'm still pondering that one. As a teenager, and as an adult, the happiest memories that come to mind are actually the most *peaceful*. For whatever reason, I equate happiness with *peace*. I noticed that, as I looked back, I found that every peaceful moment seemed to involve being outside enjoying nature. The sad thing is that in each of these memories, these flashbacks, I am *alone*.

The more I think about it, the more I realize that I'm *never* truly at peace when I'm with other people; *especially* when there's a group! So often, when people gather, everyone talks at once! (And no one ever really listens!) It drives me crazy!

Lyle asked me what I'm obsessive about, but I couldn't bring myself to tell him the truth. I've been obsessive about *food* for as long as I can remember! As a child, I'd sneak out of my room at night and eat anything from cake mix to brown sugar. I hid food in my closet and under my bed. I even kept some *buried* in the back yard! I think the *hoarding* started because I knew that if I didn't eat something right away, one of my siblings would! One year, even my candy-filled Christmas stocking got snatched! (Before I could eat any of the goodies!) When I told my mom and dad about it, they just said, "Oh well."

I remember a few times when my mother took some of us kids with her to JC Penney's and on each visit; she'd buy herself some chocolate covered orange sticks. And even though I hated the taste of orange and chocolate together, I'd follow her around like a little puppy, hoping she'd either share some or maybe drop a piece. How pathetic!

I'm also obsessive about my weight, but I don't want Lyle to know that. I don't want *anyone* to know. I'm sure that the weight issues got started because of always being known as the "Fat twin." I weighed two pounds more than my twin at birth and I continued to be heavier throughout childhood and into adulthood. As teenagers, the boys always liked my sister better. She was blond, blue-eyed and skinny, while I was brown-haired, brown-eyed and chubby.

Even though I'm obsessed with my weight, I still eat *huge* quantities of food! Mostly sweets. I've *never* actually *purged* to keep the weight off, but I have gone for days without eating. I've gorged on as many as 5,000 calories in single *sitting*. I could never confess that to Lyle or to anyone else. It would be too humiliating. I'll go to my grave with that shameful secret.

Had a great heart-to-heart with Sue today. Even though she's my husband's aunt, she feels like *my* family. We have so much in common. She's becoming one of my dearest friends!

Appt with Dr Stoune today. He was in complete agreement with Lyle's suggestion to add a second medication called Buspar. This one is for anxiety. Great! Not only am I *psychotic*, now I'm an *anxious psychotic!*

Dr. Stoune gave me a really nice compliment today at my appt with him. He said that I was the lab's most valuable employee! And to think, that only yesterday, I was talking to Lyle about how Dr.Stoune was angry at the lab. (And how I was trying *not* to take it personally!)

I feel so good!!! The Buspar must be working! I didn't feel any agitation at the usual stressors this morning. I kept waiting for the anxiety *or* the rage to appear, but neither one did! Yeah!

WELL IT FUCKING SHOWED UP LATER! WE'RE SO SHORT-STAFFED AT WORK AND OUR BOSS WENT AND FIRED AN *EXPERIENCED* EMPLOYEE THAT WORKED AT ANOTHER SITE. NOW WE HAVE TO SEND ONE OF THE FEW REMAINING TRAINED EMPLOYEES TO COVER, AND THAT MAKES *US* EVEN MORE SHORT STAFFED!!!! AND THEN TO TOP IT OFF, I COME HOME AND THE ONLY THING BILL HAS TO SAY IS "YOU DIDN'T SHUT THE GARAGE DOOR RIGHT." YESTERDAY, IT WAS THAT I DIDN'T PUT WOOD IN THE STOVE. SO WHAT?!?!?! WHY DOES HE *ALWAYS* HAVE TO FIND THE *ONE* THING I DID OR DIDN'T DO? IT PISSES ME OFF TO NO END!!!!!!!!!!!! I COME HOME FROM WORK AND THE HOUSE IS A FUCKING MESS. BOTH HAVE SHIT ALL OVER THE PLACE. DO THEY THINK I'M THE FUCKING MAID? (Of course I don't say anything out loud. I just paste on a smile and hide behind one of those masks that Lyle talks about.)

Lyle and I talked more about the borderline today. For some reason, between the ages of 12 and 20, I failed to gain my *own* sense of identity. Without my *own,* it became necessary to latch on to the identity of others. It was the only way I knew how to be someone.

The DSM-IV CRITERIA for Borderline Personality Disorder is as follows:

A pervasive pattern of instability of interpersonal relationships, self-image, emotions, and control over impulses, beginning in early adulthood and present in various contexts, as indicated by five of the following:

1. Frantic attempts to avoid real or imagined abandonment.

2. A pattern of unstable, intense relationships in which the individual first idealizes another person as perfect in every way and then completely devalues him or her.

3. A markedly unstable self-image or sense of self.

4. Impulsivity in at least two potentially self-damaging areas (e.g., spending, sex, substance abuse, reckless driving or binge eating.)

5. Repeated suicidal threats, gestures, or behaviors, or self-mutilating behavior.

6. Frequent mood changes, with intense emotionality, such as episodes of extreme unhappiness, irritability or anxiety lasting from a few hours to a few days

7. Chronic feelings of emptiness.

8. Inappropriate, intense anger or difficulty controlling anger. (e.g., frequent displays of temper, physical fights, etc.)

9. Temporary stress-related paranoid ideas or severe dissociative symptoms.

We talked about *how* our *thoughts* eventually become our beliefs. By choosing our thoughts, we essentially choose our beliefs! I told Lyle that I've been trying, without success, to convince myself that I *am* worthy. He said that at this point in time, whenever I receive a compliment, I reject it; kick it away! The voice that claims that I'm *not* worth anything is just too damn strong right now! Hopefully, with Lyle's help, I'll learn how to kick that little voice right out of the picture!

Lyle also told me that I'm *not* responsible for the things I did in the past. He explained how the *borderline* sneaks in, and allows my thoughts and behavior to deviate from what I usually know to be moral and acceptable; throw that in with a little mania from the bipolar disorder and there's no telling *what* can happen! *But,* even though I'm *not* responsible for the past, I *am* responsible for *today*. This means that I need to continue with the therapy *and* the medication to avoid devastating relapses. But even then, there are no guarantees…

Same old argument with my husband about my wardrobe. He wants me to wear nicer, more form-fitting and fashionable clothing. You'd think he'd be thrilled that I'm so thrifty. Why is he so concerned about what I wear anyway? It's not like my clothes are totally outdated. It's more like they're nondescript. I prefer to "blend in" rather than stand out. He just wants me to be his "arm decoration." The last time I wore form-fitting slacks, Bill called them my come-fuck-me-pants. (He thought it was a compliment.) Nice huh? That comment *alone* is reason enough to *not* wear anything that shows off my figure! I'm *not* a piece of ass! I want desperately to be valued for the person I am; *not* for my body. That's asking a lot though, since I don't know who the hell I am.

On my way to town this morning, I started to feel hopeless, tearful and worthless. And then I got mad! Downright *pissed*! At God! At myself! At the *world*! Alone in the car, I started screaming at the top of my lungs! I cursed God and shouted "Why me?" Over and over I yelled, as loud as my voice would let me! I was *screaming* at God; challenging him, "If You really *do* exist, then help me! God-damn it, **HELP ME!** I didn't know how much more I could take. The internal violence from the war inside my head was dragging me deep into the darkness; so deep that I feared I would never get out. I screamed hysterically, until my throat was raw and my voice was nearly gone.

I'd rather be *dead* than to go on with this constant monologue, the voice within my mind, stating my worthlessness day in and day out. I am so *fucking* tired of this goddamned bipolar shit! Or borderline shit! Or *whatever* the fuck it is! I can't shut off my mind for two fuck-ing seconds! I'm so fucking tired of trying so damn hard, over and over, only to be knocked down again and again and again and again! I never know *when* it's going to hit; this agitation that drives me to self-destruction. I don't know how much longer I can keep getting back up. No one knows how bad it is inside my head. I can't even begin to explain it! But... if anyone had witnessed the blood curdling screams coming from me today, from the hell within, they might have known a small measure of what goes on inside my broken brain. The trouble is that if I were to let anyone *know* just how bad it is, I'd be locked up in a heartbeat. But then again, what does it matter? I'm already serving a *life sentence* in my own private hell.

When Bill picked me up after work, I could tell he wasn't pleased with the outfit I was wearing. Instead of the come-fuck-me-pants he'd want-ed me to wear; I'd selected a nice, but conservative, blouse and skirt. I knew he was disappointed and by the time we got to the dance, I was miserable. I had failed Bill again. It didn't help either, that I couldn't stop thinking about how everyone at the dance probably knew about my suicide attempt. I'm sure I'm a huge embarrassment to Bill. I tried to act like I was having a good time, but I didn't fool my husband. When we got home, he said "Sorry you had a bad time. I'm going to bed." I tried to talk to him, but it didn't go well. Bill thinks I'll leave him as soon as Rachel goes off to college. I don't know what I want. I feel alone, empty, unloved. I'm a burden to all who are unlucky enough to know me, but especially to my family.

Whenever Bill asks me how my session with Lyle went, I draw a complete blank. The same thing happens when *Lyle* asks me to recall something, like a recent incident with Bill. It's as if the only moment I've ever existed in, is right now. I can't seem to draw on past experience to help me with the present. I can tell Bill something one day, and the very next day I'll contradict what I said before because I've already forgotten it! My view of everything changes minute by minute. There's no stability or sense of continuation. My *sense of self* is completely at the mercy of the tides of my ever changing moods.

I told Lyle that what I want most out of life is to be loved. Lyle told me that *I'm* the only person who needs to love me. I don't see how that's possible. I wish Bill would say, "I love you and I will always love you no matter what, whether you get well or not, I'll love you forever." But he'll never say it and he certainly won't feel it. He's already told me that he's waiting for me to get better, before he invests anymore in me emotionally.

I ran into a good friend of mine the other day. I hadn't talked to her in five or six weeks, so she didn't know about the OD. While we were visiting, I felt awkward because of this big, dark secret I was hiding. When I finally told her, she felt horrible for not being there for me. I assured her that she couldn't have been there for me, because I had never let on to her that I was having any problems. As far as she knew, I was perfectly fine! Actually, *no one* had a clue that there was anything wrong with me at all. I was pretty damn good at keeping the dark side hidden!

I'm really missing my highs. I've been thinking about ditching the *meds* and having some fun! At my counseling session today, we talked about my lack of interest in *intimacy* with my husband. Apparently it's a direct result of *not* feeling loved, or even liked, by my husband! I *need* to feel valued and appreciated and until I do, it's unlikely that the *spark* from the early years will ever rekindle.

Work was *awful* today! There wasn't enough staff. The phone wouldn't stop ringing! Orders for STAT draws kept piling up! *Everyone* wanted a piece of me! I could feel my anger building as I ran all over the hospital. The exercise helped some, to burn off steam, but it couldn't stop the agitation completely. I finally gave into the mounting rage and slipped into an empty restroom. After a few good punches to one of the stall doors, I began to calm down. As I looked at my puffy and discolored knuckles, I thought back to the *last* time I had bruised my fist this bad. It was the day I took the overdose.

By the last two hours of my shift, I felt myself spinning out of control. Being *forced* to do a half-assed job because of a lack of employees and a crappy manager, pushed me to the breaking point. I could no longer contain my fury. Cuss words exploded like angry bullets as I vented my frustration loudly and without sensor! *Now*, as I sit in the comfort of my own home and reflect on the day's events, I'm exceedingly embarrassed by my behavior. It's not who I want to be.

I'll be 43 next week. The best gift I could give myself would be good health; both physically and mentally, but can I do it? I'll try. I just need to take my meds, go to therapy, get enough sleep, etc. *Sounds* easy enough.

Got agitated at work again. New bruises. Called Dr. Stoune's office and left a message for him about increasing my meds. I missed his call asking me to stop by his office. It doesn't matter though, because I've changed my mind about taking a higher dose. The agitation isn't getting any better, but my energy level is through the roof! I don't think I want to quell it; not yet.

Energy level and mood continue to climb. Feeling very good! Very up. Needing less sleep.

I'm sure my family can tell that I'm on top of the world. I've laughed a lot with them and spent quality time with my husband. I've decided *not* to make an appt with Dr. Stoune to talk about meds, because I'm really enjoying myself and I don't want to rein-in these awesome feelings! If the dose is high enough to prevent a suicidal crash, then I'm willing to live with the agitation and mild depressions that will develop from time to time. I just feel so wonderful! So alive! So fantastic! I think it's worth the risk.

I saw Lyle today. He instructed me to work on behavior modification. He said that I need to find a way into the "normal" or "middle ground" area. I hide behind the mask of *cheerfulness* too often.

Do I really *need* this damn Seroquel? Isn't it just a crutch? A big fat sign of weakness? Working on this *stupid borderline crap* should be enough! Maybe the doctors are wrong? Maybe I'm *not* bipolar? But what if I am? Will I get better as I get older? Will I get *worse*? Will I *always* have to take meds? I asked Lyle, but I didn't like his answer.

You know, I'm really not worth all this trouble.

I ran into Dr. Stoune today in the CCU. He said, "I know you have a question." He kept the statement generic to protect my privacy. I told him that I had been thinking about increasing one of my meds, but I had since changed my mind. Since there were people milling around, he let the subject drop. But *later*, when he called down to the lab regarding a patient, he brought the subject back up. I told him about my recent trouble with rage. I assured him I was feeling much better; maybe even *too* much better! I wasn't sure, but I knew that I liked being "up!" I told him that I was going to work on behavior modification. He said that was fine, *but*…there was still the possibility I would need to *increase* the Seroquel. I promised Dr. Stoune that I'd call him if I needed to. I also told him that I really, really missed the "highs" I used to have. He reminded me of how I ended up in the *unit*, because of one of those episodes! (How quickly I forget.)

11pm - I should go to bed, but there's so much I still want to do! Bill got mad at me tonight because I spoke up about a chore list he made for Rachel. He just kept adding to it! It seemed excessive, so I spoke up. Bill got mad and stormed off to bed without saying goodnight to either one of us. Later, he told me that he was angry because it felt like I had been undermining him, when he was only trying to get me help with the housework. I told him that the chore list reminded me of *my* childhood and *my* never-ending chore list. He said this isn't *my* childhood! He's right, but I *still* think the chore list was too long!

Feeling very agitated! Been thinking about what I did two months ago. *Why* didn't the overdose work? I have no memory of that afternoon. Apparently, while I was drugged, I talked to several people, but the drug I took caused amnesia. *Who* did I talk to and what did I say? I've been thinking about suicide a *lot* today. But why? The rage is building again and I don't know where it's coming from! I found an old bottle of Prozac in my drawer; a three month supply. Could *that* kill me? I looked it up in the PDR but it's not lethal. I wonder if potassium would do the trick? Carbon monoxide poisoning? I have that damn feeling like I *need* to jump out of my skin!! My thoughts are racing. My mind won't shut off, or even slow down! **I am soooooo fucking sick of this!!!!** I feel like it's only a matter of time until I end it all.

I know that it doesn't matter whether I live or die; people will still be hurt. It's best to distance myself *now* from those I love. I find this all so depressing, but I feel the need to *protect* them from me. (And what could happen if I "snap" again.) I wish I could promise that I'll never do "it" again, but I can't. I know there's a very real possibility, that if the conditions are right, I might *not* be able to control the impulse to kill myself.

I'm feeling so hopeless. So unstable. Who knows what the next day will bring? Or even the next hour! I *hate* having to spend so much time on trying to get better. The reading, the journaling, the therapy. I wish I could somehow get away from *me*.

I called Dr. Stoune today. I realized I needed to make the call when I started entertaining thoughts of *how* to make my death look like an *accident*! (I thought an "accident" would be less hurtful to my loved ones.) But I didn't tell Dr. Stoune that. I just said that I thought I needed to up the dose of Seroquel to quiet some of the agitation I'd been feeling. He agreed and increased the dose to 200mg.

A supervisor paid me a nice compliment on my work today, but later, when I tried to relay the conversation to my husband, I got tongue-tied and nervous! That happens a *lot* when I try to share something with Bill, because he gets really inpatient when I don't "spit it out" quickly enough! It's not just me though. He's that way with everyone!

After getting the chores done for the evening, I sat down to watch a show on TV. Just as I was getting comfortable, Bill started asking me questions about some of our (my) medical bills. I really, really just wanted to enjoy *one* TV show! I knew though, that if I was honest and told Bill the truth, he'd say something belittling! (And he thinks my Dad is the "belittling" king!) After spending 30 minutes looking for the statements, I finally got a chance to sit down to relax. At that time, my daughter came downstairs and asked me to mend her jeans for the next day. It took me an hour to find the sewing kit. I don't know *why* it's so hard for me to just say *no?* To *anyone.* Maybe it's because I feel like it's the only way I'll ever have *any* value as a person; by doing what other people want me to do. I'm not liking myself right now. I have such conflicting feelings about this issue. I know that *I* would be uncomfortable asking Bill or Rachel to do something for *me* and even *more* uncomfortable if they actually did it! Maybe that's why I feel so annoyed that they're perfectly fine with being "waited on." It makes me feel like their love is conditional on my servitude. On the other hand, maybe I don't feel worthy of being waited on? (Or of being loved.)

Bill always asks me how my sessions with Lyle went. He wants me to *hurry up* and get well! I wish I could. I really do. I have to remind Bill of how fortunate we are that Lyle is seeing me for only $25.00 a week. (Whenever I want to stop therapy, I think of this generous offer and I feel obligated to continue.) I also feel fortunate that Lyle's willing to treat me at all. Most therapists choose *not* to take on patients with borderline personality disorder. The bipolar is a "piece of cake" compared to the borderline! And most *borderline* patients need 3 to 5 *years* of therapy to repair the thought processes that have been damaged at some point in their lives. Most people with this disorder will drop out of therapy long *before* they are healed. And even with counseling, some *never* do get well.

I'm discouraged about my marriage. I know Bill is disappointed in me, but I'm also disappointed in him! He wasn't there for me in my darkest hour. (I guess he could say the same.) When I was in the CCU, Bill seemed completely indifferent. I felt lost and incredibly alone. My *boss* was more supportive than my own husband! When *he* came to see me in the unit, he said he'd help me however he could. Why couldn't my *own* husband do that? I don't know if I will *ever* get over the dismay of being let down when I needed so desperately to be held and loved and cherished by the man I call my husband. Maybe he never did love me?

I really don't know if my marriage is repairable. If I *am* able to get well, Bill may not *like* the person I become. If I get strong enough to stand up for myself and *not* jump through his hoops, he may not want me anymore. What do I have to lose though? He may not want me either way. I have *never* felt good enough for him; *never* felt his approval; *never* measured up to his expectations. I feel like he disapproves of *everything* about me! Of course, *no one* measures up to Bill's standards. Wow! It's *not* just me! *Everyone* lets him down! *No one* is good enough in his eyes! (This feels like one of those "Light bulb moments.")

My boss talked to me about a new work schedule. How would I like working 11:00am to 7:30pm, with Wednesdays and Saturdays off? I told him I would love it! I've never liked working 5 days in a row. I would prefer to have my days off split. That way I only work 2 or 3 days at a time before getting a day off. I've read in books, on bipolar disorder, about how this kind of a schedule can actually help with stability in someone like me.

I'm not feeling suicidal anymore. It still worries me though, because my thoughts and feelings can be so *intense* and being impulsive continues to be a problem for me. Bipolar and borderline definitely feed off each other, creating the perfect environment for *disaster*. I read once, that being borderline is like having a form of "emotional hemophilia." The therapist described it as a condition, in which the individual lacks the clotting mechanism that controls spurts of feelings in normal people. Apparently there is no such thing for the borderline person to feel a *little* angry or a *little* sad. *Every* reaction is extreme. I can vouch for that!

I feel so puffy today! Even my shoes are tight! Everything aches! I ate like a pig yesterday! I don't know *why* I do it. It just makes me miserable! I binge on *huge* quantities of junk food, mostly sweets, and yet I *never* get full, *never* feel satiated. I don't know why I have so little control over food. It's ridiculous!

Lyle and I talked about motherhood. Having a daughter changed the way I saw my husband and the way he treats women in general. Before we became parents, I hadn't realized how *often* he refers to women by their body parts! I thought his crudeness would dissolve when he realized his daughter would one day be a *woman*, but it didn't. Being exposed to Bill's degrading talk of women has actually made me *embarrassed* to be a woman, or even associated with women in general! Of course, if I'd been a mentally healthy woman when we met, I would have demanded to be treated like a lady. (Or the relationship would have ended.)

MY HUSBAND IS A FUCKING ASSHOLE! He thinks *everything* about *me* is *wrong*! I was really excited about my new work schedule. My shift includes working Sunday through Tuesday and Thursday and

Friday. When I told Bill, he said, "Hon, you can work all the Sundays you want." I thought he was being sweet and sincere until he uttered the next sentence, "That way you'll never have to go camping with me again." WHAT THE FUCK?

Sometimes I swear Bill wants a carbon copy of himself for a wife. He sure as hell doesn't want *me*! (At least not the way I am.) I've tried to be a good wife, but I fail every time. I'm not good enough for him or anyone else.

I can feel *it* building again. The self-directed anger is rising up in me like a wild beast, but I know how to tame it. At least for a little while…

Later--- I'm calm now. It took 7 or 8 strikes to my head and a few minutes with the straight edge. This time I left a goose egg above my right ear and a gash on my ankle (hidden beneath my sock and blood-soaked bandages.) I wonder how hard I would have to hit myself in order to put myself out of everyone's misery? I'd have to use something hard. A hammer?

Bill asked me recently why I don't tell him when I begin to feel suicidal. I said, "Because I don't want to see the look of disapproval and disgust on your face." He couldn't argue with that. And for those same reasons, I know it's not *safe* to share *any* negative feelings with him. Everything seems to make him angry with me. Doesn't he know that I'm angry enough at myself for the both of us? I wonder if he'll ever forgive me? I've gone from wanting my husband to feel compassion for me, and my troubled mind, to just hoping he can forgive me. Screw the whole notion of being loved unconditionally. *Not* gonna happen!

2

March 16th 2006 thru July 31st, 2006

Per Lyle's instructions, I've been keeping track of my feelings. It's like a damn rollercoaster ride and I want the heck off! Still short-staffed at work. What's new? The staff in CCU was pissed when I went up for a draw. I had just gotten to work, but apparently they'd called down to the lab 45 minutes earlier. Even though it wasn't *my* fault, I felt bad; like I was somehow responsible. Bill's been after me to leave work on time, but that's not always possible. I feel so pressured, by both work *and* my husband! Tonight I was actually able to leave work *early*! I thought Bill would be pleased, but when I got home he wasn't even there! He'd gone out with his friends. I'm frustrated and confused.

Bill said we need to rein-in our use of the credit card. That really irritated me because he always has cash from the business, while I have to ask for every penny; even to buy groceries! And on top of that, *I'm* the frugal one in this marriage! It isn't like we don't pay off the credit card each month, so I don't know what the big deal is.

Felt very anxious and uncomfortable tonight. We went to a party and in order to please Bill, I wore a very form-fitting outfit. I hated every moment of the evening! I wish I'd worn something that *I* liked. My therapist told me that there will come a day when I will *want* to show off my figure. He said it will be a sign of *healing*. Why the hell do I have to show off *anything*? It really pisses me off! Male chauvinist pigs!

Feeling very hopeless ...about life ...about my marriage ...about *me*! Suicidal thoughts are rampant. Can't seem to shake this dark cloud. I'm afraid of so many things, but mostly my instability. There's no telling what impulsive, dangerous thing I might do! I'm also terrified of losing my therapist. He's truly my lifeline right now and that dependency scares me. Why though? Isn't death what I want most of the time anyway? But what if Lyle *can* help me? Do I *want* to be helped? Maybe I'm too scared to be healthy, to be happy. Being *ill* is all I've ever known, and to be something else...

Been trying to lose weight. Getting discouraged. Only ate 400 calories yesterday and I *still* weigh 116 lbs! It seems I have no control over *anything*! ...my weight ...my mind ...my life.

Lyle's fucking crazy! He accused *me* of being anorexic!!!! That's fucking ridiculous!!!! How can he *not* see the fat? I'm *at least* 16 pounds overweight. Maybe even more. I was 94lbs once and I felt really good at that weight. Most of my fat rolls were gone then. He also said that I'm afraid of something. Afraid of what? He didn't say. As pissed as I was at Lyle, I still told him about my fears of losing him. I confessed that I was afraid he'd dump me. He promised me he would never do that. But what if something *else* takes him away from me? As disturbing as these thoughts are, they point to the possibility that maybe, just maybe, I *do* want to live!

Lyle talked to me about courage, including *dis*courage and *en*courage. We also discussed some of the problem symptoms of both bipolar and borderline. The *bipolar* mood swings help to facilitate the *borderline* in wreaking havoc. Thankfully the meds are controlling the *major* moods swings, but I still have to work on relearning how to think and how to behave. Being borderline for so long has really messed with my brain and how it works; or *doesn't* work!

When I told Lyle about my discomfort at the party, because of what I wore, he insisted that we explore my "discomfort" about revealing my figure. That's *not* what I wanted to hear! I wanted him to tell me it was perfectly okay to hide my figure, but he wouldn't side with me on this issue. I don't see anything wrong with wearing clothes that hide my curves. My wardrobe is *my* business! I'm really getting sick of people telling me how to dress!

Lyle warned me, that even though the bipolar can be treated with meds, I *still* need to be aware of bipolar *triggers* such as not getting enough sleep or scheduling too many activities. He also said that it's time to work on the borderline personality disorder. (There's no pill for that.) He said that we have a lot of hard work ahead of us, and that there will be times when I will leave his office "Hating him!"

I bought a book titled *An Unquiet Mind* by Kay Jamison. She's been on lithium for years to control her manic depressive illness. As I read about her struggles, I continually thought "Wow" because I saw so much of *myself* in her story!

Been on an upswing lately. Really liking it! Stayed up for 40 hours straight. Got a lot done. Bill gets worried when I won't come to bed at a *reasonable* time. He says it's a *sign* that I'm getting "bad" again. I think I'm doing fine. I'm still taking my meds and I haven't felt suicidal in over 2 weeks!

I felt happy at work today; giddy even. My boss asked me if I had been taking my meds and it pissed me off a little bit. Since when does a happy mood have to be a sign of illness? I felt a little shaky in the afternoon, but my blood sugar was fine. Energy continues to climb. I *love* running all over the hospital! It's like I'm a little lab *rat* who gets to run through a maze all day! I'm happiest when I'm in motion.

I did have a little incident today when a coworker got pissy with me! (I know that I'm supposed to stay and "fight" when I'm angry, but it's still so much easier to *flee*!) I felt the agitation building in me, but instead of confronting the grouch, I stormed off! After unleashing my fury on a nearby file cabinet, I looked around, hoping that no one had witnessed the attack. Shame washed over me as I took in the damage. Several very noticeable dents now marked the metal box.

Good therapy session today. I need to figure out what *my* beliefs are. For so long I've tried to be what other people want me to be. Because of these unhealthy attachments, I have absolutely *no* idea of what *my* beliefs are (about myself or about the world.) I've relied on cues from the people around me to tell me what to say or do, or even what to *think!* And without my own identity, I've become dependent on other individuals to provide me with one; albeit borrowed and temporary. And because of the fragile state of this identity, it can be taken away without notice! It's not solid. It's an illusion. No wonder I try so hard to please everyone. If I don't please them, they'll reject me and I will be *nothing*.

Lyle insists that I need to *stop* wearing the masks; *especially* the cheerful one! That one mask alone is like a big neon sign saying, "I'll be or do whatever you want. You can walk all over me and I'll just keep on smiling, keep on hiding the hurt, the anger, the sadness." Another thing that really must stop is my *need* to *justify* everything that I do. Lyle's right. It's as if I'm trying to justify my very existence!

I'm frustrated with my husband! I *love* my new shift at work and it hurts me that he is so against it! I asked him again *why* he's so opposed to my new schedule, but I got nowhere with him. (Although he did say that *normal* people want Saturday *and* Sunday off.) It feels like he disapproves of so much of what I am and what I do. There *was* a time when I would light up every time he walked into the room. Now I just feel dread, because I wonder what I've done *this time*. It feels like he truly hates me.

Bill has racked up some enormous bills lately on home improvements and yet he goes on and on about how broke we are! I get tired of hearing about it; especially when I'm *not* the one who keeps spending! I know I'm really going to hear about it with these latest bills, and I'm already dreading it. *My* need for material things is practically zilch, but Bill is *never* satisfied! He knows that I've always wanted to have the house paid off. In fact it *should* have been paid off already, but Bill keeps refinancing it to make it fancier and to buy more stuff. If the house were paid off, we'd have a little cash to play with! We'd be able to buy gifts or go to a show or a play together, maybe even take a weekend trip or an actual vacation. But our money just goes into the house and for what? So that it can be worth a lot when we *die*? I feel sad and empty. I'm trying to keep the darkness at bay, but I feel the storm clouds moving in. I keep thinking about suicide and how *not* to mess it up this time!

‿◌◌‿

I'm so angry! We're short-handed at work again and when I finally sucked up enough courage to ask the boss to help out, he said that I had two other people on shift with me, so I didn't *need* help. THE TWO PEOPLE ARE FUCKING *NEW!* THAT'S NOT *HELP!* IT'S A HINDRANCE! WHAT A JERK! I've only asked for help *twice* in the 3 *years* I've been at the hospital! Both times I was denied. What *really* pisses me off about this is that in one of my yearly evaluations I was told that I *need* to ask for help when it gets too busy! Then when I do, I'm belittled? They're all fucking jerks! I ended up punching a stall door in the restroom. Bruised again.

Hurting myself keeps me from crying. I don't have time for tears! I've been thinking *a lot* about suicide. It's *always* in the back of my mind. It feels like it's *not* a matter of "*if*" I kill myself, but "*when!*"

‿◌◌‿

I was thinking about the events of January 4th, the date of my attempted suicide, and I was wondering *why* I've been torn about *faith* ever since? I remember praying to God as I took the pills; asking Him to take me home *or* to get me the help I needed. So the fact that I'm still here, and the fact that Bill ran into Dr. Stoune that day, *seems* like divine intervention. Without Dr. Stoune, I might not have received the right diagnosis and medication *or* the emotional support of a caring and trusted doctor. So if it *was* divine intervention, then *why* is my belief in God so shaky? Is it because this path, leading away from suicide, feels impossible to stay on? Is my fear of *life* greater than my fear of *death*? When I *attempt* to pray, it feels empty and hollow.

I tried to set the sprinklers this morning and got very angry with myself because I'm too stupid to figure the damn things out! I suck at so many things! (Years later I would find out that I have a type of "spatial" dyslexia that has nothing to do with my *intelligence*.) Still thinking about death. I did some reading on famous people with bipolar disorder. Some of them were actually schizophrenic. (The two diseases are very similar.) It's amazing how many of these deeply talented individuals ended up taking their own lives.

I'm gaining weight because of the damn medication! As it reins in my hyperactivity, it also slows my metabolism. I feel like a big fat slug! I changed my screen saver at work. Now it's the title of one of Kay Jamison's books, *Night Falls Fast*. (It best describes my instability.) Today at work, I found the original ER lab orders for me, from the day of my failed suicide attempt. The diagnosis was entered as an *accidental overdose*. Someone was trying to protect me! Lyle asked me once why the police weren't involved in my case. *Now* I know why! I wish I knew who to thank.

Other than being shaky a few times, I've been doing fairly well these last few days. I don't think I need therapy anymore. I can do this on my own.

I told Lyle that I had a good *7 days!* A whole *week!* We talked about my unhealthy attachment to Bill and how I need to set boundaries with him. This was after I told Lyle that I really hate it when Bill gropes me and uses crude language. I am so disgusted with the way Bill and his friends talk. I chickened out on telling Lyle that I thought I was ready to quit therapy.

I'm still feeling shaky. It's mostly an *inner* trembling. I wonder if it's a *sign* that a manic or mixed episode is coming on. It's *feels* like low blood sugar, but whenever I check my glucose, it's fine. It's probably just stress. I notice it's worse at work. I've also noticed that the normal lab sounds, of the machines and ringing phones, seem much louder than usual. Hopefully it's nothing.

I had a ton of energy today! I couldn't sit still and I found myself talking too much about nothing. I know these aren't good signs, but I sure as hell don't want to increase the meds. I'll end up obese.

I "lost it" at work. When I started my shift, I saw a waiting room full of patients and not a single employee in sight! As I tried to answer the phones and check-in the patients, I became increasingly agitated because I couldn't get away from the front desk long enough to draw anyone's blood! As the waiting room continued to grow more crowded, my boss showed up long enough to say that he'd sent the other employee home because she had too much overtime! And then he left! By the time the assistant supervisor showed up, I'd had it! I threw my collection tray across the room and started shouting that I was sick of being forced to do a half-assed job because of short-staffing. As I continued to rant and rave, the supervisor repeated the word "settle" over and over again. In a calm and steady voice he chanted, "Settle, settle, settle." It was as if he was trying to calm a wild animal. And maybe he was.

❧

I had very difficult session with Lyle today. I told him about what happened at work. When he asked me about how I'd been feeling in the last week or so, I looked back at my symptoms and realized that my anxiety level had gone up, along with some agitation. I was constantly seeing things out of the corner of my eye. I heard my name often, but when I *looked* no one was there. I had begun to ramble. Normal everyday sounds were excruciatingly loud. My soft comfortable clothing had become scratchy and constricting. I was easily distracted and the list continues. Lyle and I talked about the hypersensitivity of a bipolar person as they escalate into hypomania, mania or mixed episodes. It's a type of *sensory overload*. Too much sensory input and we become *hypersensitive* to everything! (Over-stimulated by our own environment!) I shared with Lyle the poem I wrote, about losing it at work:

There's a darkness in my soul
That closes in on any light
Will it always be a struggle
And will I always fight

With the shadows hanging over
And the darkness closing in
The chance I had at peace
Is lost to me again

My heart is truly heavy
With the burden of my ways
Can't count how many times
I regret what I did say

Was feeling rather manic
When something pushed me to edge
I was like a wild animal
Trapped and scared to death

A supervisor calmed me
By repeating just one word
"Settle" "Settle" "Settle"
Until at last I heard

But now the shame has hit me
I've lost it once again
This fight is too damn hard
As the darkness closes in

I cried through most of the therapy session. Lyle asked, "Why so sad?" I
didn't have an answer for him, but I think it's a combination of things.
I'm embarrassed by my behavior at work. I'm angry at myself for not
having more control. I feel frustrated because I can't seem to do the
things Lyle tells me to do; like taking a break when I need one. (He
makes it sound so simple!) I'm also sad about not being able to do my
job well. I know I'm good at what I do, but I'm only *one* person and
I can only do the job of *one* person! My employer is making it impossible to get my work done! We don't even have a receptionist! I love
the patients and drawing their blood. I enjoy putting them at ease and
making them smile. Being forced to do a half-assed job, because of the
situation in the lab, is disheartening.

I told Lyle that there was one more thing was really bothering me. I
don't know what's *me* anymore and what's the *bipolar*? He said we'll figure it all out. It will just take time. He did think that I should increase
my meds, so I called Dr. Stoune and he agreed. I have an appt with Dr.
Stoune in 2 weeks, but he said to call him sooner if I need anything.

❦

I'm feeling pretty stable on the 300mg. Weight's up to 123 lbs though, so I'm not sure about staying on this higher dose. Of course I realize that taking my meds is an important aspect of therapy. In order for the *counseling* to work, I need to have the worst of the bipolar mood swings under control. Lyle talked with me about "building a rope." As I figure out what *my* beliefs are, as well as my likes and dislikes, I add a little more to my rope (or my *core*) with each revelation. My "rope" at this point is like a thread; it's very fragile. I need to add *layers* to the thread, so that eventually it will become a strong and stable *rope*.

I also learned that I need to *retrain* people on how to treat me. I've inadvertently allowed mistreatment of myself because of my lack of respect for *me*. Another area that needs work is my preoccupation with weight. I know that some of my hang ups on this issue stem from being the "fat twin." My twin sister was so much smaller than me at birth. She only weighed 4 lbs 14 oz., while I was nearly 7 lbs! From the very beginning of my life, I was known as the "fat twin." By the time I met my Bill, when I was 20, I already had it ingrained in my mind that I was overweight.

What didn't help, at this point, was my husband's own preoccupation with weight. Only it wasn't *his* weight he was concerned about. He had an opinion about *every* woman he saw and what he thought of her size! It was obvious from his comments that he found very thin women to be attractive. On the other hand, if a woman was a little chubby, or even *average*, he saw her as fat. He's still that way. He'll say, "Look at her huge butt!" and I'll turn to look at what inevitably ends up being a very average size woman. I know that his behavior has reinforced my own obsession about fat and what constitutes being "overweight." Lyle recently made a very good point about me being the "fat twin." He asked me if I really thought that a 7 lb baby would be considered "overweight?" Would a diet be necessary for a baby weighing a "fat" 7 lbs? I'm finally realizing how messed up my thoughts are on this subject. Lyle definitely knows how to help me to see things in a new light.

Still on the 300mg. Feeling pretty content with life. Hopeful even. I've noticed that the bipolar symptoms have once again receded and I'm back to *normal.* Therapy seems to be going well. I'm realizing that I get *way too much* of my sense of worth from work. I'm very good at what I do; very competent. I get a lot of compliments from nurses, patients, co-workers, even doctors, but I *know* that I need to value me for just being *me!* Too much of my identity is wrapped up in my job! When things aren't going well because of staffing problems, and suddenly I can't get my work done in a timely matter, my self esteem takes a nose dive. I have to get away from that mentality! I know, intellectually, that I'm worth more than what I *do,* but I'm having a hard time convincing myself of that.

Had an appt with Dr. Stoune today. I told him I was so embarrassed about my behavior at work last month. He told me not to be embarrassed, or ashamed, because it was the *disorder* causing the uncharacteristic behavior; not *me.* He compared my situation with that of a diabetic. He said we wouldn't blame a diabetic for behaving abnormal if his glucose was out of control. He said this was no different! Maybe it really isn't my fault?

I started to feel shaky and restless this afternoon. It made me nervous because I never know *what* is going to end up being a sign or symptom of the bipolar returning. I started to panic. What if I'm *already* cycling back into a manic or mixed episode? Next thing I knew, I was thinking about *death* and "ways to go." What the hell is wrong with me? I feel hopeless, agitated and afraid. What if the meds stop working? If they do, I'm dead.

Today at work, I felt the dreaded shakiness returning. Before I panicked, I decided to check my blood sugar. It had fallen from a normal *fasting* reading of 90 to a very low 46! No wonder I was trembling. I just needed some food. I'll get this all figured out someday.

I'm getting frustrated with the meds again. They make me sleep too much and I don't have as much energy as I used to! I wrote a poem about my frustration:

I really miss the *highs*

The highs that made me, *me*!

I miss bouncing off the walls

And the endless energy

I miss the constant chatter

And all the thoughts that filled my head

I miss the friendly banter

I might as well be dead

I want to stop this drug

It numbs me to the core

But I know that with the "highs"

Comes the risk of something more

The price I'd have to pay
Just to have my highs again
Could very well be death
Am I ready for the end?

I showed Lyle my latest poem and he discouraged me from trying to recapture the *me* I remember from my "up" days. He said I was wearing too many *masks* back then, but I don't agree. Sometimes I just feel happy and social and outgoing.

Work was wonderful today. I was on cloud nine! It was a great day. A fun day. An *alive* day! I felt like the old me. I was energetic and talkative and flirty and high on life. But, it was short-lived. As soon as I got home, and tried to share some of the funny stories with Bill, his reaction took the wind out of my sail. His responses were so muted and stoic that I instantly came crashing back to earth. I don't think it's a bipolar issue, although it might be related to the borderline problem. Maybe it's a *husband* issue? I don't know why he always acts so bored with me! It really hurts. No wonder I feel more validated at work; people appreciate me there.

Bill and I had a long talk yesterday. He doesn't see *any* improvements in me! I was shocked! I've been working my butt off to get well, and yet he doesn't see *any* improvement? I've been in therapy *and* taking my meds *and* journaling! Why am I working so hard if it's not making a difference? I'm more confused than ever! I finally asked him if there was *anything* he even *liked* about me. He said *everyone* likes me;

everyone adores me. He never did answer the question. I asked him what bothers *him* about me, and he said that I sleep too much and I'm not active enough. He also wants my help in improving our house and our yard. (Like our neighbors have been doing.) To *me*, a house is just a house. I don't see the point in tearing out cupboards or ripping up carpet just because it's old. If something is still functioning, why on earth would I want to spend money replacing it? And besides, when we *do* improve something, Bill still isn't satisfied! He still wants to keep changing things, spending more and more money. No amount of house improvements will *ever* be enough. He *always* wants more! With *everything*!

We also talked about Bill's anger at me for the overdose and how selfish it was of me to attempt to end my life; to not consider what it would have done to him and Rachel if I had succeeded. I tried to explain to him, that in my state of mind at the time, I honestly thought they would be better off without me! He wanted to know *why* I didn't tell him how I was feeling in the days leading up to the overdose. I told him it's not *safe* to share my thoughts or feelings with him. I don't think he's even aware of how he belittles me! If something's not important to *him*, then it's *not* important.

Been thinking about what Bill said about me sleeping too much and not being active enough. He was also upset that I snack and watch TV at night. He doesn't like this extra weight I've gained. I don't like it either, but it's especially upsetting because I know he's disgusted by fat women. Anyway, the only way I know how to sleep less *and* be more active, is to reduce the dose of my meds. I just hope that the bipolar doesn't rear its ugly head.

Lyle and I talked about my inability to accept love. I reject people, and their love, before they have a chance to reject me! I don't even know if

I'm *capable* of giving or receiving love. I certainly never feel it. We also talked about my need to justify everything I do, as if trying to convince anyone who will listen, that I just might be worth the space I take up.

I cut back to 150mg of my Rx about a week ago. Bill doesn't know about it. But he *did* notice, and thank me, for being more active and for getting up earlier. I've been the *energizer bunny* for the last few days. I know I shouldn't mess with my meds, but I have to admit it's been nice to have some energy again. I was washing dishes and vacuuming at midnight last night! (That's definitely not sluggish or lazy.) I feel so good! At times, I can actually *feel* a "high" permeate my entire being! At those times, a warmth and giddiness flows through me. I feel *drugged* somehow; in a good way! It's like I'm high on something, but it's the opposite! Instead of taking drugs to feel high, I just *stop* taking them! It's really kind of funny, in an ironic sort of way. Also, with less medication, I don't have to waste my time sleeping! In fact, I hardly need to sleep at all.

I went to my session this morning bursting with energy! I could barely contain my enthusiasm for *everything*. Lyle seemed very concerned right from the start. He asked me if I'd stopped my meds. I admitted that I'd *adjusted* the dose… but no, I hadn't *stopped* them. He warned me about how dangerous it was, and that I was taking a very big risk! I told him that I felt *great*! Absolutely wonderful! Never better! He said, "Yes, *but* …" Then he went on to say something about the "crash that always follows the high." Blah, blah, blah! I just don't care. I'm up, up, up! And I love it, love it, love it! I promised him that I'd increase the dose at the *first sign* of any *bad* symptoms. He said that I won't recognize them "in time" or some other crap like that! *Why* would he want me to give up these wonderful, glorious feelings? And

I have energy again! Lots of it! I can hardly contain my excitement at just being *alive!* I feel like I can *do anything!* Anything at all! Lyle kept trying to bring me down with a list of reasons *why* I shouldn't mess with my meds. Blah, blah, blah. You need six hours of sleep a night. Blah, blah, blah. Something about my body breaking down if I don't rest. Blah, blah, blah. Instability will rise. Blah, blah, blah.... impulse control problems....blah, blah, blah.

I had a tough time focusing on anything Lyle was trying to tell me at our last session. When he asked me for the *real* reason I had messed with my meds, I said something about needing to lose weight. He accused me of getting back into "an unhealthy attachment mode." (Because I want to be thin for Bill.) Finally, at the end of the session, I promised Lyle that I'd go back to my regular dose. And I will...*eventually.*

My new nickname at work is *butterfly* (for *social* butterfly.) I guess that would have something to do with my non-stop jabbering, and because I can't seem to sit still. I'm in constant motion! I've been thinking about what Lyle said, concerning the "depression" that always follows a "high." I don't think there's anything to be worried about. I know I won't attempt suicide again; mostly because I no longer have access to killer drugs. And there's no way I would ever shoot myself because of the mess it would make.

Does Bipolar really *need* to be controlled with medicine? What's wrong with having extreme moods? Why isn't it okay to enjoy the highs while they last? Lyle said he can't help me if I refuse to stay on the meds. He even threatened to tell Dr. Stoune that I was being non-compliant! I'm feeling really torn about this. I almost took the correct (and higher) dose tonight, but at the last minute I remembered that Bill had asked me to do some extra chores tomorrow... soooo... if I'm going to have enough energy....

⚭⚮

I disappoint Bill constantly, just because I don't want the same *exact* things that he does! For so long I've *tried* to be the wife he wants, but I'm always failing. Always falling short. I don't even know who I am. Maybe, I never did.

⚭⚮

I've been thinking about what Lyle said, regarding the need for medication if therapy is to work. I don't *want* to be reined-in, but maybe it *is* in my best interest. Lyle was so adamant that I stop messing with my meds; stating that it was extremely dangerous! I had said to him, "But... I *like* being hyper and driven!" He said that it could lead to "hyper and *dead!*"

⚭⚮

Had a session with Lyle today. I told him he's right! As usual. I *do* need to be reined in if therapy has any chance at all. We talked again about the poem I wrote. The one about missing the highs "that made me, *me!*" He disagreed that the "highs" were me. They are actually a part of the *disorder*. He asked me if I *really* missed bouncing off the walls. Of course I didn't really bounce off any walls. It was more like I walked in circles, but that's not the point! I miss the *energy*! I don't feel like myself when I'm reined-in. Lyle said that *eventually* I will stop missing the highs. I will learn to accept, and maybe even *like*, my new normal; the *me* without the rollercoaster ride! To reinforce what he was trying to teach me, he told me the following story:

There once was a man who was tired all the time. He couldn't remember a time when he wasn't tired. He had grown used to feeling this way, so it became his *normal* way of feeling. Finally, a routine physical showed that he was very low on red blood cells. After receiving a transfusion, he went home. A few days later, he called his doctor because he was convinced he was dying! The doctor asked him why he thought that, and the man told him that he just didn't *feel* right. *Something* was wrong! He wasn't *himself.* He didn't feel *normal.* After more questioning, the doctor realized, that with more oxygen-carrying blood pumping through his body, the man was actually feeling *well* for the first time. But, because the man wasn't familiar with good health, he thought he was dying!

Lyle pointed out that my bipolar symptoms have been my "normal" way of life for so long, that anything else feels uncomfortable at best. And yes, I will miss the highs, but *eventually* I'll see the good in my *new normal;* like not having the crashing lows that always finds their way in! And having more control over my life and being able to make *plans* without the fear of what mood may strike! Eventually, *stability* will become the new norm. Eventually. Sigh.

Lyle's going on vacation and I won't see him for two weeks. I'm freaking out! I don't want anyone to know how *needy* I am, but God I *am* needy! I am so needy it scares me! Without Lyle in my life, I would *die*!

I am so embarrassed by how fat I've gotten! I'm 120 lbs. Way too much. "Weigh" too much. I *have* to stop the meds. (Or at least decrease them.) It's the only way to get rid of this blubber. I'll be careful though, so Lyle doesn't find out.

Bill was trying to show me how to do something and he was being very condescending. I told him that he was making me feel stupid. He didn't say anything, so I guess he agrees. I am stupid. It seems like the only time he approves of me, is when I lose weight or when I wear tight-fitting clothes. God I feel like a slut! It makes me sad to think that I will *never* be good enough for him just the way that I am. My husband believes that I'm the whole problem in this relationship and maybe I am, but his constant criticism isn't helping. I'm realizing that the respect and love and friendship I'm craving, is never going to come from the one I want it most from. Maybe it never did. With our daughter almost grown, and knowing that my husband doesn't even *like* me, I feel that I am at a crossroad. I don't know *what* to do! This bipolar disorder *and* borderline crap has really thrown a curve into my life. I'm sick of *needing* medication, of *needing* therapy. *Why* can't I beat this? What difference does it make if I stop the drugs? No one gives a shit about me.

I'm thinking about quitting therapy. I'm tired of it! I'm tired of all the work that goes with it! I don't want to be under the microscope anymore. I want to be free to say, "Screw the meds!" If I stay in therapy, Lyle will hold me accountable for my actions. He'll also keep "harping on me" about being too thin! Is he fucking blind? If I can, at the very least, take a break from therapy, I can pretend that I'm *normal* right now just the way that I am!

Who am I kidding? I *need* therapy. I *need* Lyle. Our session today was going along just fine, when he had to go and ask the dreaded question,

"Are you taking your meds?" I told him I was, but *then* he asked, "The full dose?" I wasn't. So *now* I'm "playing with dynamite." (Lyle's words, not mine.)

Back to punching stall doors in the restroom. Very agitated at work. Boss seemed concerned. Asked me how therapy was going. I told him about *not* taking the right amount of medication. I told him that I *hate* that I need drugs to function! It feels like I'm being weak, or caving in, when I take *any* dose! He told me that it's actually "being weak" when I *don't* take the drug. (He said that it takes a *strong* person to admit when they need help.) Maybe he's right. Maybe Lyle's right. God knows *I'm* not right.

Back on track. Back on drugs. Yippy. My latest assignment is to figure out what *my* core beliefs are:

I am the chubby twin.

I am not good enough.

People let me down.

I am safest when I'm alone.

Stealing is wrong.

I am unlovable.

My body is never just right.

My husband and daughter are smarter than me.

Organized religion is *man*-made.

Nature is healing.

Animals are healing.

Fat should be hidden.

I am a good phlebotomist.

Men want skinny women.

Boys want skinny girls.

I should treat people the way I wish to be treated.

My husband doesn't love me.

My husband doesn't *like* me.

God *won't* strike me dead for cursing Him.

I'm overweight at anything above 100lbs.

I am a good mom.

I don't matter.

The next part of the assignment: If I was 12 years old again, and I could create a new me, who would I be? I honestly don't know.

August 2006 thru October 2006

If I were 12 years old again, and could create a new me, who would I be? What a thought provoking question! I've been pondering it ever since Lyle asked it last week. What would I like? What would I expect? What would I *demand*?

I've been trying to remember what it was that I used to enjoy. What did I like to do as a child *and* as an adult? I used to like writing poetry or curling up with a good book. Adventures were fun; whether it was a hike through the woods, a road trip or exploring a new city. I've always loved animals and nature. Something as simple as feeding the squirrels could fill my heart with joy. Through the years, my enthusiasm for everything has been squashed over and over again. Discouragement has run rampant; encouragement obsolete. Over the decades, I've become extremely self-conscious about so many things because of constant *put-downs*. I told Lyle that I stopped using the word "wonderful" after I met Bill, because he made fun of me every time I used it. Lyle said that *he* likes the word *wonderful* because it makes him think "full of wonder." Interesting.

I can't believe I'm still writing in a journal *and* going to therapy. I thought I'd be done by now. With both! I guess I still have a lot of stuff to sort through. I really want to quit journaling, quit therapy and quit the Rx, but something keeps me going back to therapy, which in turn leads to writing. And of course, with counseling, I have Lyle to hold me *accountable* for my actions. Deep down, I honestly don't want to disappoint him.

Lyle asked me to promise that not only would I stay on my meds, but that I would *call* him if I ever feel like hurting myself. I told him what he *already* knows; that I can't *promise* anything. My promises are empty. They mean nothing; *especially* when it comes to my health. Lyle and I talked about *why* it's so hard for me do what's in my best interest and *why* I continue to think of *suicide* as a way out. According to Lyle, the suicidal thoughts I have are from the borderline personality disorder, and it's the suicide *ideation* that can sometimes sabotage my efforts at becoming well. (The bipolar factors in also.) A part of me doesn't want to let go of the borderline *or* the option of suicide. Why do I cling to something that is so obviously wrong?

This morning, as I was trying to help Bill move a piece of furniture, I told him that I needed to stop just long enough to reposition my hands. He got irritated with me and asked our daughter to help him, because *I couldn't!* My feelings were really hurt. After I had a chance to think about it, I told him that from now on, I expect to be treated with dignity and respect. He tried to joke about it, but he could see that I was serious. He promised to try.

When I told Lyle that my husband had promised to try to treat me with respect, Lyle spoke up right away. He didn't like the fact that Bill had said he'd *try*. Lyle said, "That's not good enough. Either he will or he won't. It's like saying I'll *try* to turn off the light; either you flip the switch or you don't." At first I was disappointed in Lyle's reaction because I'd been so happy with Bill's response. But Lyle's right! It's not that hard to "flip the switch." Lyle did acknowledge that it was a very big step for *me* to even say what I said. I am making progress!

I bought a book called *Get Me Out Of Here,* by Rachel Reiland. It's about one woman's struggle with borderline personality disorder. She went to therapy for 4 years and eventually made a full recovery. I cried when she recounted her final visit with her therapist. Her book gives me hope. It also makes me acutely aware that someday, I too, will tell *my* therapist good-bye.

Yesterday, when I turned the radio on, the first words I heard were, "Let somebody love you before it's too late." It made me wonder whether or not, I will *ever* be able to *let* somebody love me *before it's too late.*

In looking back at my childhood, I've come to the conclusion that the relationship between my dad and me was superficial. I could never seem to get the love and validation that I so desperately wanted! I'm wondering if that's *why* I was so drawn to Bill. I chose a husband that was just like my father; a man who's *incapable* of giving me the love and approval that I so desperately crave. Now I can see *why* I always broke up with men who treated me like a queen. I was subconsciously trying to recreate my past by choosing men who *couldn't* be there for me emotionally. Poor Bill! He really didn't have a chance. He received *damaged goods* for a wife. He didn't sign up for that!

I've been faithful about taking the full 300mg of Seroquel for almost two weeks! I'm trying to remember that it takes a *strong* person to admit that she needs help. Lyle and I talked about something called *twisting*. He said that I do it every time I start to feel close to someone. I twist away from *them* before they can hurt me. Apparently, in my mind, relationships are *not* safe! I'm always testing the trustworthiness of the people in my life. Lyle even said that I'd been testing *him*! Evidently, as I'm learning to trust Lyle, I'm constantly "twisting." When Lyle pointed it out, and I could *see* it, I told him I'd stop. He said, "No you won't, not yet." I assured him, that now that I *know* what behaviors are forms of twisting, I can choose to stop them! He said, "Yes… but you'll find *new* things to throw at me." He's probably right.

I've been thinking back to my early years. I was 9 when my parent's separated. I chose to live with my dad for one reason only; *he* had our dog! I'm not very close with any of my family members. I never was. I preferred being *alone* to being with them. As an adult, I've maintained contact with my twin. I believe she loves me. In fact, if there's anyone in this world who does, I know it would be her. But, as usual, I can't *feel* it. Lyle once asked me if I thought my life was sacred. My answer was a quick and resounding NO!

The anger is building! I can *feel* it! Anger about my childhood. Anger at *myself*. Anger at being unloved, and unlovable. In looking back, I *can't* remember *ever* feeling loved or wanted. Most of the time I wasn't even noticed. There were too many kids! And yet, I was *alone*. Alone in a family of *nine*! I am soooooooo fucked up! There isn't a fucking chance in hell that I'm ever, ever gonna make it through therapy! Not a fucking chance! I'm a lost cause. There is no hope. There is no light. Fury is boiling throughout my entire being, and self-hatred is quickly gaining its foothold. The god-damned madness won't recede. Won't let up. I don't know how much longer I can take it! This inner turmoil toys with my very sanity. The intensity of these feelings feeds the dark beast within; fuels the fire it breathes. I'm going to explode; actually physically explode! Into a million little pieces! If I can't find a way to stop this monster…this monster called me.

Later—

I finally found a box cutter in the shop, but no matter how deep I dug, the blade was too dull to draw much blood. Thankfully, just going through the "motions of cutting" had a calming effect, and I was able to *numb out* my feelings with minimal damage.

This morning when Lyle asked me how I was doing, I mumbled, "Barely existing." Upon questioning, I told him that I didn't *feel* anything. (How ironic for someone who feels *too* much a lot of the time.) Lyle told me, "When you're feeling *nothing*, it's probably depression." Whatever.

Maybe I *am* depressed. I have no motivation to do *anything*. It takes everything I have, just to get through the day. Lyle wanted me to read a book about borderline personality disorder. It's called *The Angry Heart*. I'm trying to read it, but even *that* feels exhausting! The two or three chapters that I did manage to look at left me feeling more hopeless and overwhelmed than ever! Borderline personality disorder is a tough diagnosis to beat, and I don't think I can.

I'm feeling so angry! So *damn* angry! And horribly sad! At the same time! My tears won't stop! I'm so agitated! I feel as if I'm going to explode! I *want* to explode! I *need* to explode! I can't stop thinking about my childhood! My siblings seemed to turn out okay, so *why* am *I* fucked up? Why didn't *I* get through those years unharmed? What's wrong with *my* brain? My childhood wasn't bad. Other people have lived through unspeakable, despicable, awful childhoods, and yet they thrive as adults. Why am *I* so weak? I wasn't *abused* as a child, so what's *my* problem? Why am *I* the loser?

Lyle keeps telling me that I need to learn how to trust people, including myself, but I can't! It seems that every time I get close to someone, they *leave me*! (I even lost my favorite boss to cancer.) How can I trust *anyone*? Even Lyle isn't *completely* trustworthy. He's promised me that he won't leave me, but at the same time he's also told me that if I won't take my meds, he can't treat me. So which is it? *How* can I trust him if his guidance is *conditional*?

Lyle keeps telling me that I need to learn how to trust people, includ—

I've been on the 300mg dose for 4 weeks now. I'm still having mood swings, but the depressions are no longer suicidal. God, I miss the "highs." I really, really, really miss them! Oh well, at least with the bipolar symptoms reined in, Lyle and I can finally get to work on the borderline issues. It's sooooo depressing to think of all the work that lies ahead. How will I ever make it? Can I make it? Although I'm *not* able to love myself, not yet anyway, maybe I can start by taking care of myself? That would mean sticking with therapy, journaling, medication, exercising, eating right...blah, blah, blah.

❦

After reading more of *The Angry Heart*, I can see that I really need to apologize to Bill. I'm beginning to understand how difficult it's been to live with me. I know he's not a saint, but I'm truly impossible to predict. My poor husband never had a chance! My moods are all over the map without rhyme or reason. Acknowledging this to myself is painful. Excruciatingly so.

❦

Lyle told me that after the *borderline* is healed, I may be able to *reduce* my meds for the bipolar disorder. (We're talking *years* from now.) He also wants me to figure out what it is that I'm afraid of? I don't know the answer to that one. *Am* I afraid of something? Does Lyle know something I don't? He keeps reminding me that I'm an *attractive* woman who looks years younger than she is! I want to believe him, but I can't. *Every* time he brings it up, I start crying. Not out and out bawling. I just tear up and my chin quivers, and I'm sure there's nothing *attractive* about that! And, as he hands me yet another tissue, I'm exceedingly embarrassed.

❦

I recently told Lyle that it's hard for me to get out of the house in the morning because I spend so much time trying to look decent. Not good or great, just decent. But, no matter how hard I try, I don't look nice, or decent, or even *good-enough*. I'm always repulsed by what I see. I even shared with him something I've never told *anyone* before. When I first saw my wedding photos, back in 1987, I was so disappointed! The photographer didn't do anything wrong. It's just that, at the wedding, everyone kept telling me I was a *beautiful* bride and I actually believed them! But later, when I saw the pictures, I only saw *me*: a plain

Jane. I was crushed. I felt betrayed. *Everyone* had lied to me! I felt like the butt of a cruel joke.

"Let somebody love you before it's too late." That song again! What's the deal? Is God trying to tell me something? Well I *can't* "Let somebody love me." Not yet. I don't deserve to be loved.

I'm so pissed at Lyle right now! I keep thinking about the last session and what he said about reducing the bipolar meds. Does he think I'm *not* fucking bipolar? Is that what he thinks? I've spent the last six months trying to come to terms with the bipolar disorder and the fact that there's no *cure* for it. I even told Lyle that now that *that* disorder is controlled, I'm ready to work on the more difficult task of overcoming my borderline personality "problem." Then he drops a bomb like that? What the fuck am I suppose to think? Does he really think I'm just a fucking loser who can't control her god-damned moods? Is that what he thinks? That I'm fucking lazy? Well, I'll show that bastard! I'll just fucking quit therapy and he can know that *he* failed. Not me! Jerk!

I left a message for Lyle stating that I needed a break from therapy. I put on my mask of professionalism and left a pleasant voice mail for him. I really want him to call me though, and ask me to come back or at least ask *why?* Although… I really *do* need a break from all of this psycho-analysis crap! I'm tired of all the thinking and hurting and work that goes along with it; not to mention the *time* involved! My entire world has revolved around bipolar *this* and borderline *that*. I'm worn out!

It's been over two weeks since I last went to counseling. I've been up, down, pissed off, and everything in between! I was very angry with Lyle for wanting to take away the bipolar diagnosis. I'm *still* angry! I think that part of this anger is from *not* wanting to deal with the *borderline personality disorder*! Knowing that the *bipolar* disorder is a physiological disease made it easier to accept that it *wasn't my fault*. *Borderline*, on the other hand, is entirely in *my mind*. "It's all in your head, Mrs. Anderson." Just some weak-willed wacko woman! I wasn't tough enough as a child and I'm still not as an adult. It's a big fat sign of personal weakness and I'm not strong enough to beat it.

My husband, and his friend, just bought two new 4-wheelers. They're huge and I hate them! Why weren't our smaller ones good enough? I still have mine, but Bill said that we're *not* taking it on our upcoming camping trip because there isn't room! I'm so upset, but I don't feel like I have the right to speak up and spoil their fun. I don't want *anything* to do with those new 4-wheelers! As far as I'm concerned, they're too big to be safe.

Later—

I got so angry at myself over Bill's decision! I couldn't stop shaking from the fury, the self-hate. I slipped away into one of our bathrooms and desperately looked for something, *anything*, that I could use to slice open my skin. I *needed* a fix. I *needed* to see blood pool up; to run down my skin. But I couldn't find anything sharp. So I beat myself with the hairdryer until a goose egg formed on my head, and bruises appeared on my legs and chest. Finally I was spent. I emerged from behind the closed door… calm, cool and collected. No one knew. God, I *am* crazy! No wonder I can't be loved. I'm not worth the fucking space I take up! This all makes me terribly sad. And it makes me physically sick to my stomach to know that I'm truly *borderline*. I have absolutely no hope for me now.

I hate to admit it, but I need Lyle. I wasn't going to go back after that last session, but I've calmed down in the past few weeks. I called and left a message for Lyle, telling him that I'd be there on my regular day at the normal time and to call me if that doesn't work. Well I didn't hear anything, so I guess he's taking me back.

Lyle acted like nothing ever happened! I still expected him to ask me *why* I'd cancelled, but he didn't. (Or wouldn't?) Couldn't he *feel* how angry and confused I was? Did he honestly *not* know why I was so upset? Finally I couldn't stand it any longer and I blurted out how discouraged I was by his comments last session. He immediately apologized for any misunderstanding. He tried to explain, from another angle, what it was that he meant about reducing the medication down the road. From a medical stand point, I am bipolar and I need medical help for it; at this time. However, once the psychological issues of borderline are resolved, the bipolar *could* go into remission.

We talked about other things too. I told him about the self-injury due to the anger at myself, and at my husband, regarding the 4-wheelers. I was so hurt that Bill didn't want to take *my* 4-wheeler for the trip. I'm *still* hurt! When I told Lyle that I don't think anyone truly cares about me, he said that *he* cares about me! I told him I didn't know if he meant it or not, but it was a nice thing to say. He asked me what I thought he'd have to gain by lying?

I saw my reflection in a freezer door at the grocery store and I *wasn't* repulsed! I didn't see a fat person or a skinny person. Just a person! Definitely a step in the right direction!

Yesterday, I told Lyle that I can't figure out what it is that I'm afraid of. He asked me if I wanted some help and I said, "Yes!" *Abandonment* is the fear I couldn't put a name to. I think he's wrong. I don't sit around worrying that Bill is going to leave me. Although maybe I should? According to Lyle, there are many faces to abandonment. I'll give it some thought.

I'm so **ANGRY!** I've tried to be available to my daughter for the last 4 *hours*. Being a good mom is very important to me, but I'm learning that it's okay to have a little *me* time, so I told her I was going to read for awhile. But, as soon as I sat down and picked up my book, she decided she wanted to visit! Didn't I *just* tell her I was going to read? It's hard for me to speak up anyway and then, when I finally do, it's ignored? I stormed off and I'm sure she could tell I was irritated. I'm really pissed because it seems like she wants me to *fix it* when she's bored. It's my own fault though. I've always assumed responsibility for entertaining her. I've spent so many years trying to make sure she's happy; that *everyone's* happy. I never realized that it's okay to make *me* happy! (At least once in awhile.)

Lyle has been pressuring me to do what's in *my* best interest. Why in the hell is it so hard for me to just be a *normal?* I'm sooooo sick of everything! *Especially ME!* I *hate* me! I'm worthless! I have so much **rage** inside of me! I'm pissed at myself for being so selfish! The anger is rapidly boiling to the surface. It's only a matter of time before I explode! But I can't let anyone know! I can't let them know that I'm totally engulfed with anger. *Where* does this fury come from? This raging fire within? One minute I'm fine and then *wham!* I'm so mad, so furious, that I strike myself over and over and over again, but the anger's still there! It won't go away. I'm afraid to be writing this down because someone might read it! Can I really open up? No! Can I trust anyone? No! It's just me and I **hate** me! I hate me with a passion! I hate me with a vengeance. I am bad to the core! I'm fake to the world! I want to be good, but it's impossible when these rages hit! Such fierce anger! Unprovoked! Unpredictable! I **HATE** ME!

Later—

Found a straight-edge. All better.

At work I feel somewhat accepting of my appearance, but as soon as I'm around my husband, I feel repulsive. For 23 years he's pointed out every attractive woman he sees. And every one of them makes me feel inferior! It seems that they're always tall, big-busted and extremely thin. Why on earth did he marry a short, squatty woman? I asked him once and he said, "Because you were easy." He thought he was being funny. I've always been fragile about feeling overweight and unattractive. My twin sister was the thin, popular, *pretty* twin and all the boys liked *her*, not me. I was 20 when I first met my husband-to-be and I had just be-gun to feel good about my body. My sister and I lived in separate cities by then and I no longer had the daily "visual" reminder that I was the *fat* twin. Before I met Bill, I'd dated several young men who all seemed to find me very attractive! As a result, I had started to think that maybe, just maybe, I wasn't fat after all. But all that I had *gained*, in the form of self-acceptance, disappeared quickly. I know he never meant to hurt me, but oh my God he did. For our entire married life, I feel like I have *never* measured up in my husband's eyes. At the same time, I feel so much anger toward him for treating women like sex-objects! I've grown to *hate* being a woman, or even associated with women in general. I constantly feel the need to apologize for my gender as if I'm somehow less-than by being female.

❧

Feeling down. Uninterested in life. Empty. Numb. Blah. When will it all be over? What's the point? I'm so tired of *trying*. Trying to get better. Trying to figure out who the hell I am? What do I like? What do I believe in? I don't have a fucking clue! Not a fucking clue. I want off the ride. It's not fun anymore.

❧

I told Lyle about the cutting. We talked about the triggers and how I can better manage them by being *aware* of my thoughts and feelings. For example: If I need a time-out from someone who wants a piece of me, I *need* to speak up! Nobody can read my mind! So how can they know what I want? I feel like a bad mother when I don't make myself available, at all times, to my child. Lyle asked, "Why?" I think it stems from the fact that *no one* listened to *me* when I was growing up. I've gone overboard in trying to make sure that Rachel always feels loved; that she matters! But she *already* knows! It's *me* who is still a hurt, lonely little girl.

When Lyle asked me *who* I turned to as a child, for listening, I got choked up. My eyes filled to overflowing and I whispered, "No one." As the tears streamed down my face, I told Lyle that our sessions have been the *only* time, in my entire life, that I've had someone to listen, *actually listen*, to me! This makes me think about how much I *despised* family gatherings when I was growing up. *Everyone* talked at once and *nobody* listened! It was (and is) a lonely feeling. Lyle acknowledged my sadness and anger at not being listened to as a child. He didn't belittle me or tell me I was wrong. Memories, no longer pressed down, emerged from the deep, dark recesses of my mind. Lyle validated my feelings as they rose to the surface. Naked and raw, I laid them out there under the psychiatric microscope. I felt the pain as I put my trust into Lyle… my confidante, my mentor, *my friend.*

What should I look like? When Lyle asked me that question, I started to tell him what Bill wants, and Lyle stopped me with, "What do *you* think you should look like?" I've given a lot of thought to his question. For so long, I've tried to be what *other* people wanted. I don't know *how* to begin discovering what *I* might want.

Bill told me that money is tight. He just bought two fricken gigantic 4-wheelers! And he's telling *me* money is tight? I'm the most frugal person I know! I hardly spend a dime on myself, and he's telling *me* money is tight? Lyle asked me once, *why* I don't spend money on myself. I told him that I don't need material things, but Lyle thinks it's more than that. He believes that I think so little of myself, that I don't believe I'm entitled to enjoy "material things." Maybe he's right.

I really wish I could open up to Bill about my deepest feelings, thoughts and fears. But it's not safe. He's asked me more than once, *why* I don't open up. How do I tell him that the second I begin to share my "demons" with him, I can *feel* his disapproval? It somehow emanates from him; a negative energy if you will. It's hard to explain, but as soon as I start to talk, I feel judged, convicted and hung. Without the jury. Without being heard.

I had a productive session with Lyle. We talked about the little girl in me who still feels hurt and lonely. I told him that I wished I could go back in time to get what I needed. He said that it's possible to get what I needed back then, *now* in the present. He told me about *how* we "replace" people as we grow up. As children, we begin the process of replacing our parents as we develop friendships with our peers. And later, we replace friends with a spouse. And since I can't get the love and validation I so desperately need, from my husband, I'll need to get it from a platonic friend. Or something like that. From Lyle, I receive unconditional acceptance. He's someone I can bounce ideas off of. He validates my feelings, empathizes, and cheers me on. He's truly a light in this darkness.

Today I did things for *me*. I took my beloved dog, Belle, for a ride in the car. (Bill doesn't allow animals in the car.) I spent $20.00 on a much-needed watch for myself. I rented a movie I'd been wanting to see. And last, but not least, I made cookies! I love baking, but since Bill doesn't want sweets in the house, I usually don't bake. I feel like there's hope! I did one more thing for me …I prayed. And afterwards, I sent a note to Lyle that read:

> I said a prayer today.
> A truly heartfelt prayer.
> The first in nearly a year.
> I thanked God for you.

I told Lyle that I'd been thinking about his question regarding what *I* think I should look like. I've been trying to form my *own* opinion and it's more difficult than I had anticipated! He talked to me about the fact that I *don't* see a beautiful woman when I look in the mirror. I told him, once again, that I *hate* it when he uses the word *beautiful* when talking about me! I *hate* it!!! I asked him to please, please *not* use the "B" word with me. He finally agreed, but for a split-second, I thought I saw sadness in his eyes.

⌘

I saw an ad on TV for a women's fitness run, and some other women-thing like shopping. I instantly dismissed the program as worthless because it was about *women*. In my head, being a woman is a *bad* thing; not at all something to be proud of. In the eyes of men, like my husband, women are for one thing only and *that* makes me feel dirty and used.

⌘

Bill and I were lying in bed when I mentioned to him that my mom would've been 69 today. He said, "Wow, has it really been 9 years?" I started crying and it suddenly felt like there were 50 yards between us, instead of a few inches. I wanted so desperately to be held, but I couldn't bring myself to ask for a hug and he didn't offer. How can I be married and yet *so alone*?

⌘

This morning, my husband started listing all of the chores he wanted our daughter to do. There seemed to be no end, so I finally spoke up and light-heartedly asked him to wait, until I left for work, before adding anymore chores to the list. Bill got pissed at me, so I tried to explain my discomfort at such a long chore list for Rachel. It stems from my *own* childhood and the never-ending chores *I* had to do. Bill verbally attacked me with, "This is *not* your childhood!" I agreed and told him that I was only trying to let him know *where* I was coming from. He accused me of spoiling our child *because* of my childhood and that's probably true, but it sure hurt to be cornered like that.

It's definitely *not* safe to be honest with Bill. It always backfires. I'll never be the person he wants me to be. He's forever disappointed in my efforts. I feel emotionally drained. He's so judgmental. I used to worship the ground he walked on. Now I'm just numb. I know that if I were to tell him that he treats me like crap, he'd counter with, "I don't beat you." But, *verbally*, I have been beaten; first by my father and then by my husband. Most of the time it's been subtle, but it hurts just the same.

In looking back at what I wrote yesterday, I feel the need to mention that Bill has done a lot of very kind and thoughtful things for me over the years. I just get so hung up on the rejection I feel, that sometimes it clouds my perception. Although I do think it's accurate to say that my relationship with everyone, including my husband, is superficial. It's not anyone *else's* fault. And, in a way, it's not my fault either. It's that damned borderline personality disorder! I can see how this disorder has affected the people around me, through some of my own behavior. I'm *damaged goods*. I know Bill deserves better. I'm feeling very hopeless about our marriage. I know Bill is frustrated with me.

I was so angry and hurt by Bill's comments yesterday, regarding the chore list for Rachel. I knew that I couldn't *show* my anger, so I directed it at myself in private. Now I have a 7 inch gash on my leg to show for it. I wish I wasn't such a fuck-up. I hate myself more than words can express! Perhaps the scars I leave on my body, paint a fairly clear picture of just how *deep* my hate for me goes. I've never hated anything, or anyone, like I hate myself. I wish I'd never been born. I wish there was a way to cease to exist. Both physically and spiritually. A final end to this person I hate with a vengeance!

I tried to share with my husband, my negative feelings about women. His response: "So you want to be a man?" I tried to gently express my view on how I thought this all started, but before I could even get to the part where Bill, and his Dad, shaped a lot the negativity, he quickly put the blame on *my* Dad. The more I tried to explain, the more he defended his views *and* his behavior. He blamed *me* for being too sensitive. According to him, *normal* women are fine with crude comments about their bodies. Later, when Lyle and I discussed this issue, he asked me about Rachel's appearance. I said she's beautiful, and when I think of her as a young woman, it's the only time I don't feel negatively about women! Maybe I need to start *there* to heal my distorted views?

Late last night I sat alone on the couch, in the dark, feeling completely forsaken. Eventually the tears came as I thought of ending this empty marriage. I cried even more when I thought of how *alone* I felt. There was absolutely *no one* to turn to. And so I sat there, in the dark, feeling the sadness and aching for someone to hold me.

Rachel wanted to go shopping and even though I felt down, I knew I needed to spend some quality time with her. As I was getting ready for our day, I became more and more agitated because I couldn't stand what I saw in the mirror! I grew uglier and fatter by the minute! By the time Rachel and I left, I was in tears. When she was growing up, I made it a point to *never* put down my looks or my weight. (Or hers.) I wanted her to grow up with a healthy self-image. I didn't want her to suffer as I had. Now that she's grown, I've started letting it slip that I hate my body. Hopefully, she doesn't know that I also hate *myself!* I need to keep my mouth shut! I've always prided myself on being a good mom, but lately I've been failing. Sometimes I feel like my poor kid is the *mom* and I'm the child. It shouldn't be this way and yet I can't seem to help myself. My daughter and my husband deserve so much better. I am truly a curse to all who know me.

—◦◦◦—

I've decreased my meds because I just can't be fat anymore! 120 lbs is too much! I did well on my diet today. One day down and a zillion to go! *sigh*

—◦◦◦—

I've been trying to remember what it is that brings me joy. Holidays were fun. I enjoyed writing at one time; mostly poetry. (Although I did have a short essay published about 20 years ago.) I used to enjoy reading. It seems that I've lost interest in *everything*. Lyle has told me that I need to make the decision to get out there and become active in my life; not just sit passively and watch it go by. It's up to me to *choose* happiness, and to *choose* to be a participant in life. No one can force me. The choice is mine. But how can I participate, when *nothing* sounds worth the time or energy?

—◦◦◦—

I've been thinking about the gender issue; my *conditioned* dislike of females. I've started thinking of individual women that I know and I'm realizing that I actually respect, and like, some of them! Maybe *eventually* I'll see women, as a whole, in a positive light!

—◦◦◦—

Lyle and I talked about my stress level at work when we're short-handed. I need to remember that *I am not my job*. I already have a good reputation at work. If I'm late on something, hospital employees who know me will know it's *not* me personally. And even if someone does blame me, *I* need to *not* personalize it. Apparently we all have a certain stress level, and it's our *perception* of the incoming data that can overflow the cup. *We* decide what goes into that cup. *We* can choose to filter-out the less important stuff. And the good news is… *we* can decide what's important and what's *not*! Perception is such a huge factor in everything! And what's awesome about that is that *we* can continue to change our perception by gaining knowledge and awareness! Cool.

⸺⊙⸻

Yesterday didn't go too well. One of the girls from work, and I, had made plans to go out for a drink after her shift. (On my day off.) I'd been looking forward to it all week! In fact, I was so excited about spending some time with my new friend that I woke up at 6am without the alarm! I spent two hours trying on clothes in anticipation of my "girls' night out." Anyway, I was waiting for her to call to let me know what time to meet her. I'd already gone to town to pick up a pizza for Bill and Rachel's dinner, and I'd warned them both that I was going out and I didn't know how late I'd be. Finally, the phone rang and I heard the voice on the other end say, "I'm really sorry, but I can't make it today. I don't feel well." I said, "You're kidding, right?" But, she wasn't. I was crushed. She had also cancelled the time before, but I just thought it was a fluke. Now I know it's *me*. I really thought I'd made a friend. I was devastated. I felt totally abandoned and completely alone.

I knew I needed to somehow pull myself out of the dark place I was rapidly descending into. I knew the quickest way would be a straight-edge, so I locked myself in the bathroom and set out my supplies. I sat on the floor and pulled the razor across my skin, digging the corner of the straight-edge deep into my flesh. I felt nothing. I'm not sure *what* made me stop, but when I did, I was horrified! At first there was no blood, so I could see just how deep I'd gone. The only way I can explain it, is to say that it looked like the parting of *The Red Sea* in the movie *The Ten Commandments*. I could see the fatty tissue all the way to the bone and seconds later, the "sea" came rushing in; only it was blood, and lots of it! I kept whispering, "Oh my God, oh my God, oh my God," as I scrambled to reach the bandages before the blood poured out of the gaping wound. Bright red blood flowed everywhere! The bathroom was a mess. I was a mess. I struggled to pull the skin closed, to stop the blood, but it kept flowing. Of all the times I've cut myself, this was a first! I applied a pressure bandage, but the blood soaked right through it. I knew I needed stitches, but I couldn't let the hospital personnel know what I'd done! Surely I'd be locked up! So I just sat on the floor, rocking back and forth, while putting pressure on the laceration and chanting, "Oh my God, oh my God, oh my God." I was scared, and I didn't know what to do, so I called Lyle, but I got his voice mail. I didn't leave a message. I used my cell phone, but it doesn't leave a name on the Caller-ID, so Lyle wouldn't know it was me who had called. Eventually, the bleeding stopped and I calmed down.

A few hours later, Lyle called without knowing *who* he was calling. When I answered, he said, "This is Lyle. Did you need something?" I let him know it was me. I told him the crisis had passed and that I was fine. I don't think he believed me because he said he would call me again in an hour, and he did. I told him I was fine and that I would talk to him at our regular visit the following week. He said that wasn't okay. He wanted to see me sooner, as in *an emergency visit.* I tried to assure him that I was truly okay, and an earlier appointment was *not* necessary. Finally I told him I'd call him tomorrow. He asked me what time and I told him 1pm.

I called Lyle as promised. When I told him about the *trigger* for this self-injury episode, I said I knew it was stupid to be upset over something so minor. He said it wasn't stupid. Then he talked a little bit about how the borderline personality disorder can warp my perception in such a way, that even a *minor* event, such as the *perceived rejection* I'd experienced, can be blown into something too big for me to deal with. Someday, in the future, I'll be able to handle disappointments in a healthy manner. Hopefully that day will come soon, because a self-injury like the latest one could unintentionally lead to death. I guess the fear I felt was a good thing, since it points to the possibility that I might not want to die after all.

Bill asked if I was okay. He'd overheard me talking to Lyle last night on the phone. I decided to let him in on my shameful secret. I told him about the cutting and how I've used it as a coping mechanism for nearly 30 years. He was speechless, so I kept talking. I tried to explain what borderline personality disorder is, and how it factors into this particular behavior. He was repulsed and he didn't try to hide his disgust with me. When I asked him why he couldn't have any compassion for me, he said it was because I had hidden too much from him! He felt cheated. I reminded him that I had *tried,* over the years, to share some of the unpleasant parts of me, but each time I tried, I was belittled. (First by my Dad and then by my husband.) On a brighter note, he did ask me where he could go to find help for families of people like me. *People like me.*

I called Lyle promptly at 1:00pm. I assured him I was fine, but he said that he worries about me. *He worries about me!* Oh my God, someone cares enough to *worry* about *me!* Of course I didn't let on that I'd been touched by his comment. Instead, I nonchalantly remarked that I was glad that *someone* did. I'm actually very embarrassed by this whole incident! Even though I've been starved for attention for as long as I can remember, it's quite unsettling to be the recipient of such overt concern. (Although I *am* very grateful to Lyle for the compassionate and non-judgmental way he has of handling me; both in a crisis situation and during regular sessions.)

I saw Lyle today. We talked about *why* I did what I did last week. I felt tearful when I told him about how lonely I really am! (And yet, at the same time, I find it hard to be with people!) Lyle pointed out that it was very possible that the friend who cancelled on me really was sick. He told me that the borderline personality disorder causes me to *read too much into things*. He also said that some of my emotional pain, right now, isn't from last week's incident. It's due to the choices I'm facing regarding my marriage. He insisted that I deserve to be cherished by my husband. *That* will never happen.

Lyle also talked about how there is beauty in everyone. He said that I just happen to be the "B" word on the outside as well as the inside. I disagreed. He insisted that a day will come when I will look into the mirror and see a beautiful woman looking back. Why must he keep saying that? It's *never* going to happen! I feel so hopeless about all of this. Lyle believes that I *can* get better, but it'll take time *and* hard work. He reminded me that it takes *years* to *undo* the damage of borderline; usually between 3 and 5. God that's an awfully long road! I don't know if I can do this anymore.

Yesterday, Lyle told me that whenever the voice in my head starts to tell me I'm worthless, I need to talk back to it! (Maybe not *out loud* if there are people around.) He promised me that the voice *will* go away! Eventually. I just need to be persistent! He wanted to know *when* the negative thoughts, about my looks, began. I think it was about the time my twin and I became teenagers. At one point, Lyle asked, "Who do you trust?" I paused before saying that I trusted *him*. He asked, "Who else?" I could feel the tears welling up in my eyes. He gently asked me again, "Who *else* do you trust?" My answer was barely audible as I mumbled, "No one. Absolutely no one." And then the damn broke. God, I hate Kleenex!

Bill gave me a list of chores he wants me to do today and I'm really pissed off about it! I hated the dreaded *chore list* when I was a kid, and I really resent getting one from my husband! I'm not his fucking kid! And besides, I have my *own* list of chores I wanted to do. I don't need one from him too.

I've been thinking about Bill's lack of compassion for me. And his anger. I hit rock-bottom last January and when I really *needed* him, he wasn't there for me. I was ready to *die*. I didn't want to hurt anyone. I just wanted the incessant pain to stop. The mental anguish of a crazed mind tortured me daily. To have had my husband hold me, and to say that he was there for me, would have meant so much! I felt terribly alone before the suicide attempt, and even more so afterward. I'm very disheartened that my own husband couldn't be there for me emotionally.

Lyle thinks I'm getting stronger. He asked me if I had self-injured lately and I proudly told him that I hadn't. He said I'm done with that now. I don't have to direct anger at myself anymore. I don't know if that's true, but if it is... maybe I *am* getting better; becoming whole. I told Lyle that I went to a party with Bill last week and I actually thought I looked pretty nice. Bill didn't comment on my appearance, but that's okay. It's *my* opinion of me that matters. Wow! I just realized that if *my* opinion matters to me, then I *must* be someone of worth. I *am* getting better!

I've been messing with my dose again. I just don't want to feel blah anymore. I've noticed that everything seems really loud lately. I'm also sleeping less and not missing it. I'll keep tabs on any manic symptoms that may creep up. If the noise and *seeing things* gets worse, I'll up my dose.

While I was talking to Lyle today, about trying to accept my extra 10 lbs, I accidentally spilled out my ultimate goal weight. I said something like, "For goodness sake, I'm a 43 year old woman! I don't *need* to weigh 92 lbs." As soon as I realized what I'd said, I tried to back track, but it was useless; Lyle *knew*.

At the grocery store this morning, a man motioned for me to go first as we pushed our shopping carts towards the exit. I said thank you and he said, "I know you walk faster." When I looked at him with surprise, he explained that he had seen me "racing through the store." Maybe I really *do* need to slow down? (I should probably mention that I nearly rear-ended a vehicle twice today.) Maybe decreasing my meds *wasn't* a good idea. I feel shaky, irritable and physically uncomfortable. I can't focus or concentrate on anything! It's affecting my work, but I don't want to go back to feeling so blah.

My daughter told me that her friend, Ben, was nominated for the Homecoming Court and he had to write an essay. It was to be read aloud, at the pep assembly, by one of their teachers. Ben wanted to include a sentence that stated, "Rachel's mom has got it going on." The teacher vetoed that statement as well as, "Rachel's mom is hot." Finally an agreement was reached with, "Rachel's mom is very attractive." I thought it was very flattering at the time. But later, as I looked at myself in the mirror, I felt disgusted with my reflection! The longer

I looked, the more repulsed I became! The disgust was overwhelming! Self-hate oozed from every inch of me. How could I have, even for one minute, accepted Ben's wonderful compliment? What was I thinking? I'm not attractive! Who am I trying to kid? Oh my god, I actually believed that a teenage boy found me attractive! Who do I think I am? As I continued to look in the mirror, I grew more and more agitated. I became more and more repulsed by what was looking back at me. The self-hate overflowed; releasing with it unbridled anger. I couldn't hold back any longer! I began to strike myself. No one else was home as I screamed at my reflection, "You are stupid and worthless and ugly! You're *beyond* repulsive!" I punched my face and my head and my chest. Finally, the hitting slowed down and I dissolved into a heap on the bathroom floor. I was worn out, completely spent, but still trying to strike myself. Thoughts of "cutting" started to run through my head. I halfheartedly tried to stop them, but the anger at myself was all-consuming. I climbed up off the floor and I started screaming all over again. As I once again looked into the mirror, I began wailing, "I *hate* you!" Over and over I cried out, "I hate you! I hate you! I hate you!" I yelled until my throat was raw and no more words would come. With tears streaming down my face, I gathered my cutting supplies and began the process of calming myself down. In the only way I knew how.

I AM SO FUCKING PISSED RIGHT NOW!!!!!! I ALREADY HAD PLANS FOR TODAY AND BILL MADE ME CHANGE THEM BECAUSE HE CALLED THE FURNACE PEOPLE AND ASKED THEM TO COME OUT *TODAY!* LIKE MY PLANS AREN'T IMPORTANT! HE CAN'T BE HERE, SO I HAVE TO CHANGE *MY* FUCKING PLANS!!! HE TOLD ME IT'D ONLY TAKE A FEW MINUTES, BUT THE FUCKING FURNACE PEOPLE HAVEN'T EVEN SHOWED UP YET! THEY'RE OVER TWO HOURS LATE! MY DAY OFF IS FUCKING RUINED!!!!

NO ONE GIVES A SHIT ABOUT MY FEELINGS!!! NOT A SHIT! NOT A FUCKING SHIT!!!

I feel so sad. And so very alone. I'm realizing that I'm in a loveless marriage. Bill's admitted that he has no compassion for me. None at all. I really feel like it's something I *need* right now. *Especially now.* I'm going through so much upheaval, in my mind, as I try to figure out who I am and what I want. It's emotionally draining! Relearning *how* to think; unlearning all that was harmful; building new and healthy pathways in my brain. It's all extremely exhausting! I really need the support of my husband, but it's *not* going to happen. I used to treat Bill like a king; but after years of being treated as "less than," I'm completely empty. I have nothing left to give. Nothing. I know it's not entirely the fault of one person. Maybe it's no one's fault at all. It's just what it is.

I drove to the State Park yesterday and parked by the water. I sat in my car and cried my eyes out! I felt absolutely alone. I still do today. I may be married, but I am *alone.* When I told my husband that I crave emotional intimacy with him, he admitted that he's incapable of filling any kind of *emotional* need. I told him that it makes me sad that he can't offer *true* intimacy. He was completely indifferent in his reply. Apparently *empathy* is something he's *not* capable of either.

At my session today, I admitted to Lyle that I've really wanted to lose 25 lbs. *Not* 10. He said, "Thank you!" He admitted that he had suspected as much, but he was waiting for *me* to own up to it. Lyle knows *more* about me than any other human being. I can tell him *anything* because he doesn't judge me. He's truly there to help me.

I'm still not taking the full dose of my meds. Maybe, when I get down to 112 lbs, I'll up the dose. Maybe. Lyle and I talked about something he referred to as "norming" and how it's human nature to *want* to fit in. (To be *normal*.) I think it applies to weight too. When I'm feeling somewhat normal, mentally, I start accepting that I'm *fine* at this higher weight. I even start to realize that I don't want to be too thin or too fat. But *then*, when I get mentally *unhealthy*, I once again find myself wanting to lose weight! Good insight!

I'm supposed to try a new exercise in learning to accept my body *as it is*. My new assignment is to stand in front of a full-length mirror, naked, and think positive thoughts about what I see. Gonna get an "F" on this one!

Bill asked me to shop for him tomorrow. I reminded him that I had offered to shop for him *today* and he had said that he didn't need anything. I told him that I'd already made plans and wouldn't be available to run his errands. I decided *not* to change my plans, to fit *his* schedule, and the world didn't come to an end! I'm finally developing a "backbone!" My needs and wants *are* important! To *me* anyway.

I think I'm cycling up a little. Been feeling really good; maybe *too* good! I also had a weird experience at work today. The loud-speaker at the hospital plays a short lullaby whenever a baby is born, so I didn't think anything of it when I heard the music playing. But then… it wouldn't stop! It played over and over again! I considered calling maintenance, but I figured that they already knew about the problem, so I decided to wait it out. As I waited for someone to fix it, the lullaby continued to play and it was driving me crazy! Finally I started complaining to my co-worker about the incessant music! By the confused look on her face, I realized that the "music" was all in my head! And I don't mean like when you get a song *stuck* in your head. I mean it was *really* playing. But not really. God I am crazy.

Energy level continues to climb. Been feeling really good lately! I'm in constant motion! I love it when I feel like this! I can get so much done! In a short period of time. And the other good thing is that I don't need as much sleep! Time isn't wasted on slumber!

Didn't take meds. Don't want meds. Can't sleep. Socks tight. Bed hard. Furnace loud. Thoughts racing. Music distracting. What music? Pacing. Can't sit still. Need to be drugged. Don't wanna be drugged. What the hell do I do? Love the energy! Too much energy! Hate the energy! Need to be up. Can't be down. Hosted party. Disconnected. Lost in the crowd.

November 2006 thru January 2007

I'm confused. Bill has done a few things lately that make me think that he *is* trying. He seemed genuinely concerned when a friend stood me up. He took my advice about one of our bills. And he actually claimed to like my extra weight! I'm having a tough time with that one though, because he's *always* made it clear that he likes me thin; the thinner, the better. Is he changing because *I'm* changing? I'm so damn confused! Is it too late for us? I've been treated as "less than" for so long. Is love and respect between us even possible? The love and adoration I once held for him has all but died. I don't know if I can get the feelings back. I wish I could talk to my husband about this. But before I do, I need to make sure that this isn't all just a product of my unstable mind. By that I mean, my perception of his actions *now,* and previously. Everything is colored by the borderline issues. I don't want to hurt him. He's not a bad person. It's just that I feel so *empty.*

I think I'm beginning to stabilize at this lower dose. Or maybe I'm just between poles? Even if this is just the calm before the next storm, I'm willing to take the chance. I'm finally losing weight and I don't want to stop!

Therapy has helped me to see that I am an intelligent, capable woman who deserves to be treated with dignity and respect. I'm no longer willing to let anyone treat me like a second-class citizen. But how do I *erase* the years of damage? How do I forget the hurt? Lyle keeps insisting that I deserve to be loved and cherished. Cherished? *That* might be going too far.

The weight continues to come off. Yeah! My energy level is through the roof and I'm in constant motion. I got scolded at work today for not staying "put" when my boss asked me to watch the front office. I *hate* being stuck in that chair staring at a computer! I'd rather be running all over the hospital, socializing with the patients and the staff. I'm really good at drawing blood *and* public relations! One of our regional managers even complimented me recently, by referring to me as an "ambassador for the lab."

My boss asked me about my medication. I know he's trying to be helpful, but it really pisses me off! Being friendly and energetic should be considered a *good* thing! So why is he trying to spoil my fun? (I never did answer his question.) I've actually been thinking about stopping the Seroquel completely. I'm doing just fine. I really don't think I need it anymore. I know that Lyle, Dr. Stoune, Bill *and* my boss would disagree, but it's *my* life! Besides, everyone has mood swings to some degree; mine just happen to be a little more severe, and that's okay! I don't want to be drugged anymore. I'm fine just the way I am.

I'm so fucking pissed! I haven't been able to sleep without the god-damned Seroquel! It fucking pisses me off! This whole fucking life pisses me off! This whole god-damned bipolar crap pisses me off! Everything pisses me off! I'm fucking sick of work. I'm fucking sick of *life*. I'm fucking sick of *me*!

When I started the car this morning, a song was playing on the radio. It was called, "You are loved." As I listened to the words, I started to bawl like a baby. The song said something about being loved and not giving up; that you just want to be heard; to be understood. *Giving up,* is exactly what I was doing!

I need the meds. Damn it.

I told Lyle that it seems like my husband has been nicer lately and it has me confused. I'd grown used to the idea of going it alone, but if Bill really is changing in the way he treats me, I can't very well leave him. But *how* do I get the feelings back? Lyle said that if Bill is truly willing to change *and* to stick with it, then my thoughts about him will eventually change too; for the better. Our feelings are the direct result of our thoughts. Sooooo… if I develop good thoughts towards my husband, it's "possible" to regain good feelings. That's the theory anyway. Whatever I choose to do, I know it's in my best interest to continue with counseling, journaling and taking my meds. It's the only way I'm ever going to heal myself. No one else can do this for me. Embracing wellness is tough, but I'm ready to believe that it's something I deserve and something worth fighting for. I'm beginning to think that maybe, just maybe, I *am* worth the space I take up!

I've started overeating again. (7,000 calories yesterday.) *Why* do I do it? I *could* blame it on the medication, but I think it's just me. Or maybe... it's my frustration with Bill? He gets so inpatient with me about *everything*! He's impossible to please. And when he hurts my feelings, he refuses to apologize! Why is it so hard for him to say he's sorry? I say it all the time! One of the goals in therapy, as I become stronger emotionally, is that I'll apologize less and less while becoming more vocal about standing up for myself.

A few days ago, as I tried to adjust the volume, I accidentally changed the channel on the TV while Bill was watching it. After he gave me a dirty look, I told him to "chill" while I hurriedly changed the channel back. He accused me of being just like my dad; throwing out "zingers" or "put downs." I explained to him that it's a *defense* mechanism that I fall back on, when I'm not being treated with respect. I told him that as I get healthier, I'll probably do it less, because I won't feel the need to prove myself. It will be *my* opinion of me that matters! If Bill can learn to love, appreciate and value me, then there's hope for our marriage. On the other hand, if he can't treat me with respect, kindness and consideration, then I'd rather live alone.

Today I had to say good-bye to my beloved dog, Belle. I held her in my arms as she died. I know she's free from pain now. But mine, at losing her, is just beginning. I pray that she and our other dog, Kit, are together. They both brought me so much joy and so much love. I'm sure that God must have a place for them. Dogs are a lot better (than people) at loving unconditionally. If anyone belongs in Heaven, *they* do!

Feeling really agitated! I have that awful "jumping out of my skin" feeling. I'm physically restless and jumpy. I keep hearing and seeing things that aren't there! What's *wrong* with me? Maybe I'm not eating enough, or maybe I need a higher dose of the dreaded drug? Or both? I wouldn't eat at work today, but I couldn't let anyone know; couldn't let them know that I'm fasting to make up for the previous binge. I was offered food by several people, in different departments throughout the hospital, but I always had the same lie ready, "Thanks, but I just ate." If they were really pushy, I'd load up a plate just to get them off my back. And then later, I'd dump the food in the garbage and stack some trash on top of it.

Some of my co-workers have started commenting on my "thinness" and it's bugging me! A lot! Everyone seems to think I'm getting too thin. Except for my husband of course. He's loving it! He's even told me that I'm *on my way*. (To thinness.)

I've learned so much from Lyle this past year. I'm speaking up for myself and it's truly making a difference! Even my husband is beginning to treat me with respect. With all of the insight I've gained, I feel like I'm ready to fully embrace wellness. Maybe even stop the meds. I think it's time to talk to Lyle about ending therapy.

I've been a total glutton today! I'm so disgusted with myself! What the hell is wrong with me?

I'm feeling frustrated with my family. There are so many chores and they don't lift a finger to help. They probably would *if* I'd ask, but why should I have to ask? Why can't they just see what needs to be done, and then do it? Maybe the reason I binge so often, is to stuff down my feelings. Maybe it's a way to calm my anger *or* maybe the overeating is just another way for me to abuse myself.

Rachel brought her CD player to my room this morning because Josh Groban was singing "Oh Holy Night." She knows I love that song! I thought it was really sweet of her!

Today I was thinking about how I don't seriously consider suicide anymore. But instead of feeling good about it, I felt uneasy! For so long, *suicide* has been in the back of my mind as a "way out." But *now* it's not an option anymore, and for some reason it's leaving me feeling anxious and apprehensive. For my entire adult life I've been mentally unhealthy and *now* as I'm gaining *stability* (and a place in the *driver's* seat) I'm finding myself completely unnerved; terrified actually! I'm having to let go of those fantasies of being *rescued* from this life. With Lyle's guidance, I've gained the insight it takes to accept responsibility for my life; to *stop* being a child. Here I am, a 43 year old woman, and I'm just now growing up. It's embarrassing to realize how immature I've been. I suppose I could be angry that the road to adulthood had so many roadblocks, but really... it's just kind of sad. I remember being a little girl and wanting so badly for someone to save me; someone to love me. I *still* want that, but I know that *I am* the *only* one who is responsible for *me*. It's no one else's job to make me feel loved and wanted and valued. It's entirely up to me.

I talked to Lyle about my fear of being in the driver's seat; of being responsible for my own life. He reminded me of how scary it can be when we are first learning how to drive. Being in the driver's seat can cause anxiety and fear *until* we gain experience and become more comfortable. Right now I'm in the driver's seat of "the car of my choosing," and according to Lyle that should be exciting! (Albeit scary.)

Lyle asked me about the cutting. I told him that I'd been tempted once, during the previous two weeks, but I chose to look at the situation in a logical manner. First of all, I decided that I didn't want anymore scars to deal with. And second, I remembered that feelings, or in this case a lack of feelings, would soon pass. I realized that I could weather the storm, or numbness, *without* resorting to hurting myself! Lyle and I are both very pleased with my progress.

I've started to think of how much I'll have to offer my fellow human beings, once I'm healed and able to love myself. I'm learning that the only way to *truly* love another is to first love myself. I'm not there yet, but I believe the day is coming. I know that with self-love, I'll be able to love *unconditionally*. And isn't that what love is about? *Choosing* to love others, even with their less-than-desirable traits! (Mine included.) I know that self-love will afford me the patience I'll need, to give love freely and without condition; to love my family and friends just as they are. Ah, and to love *me* just as I am!

When I first got up this morning, Bill asked me if I would help him for a minute, but only after I'd had a chance to have my coffee. I was shocked that he didn't insist that I help him immediately and, because of it, I chose to help him right then! I think we were both pleasantly surprised. His consideration for *me* made me *want* to help him. Later, when I started to clean the kitchen, Rachel told me to go relax in the other room and she'd clean up! Wow! I think my counseling sessions are affecting the whole family.

I spent my lunch break visiting with Bill instead of eating. When I told him I was skipping lunch, he said that I *need* to eat even if it means gaining weight! He asked me if I'd had trouble sleeping lately and when I said yes, he asked if I was still taking my meds. I told him I'd reduced the dose so I could lose a few pounds. I reminded him that he likes me skinny, but he said that he didn't want me skinny *at my expense.* So what exactly does that mean?

My temper started to flare today at work. I wondered whether it was the borderline or the bipolar that was behind it. I decided that it was more of a borderline issue. I reminded myself that I've come too far to fall back, into my old habits, and the self-talk worked! I've had a ton of energy lately. Feeling a bit scattered. I literally ran all over the hospital today and I know that the "exercise" helped immensely in keeping me calm.

Lyle and I talked about building new pathways in my brain, and how the Rx can help with the process. We also talked about my right to be treated like a lady. If Bill and his buddies want to engage in foul language and vulgar behavior, then they can do it when I'm *not* around. I'm finally beginning to value myself enough to set boundaries!

I've been going non-stop for a few days now and I find myself wanting to skip my medicine so I won't have to sleep at all. But, as Lyle would say, that's not in my "best interest." So I'm going to keep taking the damn things. It's well after midnight and my mind won't shut off! I'm out on the overstuffed couch, because my bed felt hard again. It irritates Bill when I won't stay in bed, but I can't help it! Even with meds, I know I will still have symptoms from time to time.

Wired at work today! Extremely hyper! Nearly ran into co-workers several times! I think Dr. Taylor gets really annoyed with my "chipmunk on speed" behavior, but I just can't help it sometimes.

Rachel and I were making candy in the kitchen. It got too warm, so I tried to open the window. It was stuck, as usual, so I climbed up onto the counter to get a better angle. I was getting really irritated because we paid good money to have the window installed and it's *never* worked right! When I finally jumped off the counter, I hit my knee on the way down. It really hurt, and by *then* I was already filled with rage due to the damned window! I didn't want the day with Rachel to be ruined. So I kept calm on the *outside*. But, on the *inside*, I could feel the agitation building! I knew I needed a quick fix in order to truly calm myself. So, once again, I was off to find the straight-edge.

I've been a royal pig for three straight days. I am soooooooooooo disgusted and angry with myself! How can I stuff that much crap into my face? At last count, I was up to 14,000 calories for this latest binge. I am such a fucking loser! I feel so alone. So completely alone. I hate myself beyond words. Lyle thinks I'm getting better, but I'm wondering if he's just saying that... so I'll hurry up and get out of his life. Then again, maybe I've got him fooled? Who am I trying to kid anyway; thinking that I can be worth loving? Lyle almost had me convinced, when he insisted that I deserve to be loved *and* cherished by my husband. I don't deserve anything but the hell I've created! I'm feeling an overpowering urge to harm myself....

I told Lyle that some of the male nurses have flirted with me and it makes me uncomfortable, because I assume that all men only want *one thing*. I think I was practically boasting when I told him about the ER nurse who playfully grabbed me by the waist. I felt like I had been "hit on." But Lyle said that most flirting is harmless and actually *healthy*! My fucked-up mind has me convinced that *any* attention, from men, means they want *sex*. Bill's attitude about women has really screwed with me. So may times, over the years, I've said things that were completely *innocent* and Bill immediately turned them into something dirty! I've stopped using certain words, or phrases, just so he won't say anything nasty. I don't know if I can ever reclaim my innocence. Just being a woman makes me feel unworthy. I'm really embarrassed that I told Lyle about the men flirting with me and how I actually thought it meant they wanted to sleep with me! Now it sounds like I think I'm *hot*, which I don't think at all. I sounded so foolish! And *needy*! God, I *am* needy!

Something is really bothering me. When I told Lyle about how *suicide* is always in the back of my mind as an option, or a *way out*, he seemed to imply that I might end up in Hell! Doesn't he realize that I'm *already* in Hell? I'm so frickin tired of everything! Sometimes I think I've come so far… Then again, I wonder if I ever traveled at all? I feel so alone.

I blew up at work again. I hadn't had lunch and I was feeling shaky, but I thought I could hold off for a few more minutes, so I went to out-patient surgery to draw a patient. When I got back, I found that all of the employees had taken off for a meeting and I was left to take care of the *entire* hospital by myself! Julie, bless her heart, came back to check on me. When she saw how crazy it was, she said she'd be right back. She went to the meeting to get us some more help, but the boss made her *stay* instead! He's such a prick!

By the time everyone came back, an hour and a half later, I was ready to explode! And I did! I feel sick about it now, because I blew up at the wrong person. Jim, our assistant supervisor, asked me how it went and I let him have it; complete with a peppering of the "f" word! And to top it off, Jim had *students* with him! Now I feel ashamed and em-barrassed by my behavior. I am so fucking fucked up! I thought I was doing well enough, through therapy that it would be okay to reduce the meds. I had even gone as far as to make an appt, with Dr. Stoune, to discuss a schedule for reducing the Seroquel. And now this set back, and the humiliation of it all, has me feeling hopeless once again.

I went out to dinner tonight with my husband. I tried to look nice for him. I even wore high heels, but he didn't say a word about my appear-ance. I don't understand. I've told him that, although I don't like the "vulgar" compliments, I would *still* like to hear that I look nice. I guess if I'm not willing to accept *crude* compliments, then I won't be getting *any* compliments. Sigh.

I just got done with my therapy session. Lyle, once again, asked me to call him if I ever feel like cutting. And, once again, I told him I can't. He said that when I'm *numb*, I'm probably actually *sad* and that it would be healthy to *cry* at these times. If I were to call him, he could help me get in touch with those feelings of sadness and then I could *cry*. (Instead of cutting.) He also said that he *should* make me promise *not* to cut, and to call him instead, but he knows that I can't keep that promise. Not yet. Lyle told me that there are therapists who refuse to continue seeing their patients, if they won't stop cutting. Lyle said that's not a healthy way to deal with people who suffer from borderline. When the subject of group therapy was brought up, I vehemently declined! Lyle said the invitation will remain open, but I know that I will *never* be a part of group therapy. This is just too personal to share with complete strangers! Opening up to Lyle has been hard enough.

It seems like I'm such a downer when I'm in Lyle's office. I'm glad he's trained to *not* get pulled in when patients are depressed. I forgot to mention that when I shared with Lyle, how *abandoned* I'd felt at work the other day when everyone went to the meeting, he brought up an important point. "Normal" people would not feel abandoned by what had happened. They might be angry, and rightfully so, but they wouldn't feel *abandoned.* (Good old borderline at work.)

I acknowledged to Lyle, that there are a lot of people I could turn to when I need help. The trouble, of course, lies with *me*. It's extremely difficult for me to ask *anyone* for *anything*! I feel bad about being so negative with Lyle yesterday. I should have kept it light; especially since it's the week before Christmas.

I decided to try something out at work today. Because I'm such a private person and it's hard for me to let anyone *in*, I decided to break out of my shell a little; maybe even *stop* wearing the mask! So today, when I went to the CCU for a draw, I decided to be *real* and genuine; to *not* be fake. One of the nurses asked me how I was and before I could answer, she asked me how I *really* was. So I admitted to her that I'd been having a kind of "off" day. Her reaction was sweet, but it drew *way too much attention* to me! She hugged me and said that she hoped I'd feel better soon. This, in turn, made the *other* CCU employees look up. One of them asked me what was wrong and I quickly stated that *nothing* was wrong! I was embarrassed and couldn't get out of there quick enough! So much for being true to my feelings.

Appt with Dr. Stoune went well. He asked me *who* I could talk to about the bipolar issues. (In addition to Lyle and him.) I said nobody really, so he made sure that I had his cell phone number, as well as Lyle's. Dr. Stoune also warned me to keep an eye out for "isolating behavior" because it can be a sign of depression. We also talked about the network, or support system, we really do have *if* only we will ask! He told me that I have such a strong soul. We talked about how we both struggle with wondering if we're doing the right thing as we go about helping people through our work. We both want to serve in the best way we can; including the spiritual part of healing. At the end of our visit, he told me that I was a joy to be around! Such a sweet man indeed. He gave me a hug and wished me a Happy Holiday. After the appointment, I felt the need to call Lyle and wish *him* a Merry Christmas, so I did just that. I didn't get to talk to him directly, but I did leave a message on his machine. I also told him that I was fine, and I apologized for my earlier attitude.

❧

I'm feeling better mentally. I can see how my down mood was so "borderline." And even though it's hard for me to know *where* the bipolar stops and the borderline begins, I'm realizing it's *not* that important. It doesn't matter *which* disorder is responsible for the mood shift. What *is* important, is taking my meds, keeping a regular sleep schedule, eating right and using the skills I've gained through therapy. I also need to continue with the counseling and journaling. I may never know the *exact cause* of a particular mood shift, but that's okay. It's how I *choose* to respond that matters.

❧

I've decided on a New Year's Resolution. I want to learn *how* to fully "embrace wellness." I know it *sounds* easy, but for me... Well, it's just not that simple. I've been praying to God for help with this endeavor, because I honestly don't know if I'm ready yet. I *want* to be well. At least I *think* I do! Is it possible... that maybe I'm actually *afraid* of being well? For some reason I'm having a hard time *letting go* of the borderline! It's been "a part of me" for so long that I don't know *how* to say good-bye to it.

❧

I saw an old friend at a party tonight. I hadn't seen her in 20 years! We reminisced about the old days. It made me really sad when I realized how in love I *was* with my husband back then. A flood of memories came crashing in. I could barely hold back the tears as I acknowledged the truth to myself. My loving feelings were *gone!* Lyle has assured me, through counseling, that if I *act* loving towards Bill, then *eventually* the feelings should return. But tonight's *blast from the past* reminded me of all that I've lost. I don't see *how* it can ever be reclaimed.

We had company for a few days and I am in desperate need of some alone time. Bill hinted that he'd like me to help him at the store, but I stood my ground and told him that I needed some down time. Besides, he has Rachel to help him. I've been enjoying the day by myself, but occasionally I've felt some *anxiety*. It wasn't about being alone. It was about *how fast* my alone time was going by! I don't know *why* I find it so frikkin hard to be with people, especially my own family! I feel constantly judged when I'm with them, but I don't know if it's a *false* perception or if it really *is* happening!

I've been wondering what it is that I truly want. Not just regarding the big stuff, but *everything*! What do I *really* want to wear? What do I really want to do with my free time? How do I really want to look? For so long, I've worried about what everyone else thought of me and what they wanted from me. For years I've tried to please everyone! Now, suddenly it seems, I want to know what it is that *Terresa* wants? *Terresa* matters! I want to do what's in *Terresa's* best interest! I want to take care of her; of *me*! (God knows that no one else will.) I need to make whatever changes are necessary to be true to myself. It's like a light bulb just went on. *Hello!* I'm a person with feelings! Not someone's doormat. I matter damn it! Now I just need to figure out who I am and what it is that I want out of life.

I had a nightmare last night. Bill said I was hyperventilating and thrashing about. I dreamed that a female therapist was beating me up! She looked like my first mom. I even called her mom, as I begged her to stop hitting me! In the dream, she gave me some writing assignments that she planned to read after their completion. I told her that I couldn't be totally honest if I knew she was going to read the entries.

She started hitting me and tearing apart my house. (Where the counseling was taking place.)

Just a few hours before this nightmare, I had read that dysfunctional families will tell you it's *okay* to talk about your feelings, but *then* when you do, they will belittle or criticize you! Wow! As I continued to be *beaten* in the dream, I screamed at the top of my lungs! Soon I was pinned down by someone's foot. In reality, my husband was holding me down as he tried to wake me!

I'm guessing that this dream is telling me, that at some point in my childhood, it wasn't *safe* to share my true feelings. Just 12 hours before this dream, my mother left my house after an 18 hour visit! I know she never meant to hurt me, or make me feel bad when I was little, but inadvertently it happened anyway. I believe it has a lot to do with her *own* childhood. She wasn't allowed to share her feelings either.

My New Year's Resolution, with God's help, is twofold: I want first to embrace *wellness* and second to embrace *life*!

I was busy all morning running errands and shopping for groceries. When I got home around 2pm, Bill asked me to fix him lunch! Why in the hell can't he fix it himself? He and Rachel always expect *me* to wait on them hand and foot! It really pisses me off! Sometimes I think I'm going to explode if I hear "I'm hungry" one more time! In retrospect, I can see that I should have just said, "No." Why is it so hard for me to do the right thing? I thought about hurting myself, in response to my angry feelings, but I was able to refrain! I guess it's all about "baby steps" at this point.

It's weird to think, that at this time last year, I was entirely consumed with thoughts of wanting to die! I listened repeatedly to sad, haunting songs with lyrics about suicide. *Now* I'm listening to upbeat music about hope, love and *not* giving up. I'm getting better!

Good session today. When Lyle said something about me being a beautiful woman, I *didn't* cry! Heck, I didn't even flinch! We also talked about how I need to be true to *me*. For so long, I've been a people-pleaser. I've tried to fit in and felt bad when I didn't; like trying to force myself to be an extrovert like Bill and failing miserably. He's "*on*" twenty four hours a day! He's in constant contact with dozens of friends! That's great for him, but I'm more of an introvert. I *don't want* to socialize every night. (Or even every week!) Lyle told me there's a happy medium in there somewhere. I can say yes to *some* of the invitations, but I don't have to say yes to all of them. It's perfectly okay to let Bill be the extrovert that he is, as long as he respects my need for alone time. Lyle has told me over and over again, that I need to remember to do whatever's in *my* best interest. And of course it's *in my best interest* to go out with my husband once in awhile. It's good for our marriage *and* for our friends to see that Bill still has a wife! And socializing *is* positive for me as long as it's not too often; otherwise, it just becomes stressful.

I have the next few hours all to myself with nothing that I *have* to do! The chores can wait. Nobody's home. It's just me, myself and I. Aaahhh!

I'm feeling a little anxious about tomorrow's *one year anniversary* of my overdose. I don't know what to expect. What feelings might be evoked by this milestone? I wrote a poem earlier today that makes me think I'll be just fine. But I'm still nervous! I called and left a message for Lyle, stating that I wanted to share a poem with him to mark the anniversary. I told him that I'd just leave it on his desk if he was busy. I really hope I get to see him, if only for a minute. It's because of *him*, that I'm still here! He gives me hope. So it's only fitting that I'd want to share this commemoration with my trusted mentor.

Today was awesome! I got to Lyle's office just *seconds* before his next patient walked in! The timing couldn't have been better. Before I left my house, I'd started to tackle one last chore when suddenly I felt the need to leave right that moment! I immediately stopped what I was doing, grabbed my coat, and ran out the door. (I have no idea of *what* possessed me to run out like that.) Anyway, Lyle's next appointment walked in *right behind me!* He motioned for her to go on into his office and then turned to me. I gave him the poem and eagerly awaited his response. He put on his glasses and began to read:

Instead...

It was a year ago tomorrow
That I sat in ill-repose
With a plan to end it all
Would it be a lethal dose

I was lost and all alone
With the torture in my head
A vision of my future
Left me wanting death

I couldn't see the light
With the darkness closing in
The love and peace I craved
Were lost within the din

So I took a leap of faith
And swallowed all those pills
And prayed to God to take me
But that was not His will

Instead He sent me Angels
To guide me back to health
Through this long and arduous journey
That has brought me so much wealth

A wealth of friends and knowledge
And Blessings from above
I'm thankful for this chance
To be an instrument of Love

I had signed it, "Lyle, You are one of my Angels!"

After he read the poem, he said something endearing like a dad would say to his daughter and then he gave me a hug. I had never before, felt so safe and so cared for! The little girl in me rejoiced. *Through* Lyle, I was able to *feel*, for the first time, a *father's* love.

Lyle has truly been my "earth angel." He's seen me through so much! I've gained a tremendous amount of insight through our visits. I'm learning to be true to myself. Lyle has guided me through the depths of despair and into the light. I am very blessed. I wish I could share these thoughts with my husband, but it just doesn't feel safe. Not yet. It's okay though, because I'm learning to count on *me*! And to believe in myself. I really *do* matter. I'm a good person with a lot to offer, and I might even be....dare I say, *beautiful*? I choke a little on that word, but it is possible that *someday* I may believe it! Someday soon.

I think my marriage might not make it. I keep thinking about how sad it is that I don't want to be "physical" with my husband. It's not about his looks. He's very fit. I just don't feel emotionally connected to him. There's so much I want to share with him, but he doesn't want that kind of closeness; that kind of real intimacy. Our conversations are superficial. It's not *safe* to bring up serious issues because he just gets angry. It would have been nice to have been able to talk with him about the *anniversary* and maybe even have shared my poem, but our relationship can't handle anything *unpleasant*. I feel so *alone* with my husband. I care about him and I don't want to hurt him, but the passion is gone. Without love and emotional closeness, sex leaves me feeling *empty* and very sad. It breaks my heart to think of walking away from our shared history, but I feel like that's *all* we have anymore; a shared *history*.

In looking back over my years with Bill, it looks like a major problem began soon after we started working together. During those 7 years, I saw a side to my husband that I didn't like at all. His intolerance, of people in general, made me feel bad about *myself*! I couldn't please him. (Nobody could!) And yet... I continued to try! When he complained about co-workers, *before* we worked together, I was always on his side, but now...I'm seeing that there really are *two* sides to every story. My husband isn't able to feel compassion or empathy for *anyone*. And I don't know if those are things that can be taught. When I was in the

CCU after my overdose, I could have used a little compassion. I had sunk as low as a human being can possibly sink and when I needed him most, my husband wasn't there.

I got really angry at Bill this morning! Before I left for work, I told Rachel that there was one chore I wanted her to do before the day was over. She said no problem and asked me to write it down so she wouldn't forget. As I was writing, Bill started dictating more chores that he wanted *me* to add to the list for Rachel. He *knows* how hard it is for me to ask Rachel, or anyone else, to do *anything*, so it made me angry when he actually wanted *me* to write down more chores! I asked him if he was serious and he said yes. When I told him that I wouldn't do it, he got really irritated with me. I felt it was important to stand my ground, but I could feel the rage building inside of me. I slipped away into one of our bathrooms and began to hit myself repeatedly with a hairbrush. When welts began to develop on my face, I realized I'd better move the strikes to my trunk where the evidence could be hidden. I'm so disgusted with myself! And just yesterday, I was boasting about how much better I am at controlling my self-destructive impulses! Just when I think I've come so far.....

5

January 2007 thru March 2007

Wow! This is my 5th journal to date and here I am *still* on the quest for mental wellness! The past year was difficult. But it was also rewarding. When the song I mentioned a few months ago, about being loved and not giving up, went on sale recently, I bought it. I've listened to "You are Loved" hundreds of times since. It's very uplifting. Its words give me *hope*!

Today I had the chance to visit with my friend Andrea. It was the first time we *really* had a chance to talk about what happened last year. (She was the respiratory therapist on duty when I was brought to the ER.) She didn't realize, until today, that I have *no* memory of my trip to the ER *or* to the CCU. We had a real heart-to-heart as she filled me in on what she could remember.

I asked Lyle if he thought I was ready to cut back on the frequency of our sessions. He agreed to give it a try, as long as we continue to monitor my progress.

Been on the go all day. Haven't been able to settle down! I feel driven to go, go, go. Yesterday, I was full of energy too. Work was fun. I ran all over the hospital several times over. I love it when I'm *not* confined to the front office! Draws went well. Enjoyed people. Both patients and co-workers. I don't know if my increased energy is due to eating less, or eating less is due to the increased energy. I'm not sure what, or which, came first. I've cut back on the Seroquel and I'm feeling great!!!

Got so much done last night! (I was even ironing clothes in the middle of the night!) My diet is going well. I'm 105 lbs now, which I think is pretty good for my small frame. I've averaged 900 calories a day for the last 4 days and it's left me feeling a little bit nauseated, but I know it'll pass. I've been thinking a lot about my weight! I haven't decided whether or not I'm going to maintain it. I am aware of the fact that there's no good reason to lose more, but I don't know if I can stop. I don't know if I *want* to stop! If I *do* lose more, I'll try to hide the fact. I don't want lectures from Lyle or anyone else!

I read a funny affirmation recently. I don't remember the author's name, but I definitely remember what she said about learning to use *positive* affirmations. She had great difficulty stating the usual sentences about self-worth, so she decided to start with one that she couldn't possibly argue with: "I'm not a piece of shit." I laughed out loud when I first read it! It's true! And I can agree with it, because I know *intellectually* that I'm *not* actually a *piece of shit*.

I had a really strange dream. In it, my face was covered with self-inflicted cuts. I'm not sure what the dream means. A few days ago I was able to resist cutting myself, but I can honestly say that I have *never* had the urge to cut *my face.*

Well, I couldn't resist cutting for long. I'm feeling stressed because of the complex feelings I have about my loveless marriage and what will happen between Bill and me. I know that *endings* are also beginnings, but I feel torn; *especially* when Bill does something nice! This morning he gave me a hug and a kiss with *no* groping! That's really hard for him, so I know he's trying!

I've started thinking about Bill's lack of compassion for me. Now *and* when I was in the CCU. I just remembered something that Bill told me shortly after I came home from the hospital. He said that I had been mean to him when I was still in the ER. Of course I don't remember it. I don't remember *anything,* but I know it's possible. Heck, I might have been mean to *everyone!* I had a *lot* of anger built up in me. But I thought it was all self-directed. In hindsight, I can now see that I harbored a lot of anger towards my husband. Although my memory of "being mean" is gone, I've tried to piece together the events of that day from what various people have told me. Several co-workers stated that Bill was really pissed off and some even feared for my safety, but I *know* that Bill would *never* hurt me physically!

Awhile back, I talked to Dr. Stoune about reducing the Seroquel "just a little." He agreed to it, but asked me to keep in touch with him. I haven't followed through, with keeping in touch, because I feel guilty! I cut back on the meds *further* than the agreed amount and I'm afraid that, if I see him, he'll be able to tell. And then he'll want me to increase the dose. My goal is to further *decrease* the dose of my meds, until I'm completely without! I really, really want to try life *without*

meds! Besides, I've been in therapy for a year now and I've acquired a host of new skills that I can use whenever I start to revert back into old habits.

One of the biggest things I've gained, through therapy, is my ability to understand that intense feelings *always* pass! They don't last forever! When I'm filled with anxiety or rage, and I want to escape by hurting myself, I can now remember that the feeling is *temporary*! I'm also beginning to learn that I'm okay just the way that I am! I'm not too fat, or too short, or too dumb. I'm just *me* and that's perfectly okay!

I'm feeling angry at Bill. He turned the woodstove up, but didn't add any wood. Now the fire's completely out! I should say something to him. Lord knows *he* would if I was the one who screwed up! I'm also mad because I've *gained* two pounds! It makes no fucking sense! I've practically *starved* myself and I fucking *gain* weight?

My husband's been treating me better. I told him that I've noticed that he's more patient with me and nicer too. (He's even resisted crude language when we're out with friends!) I explained to him about my fear of his new behavior not lasting, and how I'm *trying* to believe that he *can* change, but I still find myself *pulling away*. I don't know whether this is a *borderline* issue or a basic *trust* issue. Or both?

Good day at work. I feel so appreciated by both the staff and the patients. I get a lot of positive feedback and it really warms my heart. Today I chose to listen to a co-worker because I believed she *needed* someone to listen to her. I didn't listen with the ulterior motive of wanting to be accepted by her. I listened because, at that moment, I realized a fellow human being was hurting. And somehow I *knew* that if I chose to be fully *present*, to really listen, I could help ease her suffering. It's all about reaching out; whether it's reaching out to help another person, or reaching out because *we* need help. Either way, it's a step that makes a big difference!

I feel like my insight is growing by leaps and bounds! I've learned to ask for what I need; at least in the workplace! And now that I'm *insisting* on being treated with respect, it's happening! (I've made "Expect Respect" my new motto.) As I've grown more assertive, and begun to trust my own judgment, I'm finding that people *still like me!* As Lyle would say, "Imagine that!"

I'm also gaining more control over my self-destructive impulses. I know that intense feelings always pass and that if I can just hold off from hurting myself, for a few minutes, the urge *will* pass.

Cycling into a bit of a depression. Not worried though. It'll pass. Cancelled my standing date with Deb. Don't feel like socializing. Just wanna sleep.

Had a heart-to-heart with Bill. I said that I was beginning to believe that Lyle might have been right when he said that I *deserve* to be cherished. Bill joked about not being *capable* of cherishing me and I calmly told him that I believe he's right. I may never be cherished by *anyone* and I'm coming to terms with that. Maybe I can learn to cherish myself? Lyle did tell me that *I'm* the only one who really needs to love me.

I just don't know if I can do that. I've hated myself for so long, that to *love* myself seems unattainable; a goal too high to reach.

During a somewhat serious conversation with my husband, he interrupted me to point out a spider on the ceiling! (I felt like the damn spider was more important than me!) *Why* does he do that? Is he bored or uncomfortable? Does he have attention problems? He said that he's *aware* that he does it, but he doesn't know *why*. He did admit that he does the same thing with *everyone*, so it's not me personally. I'd been trying to tell him about how jealous I'd felt when Rachel was born, because he fell instantly in love with her. Why didn't he ever love *me* like that? Nothing I ever did, or could ever do, would earn *me* that kind of love from him!

I talked to Lyle about my decision to *cherish* myself. I told him that I'm okay with Bill's inability to cherish me. (Or even love me.) Lyle said that to cherish someone is a *choice* and Bill is choosing *not* to cherish me. Lyle's right, but I'm still okay with it. I'm actually kind of relieved by Bill's admission, because now I can stop hoping for something that is never going to happen! Lyle asked me what I was going to do when someone arrives on the scene who *wants* to cherish me. When this happens, and he seemed certain that it will, I'll find myself at a crossroad.

Lyle gave me an unusual book about borderline personality disorder. It's a story about an eagle that grows up in a barnyard with chickens. He doesn't seem to *fit in* with his peers, or his family, because he's really an eagle trying to live the life of something he's not. When he finally learns of his true nature, he not only learns to fly, he truly *soars!*

I just remembered some valuable insight I gained in therapy yesterday, regarding my long-standing status as the "chubby" twin. It turns out that *I* wasn't actually fat! I was the *normal* size twin and Lisa was the underweight "skinny" twin. And to think, that for my entire child-hood, I was dubbed the "fat" twin! When Lyle referred to me as an "overweight" newborn, I finally realized how ridiculous the whole chubby thing sounded! As it finally hit me, I began to laugh at the nonsense of it all.

You would think, with my new-found knowledge that I wasn't a fat child, that I'd be less obsessed with food and eating so much! I've been an outright glutton for the last week; consuming 3,000 to 4,000 calo-ries a day! I don't seem to have an "off" button when it comes to sweets. I crave them and once I've taken the first bite, I'm hooked and I can't seem to stop. I just keep shoveling it in, cookie after cookie, candy bar after candy bar! Not only is there *not* an "off" button for me, it's as if the "on" button is *stuck*! I continue to reach for more food, even when my stomach is stretched to the limit and I'm completely miserable! Even when I manage *not* to binge, the thoughts are there in the fore-front of my mind. I'm *always* thinking about junk food and how I can hide my addiction from everyone. I would be so embarrassed if anyone knew the truth of how much I really eat. I'm not bulimic though, or at least I don't think I am, because I *never* make myself throw up. In order to keep my weight from getting too high, I just cut back for a few days or until the *next* binge.

Feeling kinda sad for no particular reason. Probably just a borderline thing. Or maybe a bipolar swing. Doesn't really matter. I'm just fucked up. So fucking fucked up. I wish that Bill would cherish me, but I don't deserve to be cherished. I'm a fucked up glutton. A real pig. I'm up to 109 lbs and my hipbones aren't sticking out anymore. I want to decrease the bipolar meds, to lose this fat, but I've been feeling kind of shaky lately and sounds are getting too loud again. I'm also constantly seeing things out of the corner of my eye. That's never a good sign, so it's best not to mess with the drugs right now.

If I can't be cherished, I wish that I could at least be loved. I want to be loved for just being *me*. But even *I* can't love me, so how can I expect anyone else to?

My extra weight is disgusting to me. I feel gross with all of this flab. My friend, Lynda, keeps telling me I'm too thin. How can she *not* see how heavy I've gotten? She thinks I have an eating disorder. If I have any kind of *eating* disorder, it's that I eat *too* much! I once told Lynda, when she first met me, that I was at a heavier weight than usual because of my meds. She chose to zero in on my choice of the word *heavier*. She thinks I'm starving myself! If she only knew. I'm sometimes shocked at how much I can pack away in a single sitting! I just ate a dozen chocolate chip cookies and I'm still wondering what else I can eat!

Lyle asked me at what weight do I *physically* feel my best? When I told him105 lbs was okay, he seemed genuinely surprised that I didn't feel better at a *higher* weight. God, why does everyone want me fat? Everyone except my husband that is. I'm never thin enough for him. I really want to lose 15 lbs. I'd love to finally be thin enough for Bill to tell me to *gain* some weight! I'd absolutely love to hear him say, "You're too thin." If Lyle were to read this, he'd say that I'm getting back into an *unhealthy attachment* mode. When I last saw Lyle, I told him I was ready to go three weeks between sessions, but he thinks two weeks is long enough. I guess he still wants to keep tabs on me and what I'm doing. I do appreciate that he truly has my best interest at heart. I know I still need his help. Even though I've come a very long way, I'm not ready to go solo just yet.

Skipped my meds last night. I paced around most of the night waiting to get tired; which never happened. I exercised and cleaned house. I tried to read but my mind kept racing! I tossed and turned when I did try to sleep. I just couldn't slow down my body *or* my mind. I'm okay though, even without sleep! I feel great and I had tons of energy for work today!

I had a really good talk with my boss today. We discussed some of the issues that people, with bipolar disorder, have to deal with. He stressed the importance of a regular sleep/wake cycle and he also stressed the major role that medication plays in keeping the person with bipolar disorder stable. He said that he can tell when I've been messing with my meds. I asked him if he thought I'd *ever* come to terms with needing to take medication for the rest of my life and he said, "Yes, to some extent." He believes that I will continue to "adjust" the dose of my meds, but that I will do it less and less with time. The main point that I wanted to make in this journal entry, is that I really needed a friend today and my boss was awesome! He gave me good advice and encouragement. He assured me that I'm going to be okay. It's weird that I can talk to him about those things. He and Lyle and Dr. Stoune are the only ones who seem to realize how hard of a struggle this journey is.

I wish that I could turn to my husband when I need a friend. It makes me sad that our relationship is too superficial to handle serious subjects. I should be able to go to him with my fears and concerns, but it doesn't feel *safe*. I don't mean to imply that Bill would ever *try* to hurt me, but his lack of empathy does cause me pain.

I'm part of a new task force at work. Our goal is to foster goodwill between various departments within the hospital. I tried to share, with Bill, my excitement at the possibility of improving the communication between the different departments, and developing an understanding of how each dept works and what we can do to work better as a team. But my enthusiasm was shot down by both my husband and my daughter. When I told Bill about looking forward to helping people learn how to get along, he teased me about how *everyone* gets along in "Terresa Land." Our daughter piped up, agreeing with him! I tried to laugh it off, pretending that it didn't bother me, but it did! A lot!

I've been trying to come up with ideas for my meeting this afternoon, but I keep hearing Bill's condescending words, "Is that how it is in *Terresa Land?*" I'm feeling like an incompetent fraud! No one needs *me* on their task force. Who was I trying to kid? I'm a big fat fake! I told my daughter that I was hurt by her, and her dad's, comments last night regarding my mission for improving employee moral. She said that they just didn't want me "setting myself up for disappointment." A little support, from either one of them, would have been nice. I guess I'm just too god-damned sensitive. I *am* the problem.

I got really down on myself, as I tried to think of what to say to the committee members, and before I knew it, I was raging against myself! The confidence I had the day before vanished, and I began to berate myself for thinking that *anything* I had to offer could be of value! Who did I think I was anyway? Panic rose up from the deepest part of my being, threatening to suffocate me! Death would be welcome, but I was afraid that I wouldn't die. Instead I would be forced to feel, even more so, the pain of not belonging.

To ease the mounting anxiety, and to keep the tears from falling, I repeatedly punched myself. I hit my face and my trunk until I was numb. I wanted the mental pain to go away and eventually it did. Soon I felt nothing and that was a good thing. I would go to the meeting, but I would "offer" nothing.

Lyle announced that it's time for me to challenge the "Truths" I've been taught throughout my life. The first *truth* to challenge is the *fat twin myth*. According to Lyle, I was never *fat*! Yes, my twin was skinny; but that, in no way, made *me* fat! Okay Lyle, I'll try to buy into the possibility that maybe, just maybe, I wasn't fat after all.

I had an odd dream last night. I was trying to drive a motor home on a dirt road, high in the mountains. I couldn't see where I was going because of the dense fog and, to make matters worse, the road was really steep and winding. The motor home kept going faster and faster, until it was careening out of control through the thick fog and into the unknown. Just as I left the road, and headed towards a certain death, I woke up.

Session today was about learning to respect myself. (I think that means I'm not supposed to hurt myself.)

Our boss announced at a meeting today, that he is transferring to another site! I was completely blindsided! He's been my mentor *and* my friend and *now*, without warning, he's leaving! I'm feeling completely abandoned! Who will look after me?

I'm a little calmer today about the news. In many ways, the boss has *not* been a good manager. In fact, he's been a crappy manager! But... he was there for me in my darkest hour and in the days to follow. He took me under his wing in so many ways. He made me feel safe and validated and cared for. (The things I *wish* my husband would've done for me.) I will survive this, but it sure hurts like hell.

I asked Lyle if I could have my first journal back now. I wanted to read it, so that I could see how far I've come. He doesn't think it's a good idea right now. I'm making good progress and he feels that I could become "melancholy" if I were to revisit that time in my life. (I originally gave him the journal for safe keeping.)

I'm going through the motions of being a loving wife, but it feels fake. Maybe, if I keep acting the part, I'll eventually *feel* like the loving wife I want to be. On the other hand, I didn't realize how emotionally attached I'd become to my boss! Now that he's leaving, I'm realizing that I have *feelings* for him! He's been very supportive these last 13 months as I've struggled with manic-depression *and* coming to terms with its implications, and the treatment necessary to live a normal life. Whenever I've needed someone to talk to, he's been there for me! To listen, to encourage, to offer advice. How can he leave me? I'm sad beyond words! I hadn't realized how deeply dependent I'd become. His friendship means everything to me. Not only is he my friend, he's also my mentor, but now he's leaving! Oh my God, I can't stand it! Why do people keep leaving me? *Why?* I felt protected and cared for by this man. He always noticed when I was a moving towards one of the poles of my disorder, and he was quick to offer insight or advice. I can't imagine not seeing him everyday at work. I'm terrified of what might happen without him here to look after me. I can't stop crying!

Okay... it's time to dry my tears and stop this pity party! My work family needs me. They need a strong, confident, capable teammate and the *new* boss deserves my best. I will rise to the challenge. Change is especially difficult for me, but I can, and *will,* embrace it!

I've been learning about the four parts of developing a positive mindset. Feelings, thoughts, behavior and attitude. When we *feel* an emotion, we choose how to *think* about that feeling. Then, that *thought* directly affects how we decide to *behave.* Eventually, the thoughts and behavior determine our general *attitude.* It sounds simple enough, but I know it'll take hard work and diligence on my part. I never knew that embracing wellness could be so damned hard. Sigh.

I'm choosing to take care of *me.* (I hope I can stick with it this time!) That means *not* messing with my meds, getting enough sleep, eating right, having structure in my day *and* setting limits or boundaries with people who want me to jump through their hoops. Respecting *me,* and my limits, is something that I *myself* need to do. If the lab continues to be short-handed, and I'm forced into too much overtime, then I'll need to speak up and calmly tell the new supervisor that I'm able to give

100% for 8 or 9 hours a day, 5 days a week, *but* any more than that will affect my health. I have to be my own advocate. No one else is going to do it for me. And really... it should be my job anyway.

Our new interim boss is actually one of our district managers. (I've worked with him off and on through the years.) Today he made a point of telling me that he notices and appreciates my work. He said that I am one of the most positive people in the entire company! (And that was *after* he saw how upset I got when our previous boss broke the news that he was leaving.) My good days must outnumber my bad days! Either that or I'm a really good actress!

So much for eating less! I polished off 4,000 calories yesterday, bringing my grand total to 15,000 in just 72 hours! *Why*, do I do it?

Ken, our interim supervisor, has been talking to each one of the employees in private, to discuss any concerns they may have. When it was my turn, I told him that my greatest concern was losing my *set* schedule. He assured me that no one will be changing my schedule, and that I fill the shift very well. We also talked about my suicide attempt last year. (He knew about it and had called me the day I was released from the hospital.) He shared with me how surprised he'd been at the news because I'd always seemed so upbeat. I told him how much it helped me to have regular hours and that, along with counseling and medication, I was doing well. I let him know that I feel very appreciated and valued at work and that, when we're properly staffed, I absolutely love my job! I told him that I look forward to coming to work each day.

I stood my ground with one of the doctors at the hospital today. She tried to cover her own tracks by blaming *me*, but I spoke up! I do believe I'm developing a backbone!

I watched a movie called "The kid," in which a grown man has the chance to spend time with "himself" as an 8 year old. He doesn't like the kid at all. He thinks he's a big fat loser. It reminded me of how I've never liked kids, including the one I was! Another part of the movie got to me too. The main character was seeing himself, as a child, being mistreated by his dad. With his grown-up perspective, he realized that his dad had never meant to hurt him! He was doing the best he could at the time. In the end, the grown up learns to love, and *embrace*, his inner child. A very powerful movie for me.

Too afraid to weigh. God, I'm *still* a big fat loser!

Went to the Basque Dance tonight. Tried to have a good time, but I felt sad. And very alone. My marriage is superficial and I'm finally accepting that I will probably *never* get the emotional closeness I crave. Even if Bill suddenly changed into a sensitive, caring person who truly loved me, I think it's too late for us. I feel *empty* when we're together. And very, very alone. It makes me cry when I think back to the days when I was so in love with my husband. Now I'm mostly numb. I think the beginning of the end, of my love for Bill, was his reaction to my overdose. I wanted him to take me into his arms and tell me that he loved me, and that *together* we'd find a way to get me well. But, instead of loving concern, I got hostility and disgust. (I got more concern from my boss than I did my own husband!) What's wrong with this fucking picture? *Now* I'm starting to feel *pissed*! Why couldn't my own husband be there for me? He deserted me, emotionally, in my darkest hour. I'd hit rock bottom; the lowest point of my entire life! *Why* couldn't he, at some point in the last year, have said something like, "I'm sorry I wasn't there for you. I love you and I want to help you." I cried a lot last night for what we've lost, or *maybe* for what we never had to begin with.

I got a wonderful compliment from co-worker today. She said she loves it when I get to work, because I bring a sense of calmness to the lab. God, I *am* a good actress!

Session with Lyle was insightful. I told him how sad I was about my boss transferring to another site. He said he'd be concerned if I *wasn't* sad. I also told him about being uncomfortable at the Basque Dance, because I had worn my shirt tucked in and you could see my figure. My eyes kept filling up with tears when we talked about it. Lyle said that, intellectually, I'm accepting my worth, but I'm still struggling with it *emotionally*. He reassured me that I'm *not* slipping back. It's just another part of the borderline that we still need to work on. We also talked about trust and respect. I'm beginning to show signs of re-specting myself by setting boundaries with Bill, and not allowing crude behavior in my presence. I'm still having trouble though, with trusting myself, especially when I look in the mirror. (According to Lyle.) My assignment, this time, is to choose 5 people I trust and to ask them to describe me physically. I'm having a hard time thinking of anyone I can trust! It's amazing to me how very little I actually trust people. Of course I know that learning to trust *myself* is what's most important in this challenge. Sounds simple enough.

I can't trust *me* just yet. My promises to take care of myself are still hollow, but in time …? One of the biggest obstacles for me, in taking care of myself, has been my struggle with the whole medication issue. The side effects aren't bad, so there's *no* good reason to stop taking them and *every* reason to stay on the meds! When I'm compliant with my medication, it's easy to forget how much they do for me! Maybe it's time to go back and check the list, to remind me of just how much they do help!

The following is a partial list of what the medication does for me:

Stops the racing thoughts.

Calms the agitation. (Mental and physical.)

Eliminates the "jumping out of my skin" feeling.

Slows me down. (So that I don't run into people.)

Helps me to concentrate.

Allows me to sleep.

Keeps normal sounds from being too loud.

Keeps my pillow-top bed from feeling like "concrete."

Keeps my *soft* pajamas from feeling scratchy.

Keeps my baggy clothes from feeling restrictive.

Stops me from "seeing things" out of the corner of my eye.

Stops me from hearing music that isn't playing. (Or my name that isn't called.)

Lyle and I talked about how things happen for a reason. Everything, including seemingly bad things, happens for the greater good. An example that comes to mind is how Dr. Stoune just *happened* to walk by as Bill walked out of the ER. The reason he walked by, when he did, was because he'd been attending an AA meeting. If he had *not* been a recovering alcoholic, he wouldn't have been walking by just then and he wouldn't have run into Bill! So even though something bad had happened in the past, it came together to help *me,* and perhaps countless others, now, in the present. I'm on the road to recovery *because* Dr. Stoune was in the right place, at the right time! (And all because of something that happened to him in *his* past.)

Lyle asked me *not* to lose any more weight. He told me that he's been worried about anorexia for quite some time. I didn't bother to tell how much I've been eating, since no one believes me anyway. And I'm *not* anorexic! Although I do constantly think about dieting and getting thinner. Lyle warned me that anorexia is a slow form of suicide, but it doesn't matter because I'm *not* anorexic! I told Lyle that he doesn't need to worry about me starving myself to death. I like food too much to ever do that! And for crying out loud, my weight is fine!

This morning, as I sat in my living room, I prayed for guidance in what to do about my marriage. About 90 minutes later, as I was cleaning out the basement, I found a graduation card from 1981. It was signed by my mom (who passed away in 1998.) I hadn't seen the card in nearly 26 years! The first stanza of the card's poem read:

You will stand many times

At a crossroad in life

Just as you're standing now

And no one can tell you

Which way you should go

Or what you should do

Or how

Mom had signed it, "Love you always!"

The tears flowed freely as I realized that Mom, or God, or *both,* had answered my prayer. (It wasn't the answer I wanted, but it *was* an answer.) And it also reminded me that my mom will love me *always.* After reading and rereading the card, I know that God is telling me that the choice of staying married is entirely up to me; but either way, whatever choice I make, He will still "*Love Me Always!*"

Lyle shared a story with me about how, years ago, he and another man applied for the same job. It seemed like bad news to Lyle when the other applicant won out, but years later, that same man was killed in the line of duty. The story shows that both good *and* bad things happen as a result of our choices, but if we can believe that all things happen for a reason, it helps to make some sense out of this life. I believe that there's more to life than what we can see. There's a bigger picture here, but our human minds can't comprehend it.

At work today, I went to the ER to draw blood from an out-of-control 16 year old girl. She was in handcuffs, which can make it hard to get to a good vein. The entire bay was crammed full of people. There were nurses, police officers, a social worker and the doctor. I looked for a vein while I waited for the injected tranquilizer to subdue the patient. At one point, one of the RN's pointed out a vein she thought would work, but I told her it didn't *feel* right, so she pointed out another vein. I felt good about that one and I was able to fill all my tubes with no problem. The reason I'm bringing this up, is because it made me realize that I'm very confident in my abilities. I'm able to tell others *no* if I need to and I'm also able to accept help if I need it. In fact, I'm actually getting good at *asking* for help! These may seem like little things, but to me, they represent *milestones.*

I think Bill's trying to connect with me, but I'm not sure. He sat with me on the couch and initiated a conversation. We talked for two hours! When I asked him if he was trying to connect with me *emotionally*, he wouldn't give me a straight answer. Sigh

Lyle and I talked about stress and how it's mostly *perception*! According to Lyle, it's about 85 percent perception. Wow! Now, if only I could remember that when I'm in a stressful situation!

I asked assorted people at work to describe me, per Lyle's request. (He seems to think, that I don't have a clear picture as to what I truly look like.) The list from my coworkers included things like, "Tiny, cutie pie, skinny, smiley, good looking, bouncy shoulder length hair, nice skin, younger than my years, etc." (A couple of people did say that I looked anorexic.) I'm thinking that maybe my view of myself has been a bit harsh over the years.

When I asked my husband to describe me, he said I was average. When I asked him to be a little more specific, he said that I'd be the person you could look right at, and *not* see! Interesting. I told him about the way my coworkers described me, but he still insisted that I was average. Then he joked that I needed bigger boobs. Sigh.

I really wish that Bill thought I was thin. *Why* does it matter so much? After all of the positive feedback I received, concerning my appearance, you'd think I'd be ready to accept a healthy weight, but I'm not. I think it's because my own husband doesn't see me as thin, and since he's the *only* one who really knows my *true* size, his opinion carries more weight! I know that Lyle would say that this is an *unhealthy attachment* issue, but I can't seem to break away from wanting my husband's approval. Maybe if I lose 15 lbs, he'll finally say that I'm too thin. (Or at least thin enough!)

Today a patient told me that he wanted to end his own life. I told him that I know, without a doubt, that something wonderful is waiting for us, *but* we have to wait our turn! We simply can't "take cuts" in the line to Heaven. It's not fair to those ahead of us. I hope my words brought him comfort.

I spent the day with my husband's aunt Sue and cousin Sara. They are more than family to me, they're friends! We had a wonderful girls' day! They both think I should condense my journals into a book, to help those who suffer from mental illness. (I'm giving it serious thought.) They also said that no matter what happens between Bill and me, they will always love me!

I'm really sad that my boss is leaving. He's been so supportive this past year and I can't imagine not having him around. But, I believe he was put in my life for a reason and now it's time for me to move on without him. I *want* to lean on him, but I no longer *need* to. I'm so much stronger than I was a year ago. I do believe that people come into our lives for a reason and, as painful as it is, they also leave. I think God places all of us *exactly* where we're supposed to be. And sometimes the reason is to help others, but just as often, it's to learn how to *receive* help. Even with these beliefs, I can't stop the tears.

As I get better, I find myself wanting to somehow *give back.* I've been doing some real soul-searching and I've decided that I want to be an *instrument* of God's love. I've prayed to Him to show me *how* I can share His love with others; *especially* with those who suffer from illnesses of the mind! I grew up in a church that taught "hell and damnation." But I know in my heart, I've *always* known, that the God I know loves me *without* condition. He loves me as a parent loves his precious child. Man-made religion has isolated people and spawned hate for anyone who doesn't fit into their narrow view of God. My faith has been tested with this illness, but my trust in God has never been stronger!

It was crazy at work! And because of it, I forgot a stat, but I didn't beat myself up! I know that I'm only *one* person and that I *cannot* do the job of three! So if my employer won't properly staff the lab, then I will acknowledge the fact, and place the blame where it belongs! No longer will I accept responsibility for the actions of others!

I messed up on the groceries. I was at the store, with the ground turkey in my hand, when I decided that I had some at home, so I put it back. Then, tonight as I started cooking, I realized that we didn't have the turkey after all. Normally I'd be so angry at myself that I'd have to slip away to literally beat the crap out of myself! But today, I was okay! I acknowledged that I'm human and that I made a mistake and that it was no big deal.

Today is my birthday and I'm planning to celebrate ME! Normally, I wouldn't want anyone to know what day it is, but this year I'm telling *everyone*! I even ordered a huge sheet cake for work, so that all of my coworkers can help me celebrate! Bill's coffee group just called and sang Happy Birthday to me. I'm really excited about having the attention on *me* today. Wow! This represents a *huge* change from the way I usually think about my birthday and the attention that it can draw. Maybe, my mind has finally accepted that I might just be worth the space I take up!

I'm beginning to think of others in a more meaningful way. One of my coworkers was having some personal problems and I called her at home to ask her if there was anything I could do to help. I *actively* listened to another person *without* my own agenda. I've been self-centered long enough! It's time to take a good hard look at the people around me.

I'm feeling very down. Very sad. Rachel's 18 now, so she really doesn't need me anymore. Soon she'll be off to college. My boss will be gone soon, so I won't have his emotional support. I don't even have a dog, for affection, anymore. I feel such a void in my heart. A gnawing emptiness. What's my purpose? What *now*? I've been eating everything in sight lately. (As if it could fix this problem of seeing the world as a bleak and joyless place.) All the food in the world isn't going to help. It's just going to make me puffy and achy and more depressed. I can't seem to shake this dark cloud.

We're going to jackpot for the weekend. Bill wants me to wear a particular outfit. When I told him that it's too tight, and that I'd have to stop eating for a week in order to fit into it, he seemed fine with that solution.

Lyle warned me that most of my "friends" at work are what he called fair-weathered friends. They aren't true friends, the kind who will be there when the going gets tough. I think I already sensed that. We also talked about whether or not I trust anyone. I told him that I trust *him* on everything *except* how he sees me physically. I told him that I think he is biased when he describes me as a beautiful woman. He said that he would *never* lie to me. He asked me what I thought he could possibly gain, by lying to me about my appearance? When I told Lyle that my husband's description of me was to say that I'm average, he was visibly irritated. It seems that my husband has a way of *undoing* whatever it is that Lyle's trying to *do*, to make me healthy.

I said I was ready for my boss to be transferred, but I'm not! I'm going to be lost at work without his support! He understands me! He was there in my darkest hour, offering support while I was in the CCU. My own husband couldn't be there for me. In fact he could hardly stand to look at me! He was just flat out pissed that I'd attempted suicide! What am I going to do without my mentor? I feel so panicky! So needy! I *need* a straight-edge!

I couldn't stand the panic I was feeling at losing my boss, so I did what I always do when I can't handle the emotional pain. As I cut myself, I went deeper and deeper until the straight-edge practically disappeared into the wound. The first cut hurt a little, but as I dug the blade in further and further, I could no longer feel it. Maybe there weren't any nerve endings that deep? Or maybe it was just me? I *still* want to cut, but I'm afraid of getting caught! The cut I have now can still be hidden under the bandages I always wear (to cover the old scars.) Bill won't think anything of that. Although, I will need a *bigger* bandage in order to cover the "butterflies" I had to use this time. (The gaping wound wouldn't stop bleeding until I did.)

Man, I really, really want to cut again! I keep trying to think of a place where Bill won't notice! I wish I had never told him about the self-inflicted wounds, because *now* he's always on the lookout. Just two days ago, I penned the words "I'm writing tonight, so I *won't* cut myself!" And *now* here I am, 48 hours later, with a deep gash on the inside of my ankle! Sigh. When will it stop?

I put on a happy face for Lyle today because I was kind of down the last time I saw him. I don't want to be such a drag!

Damn it! I thought I'd been so careful in covering my tracks regarding the cutting, but Bill found some blood on the bathroom floor and confronted me. He's really angry with me. What's new? He wanted to know *why* I don't come to him with my feelings and I told him because he'll just be disgusted. He answered in a voice *filled with disgust*, "I will not!" I told him that a part of me wants desperately for him to say, "Honey, I'm so sorry for your pain. How can I help you?" His answer to me was that until I'm well, he can't be close to me. He can't "take a chance" knowing that I could "hurt myself to death." I called him on that, and asked him about the years *before* I attempted suicide? I reminded him that he's *never* been able to offer emotional closeness. He said it was because he "sensed" that I wasn't well.

I called Lyle and left him a message asking if I could see him sooner. (My next appt is in 2 weeks.) He called me back to ask me if I was okay. I didn't tell him about the cutting or the powerful urge to *keep* cutting. I just told him that I didn't want to wait 2 weeks. I'm feeling really depressed about not having my boss to lean on anymore. I'm afraid of not having his emotional support at work. He and Lyle have both played a huge part in my life this past year! I'm feeling out of control! I can't remember *any* of the insight I've gained this past year. Panic is consuming me!

Bill asked me about my different forms of self-injury. I decided to be honest with him, and began to list the various ways in which I'd hurt myself. When I told him about burning myself with a cigarette lighter, he asked me if *he* had ever been the "cause" of such an act. I told him, that at times, his actions had prompted me to harm myself, but I assured him that it was *never* his fault; it was the *illness*. I admitted that the emotional pain, of never being able to please him, was magnified when we worked together. I told him, that because *nothing* I ever did was good enough for him, it has caused me a great deal of emotional turmoil. He admitted that nothing that *anyone* does is good enough for him. It's *not* just me.

Well, I cut again. Bigger mess than last time, but I was careful to not leave any signs. At my session with Lyle today, he asked me *why* I don't call him when the urge to cut strikes? I told him, "Because I don't want you to talk me out of it." Lyle said that out of the billions of people who have walked this earth, there is, and only will be, *one* me. He told me that I need to take care of *her,* and that I have *no* right to hurt her! A part of me thought, "FUCK YOU!" It really pissed me off that Lyle tried to tell me that I have "no right" to cut myself. It's MY FUCKING BODY and I'll do whatever the hell I want to it! I'm STILL pissed! He also thinks we need to go back to weekly sessions.

Lyle thinks I dress conservatively because the "id" part of my "ego" has been smothered somewhere along the way. Why can't I just be conservative without it being an *issue*?

Lyle and I talked about beauty. I hate the way I look and whenever Lyle tries to say that I'm beautiful, it makes me cry. I've asked him to please not use the "B" word with me. It really upsets me! He said that I need to stop comparing myself to others, so that I can see my own beauty. I will *never* see what he sees.

❧

Depression is worsening. Trying to hide it. Afraid. The urge to cut is always in the back of my mind. I asked Bill if I should lose more weight. (105 lbs is still too much) He claimed to like me at this weight. I don't think I believe him. He's always pointing out women he thinks are attractive, and they're *always* very thin and tall. Bill and I talked a little bit about the OD. He didn't think I'd make it a year. He thought that I would have attempted suicide again by now, and that I would have succeeded.

❧

The message in a movie that I just watched was that we need to learn how to love ourselves and to see our own beauty. The main character was a large woman who wouldn't be "beautiful" by Hollywood's standards, but through her own trials and tribulations, she learns to see her own beauty. By the end of the movie, I found her to be absolutely, without a doubt, beautiful! Maybe there *is* hope for me?

❧

I've been faithful with my meds, but I'm still so damned depressed! I don't give a shit about anything or anyone. It's all I can do to drag myself out of bed and go to work each day. I can't even fake a smile right now. I've been eating huge amounts of candy, probably in an attempt to brighten my mood, but it's not working. Everyday at work, I leave at lunch time to purchase a *family*-sized bag of candy to "inhale" before returning to work. In a matter of minutes, I consume an entire day's worth of calories! I'm not bulimic, so I end up gaining weight.

Lyle is my Godsend. The depression won't lift. I think about suicide constantly. I've been in contact with Lyle 4 times in the last 5 days. He's talked about putting me in the hospital, but I've assured him that I'm not going to commit suicide. Frankly I don't have the energy to carry out any attempt at ending my life. I'm grateful that Lyle's kept me on as a patient, even though I continue to self-injure. Lyle doesn't like that I'm still cutting, but he's promised never to leave me. He does say, however, that a day will come when I'm well and I'll realize that I'm ready to leave *him*. It's as though I'm a child right now and when I've grown into a healthy adult, I will do what healthy people do and leave my parents, or in this case Lyle.

This is just a setback. I'm still on the road to recovery. I've been praying to God to help me out of this depression. I believe that He always answers our prayers, but sometimes the answer is no. I guess, for now, I'm not supposed to be well. I watched another movie. This one taught me that we all have love, energy and beauty within us. Sure wish I could get in touch with at least one of those elements!

After work tonight, I decided to go shopping. Since I still have to check in at home, like a damned child, I called and left a message on the machine. I assumed that my family was outside. My cell phone was dead, but since I'd called from work and left a message at home, I wasn't worried. Big mistake! It just so happened that neither Bill or Rachel got my message because they were both out for the evening. Both of them had been trying to get a hold of me, so once again I was in trouble; like some fucking little kid!

When I got home, the phone was ringing off the hook. First Rachel called, and then Bill. I'm so god-damned tired of being treated like some criminal who has to check in with her parole officer! The rage built quickly and before I knew it, I was punching anything I could! And then the overwhelming urge to cut myself took over. I thought briefly of calling Lyle, but I knew that the reason for my rage would sound stupid, so I decided against it. I quickly got out my cutting supplies and began calming myself down. In a trance-like state, I laid out the towels (to catch the blood), the straight-edge razor, the rubbing alcohol, the bandages. As I sunk the blade deep into my flesh, I chanted the word, "okay" over and over again. For how long I sat, chanting, on the bathroom floor, I have no idea. Ten minutes? Twenty? Two hundred?

I told Bill that one of the triggers for this latest depression was my grief at losing my boss. I told him that my bond with him began after I overdosed, when he came to see me in the CCU. My own husband had offered absolutely no support while this other man, who doesn't owe me anything, shows up to comfort me at the lowest point in my life. Of course I bonded with him! He showered me with concern and emotional support when I needed it most. It *should* have come from my husband, but maybe he had his own demons to battle. After a heart to heart with Bill, about this latest downswing, he told me that he doesn't think I can be "fixed."

If I'm ever going to recover from this shitty lot I've been handed, then I need to quit with the pity party, get off my ass and do my part. The interim boss at work is willing to keep my set schedule for me, so I need to do my share by taking my meds, getting enough sleep, blah, blah, blah.

Bill told me recently that many years ago, he caught me beating the hell out of myself. The crazy thing is that I have *no* memory of it! God, I *am* fucked up! The reason I'm bringing this up, is because Bill asked me to promise to never injure myself again. He said that he can't get close to me until I'm well and that would mean I could no longer hurt my body. I may *never* be "well." I was honest and told him that I *can't* promise that I will *never* harm myself again. I wish I could, but it would be a lie at this point. I can't be trusted with promises to not self-injure. The urge is still too strong and I am still too weak.

Lyle is worried about me. The cutting is getting deeper. He said it could kill me! But they're *just cuts*! He said that because I'm going deeper and deeper, I could inadvertently sever an artery and bleed out before I could get help. He warned me that these aren't just surface cuts anymore and that I'm at risk for *death* if I choose to continue this practice. I felt like crying when he said that. "Cutting" is *not* supposed to kill!

To help me understand how distorted my view has been, regarding my self-injury, Lyle asked me if I would ever consider cutting a loved one? How about my own daughter? Of course my answer was NEVER! Not in a million years! He pointed out that *I* was someone's child and that *I* didn't deserve to be cut, or hit, or burned, or starved! His words were a real eye-opener to the amount of self-hate it takes, to be able to inflict such wounds! Definitely something to ponder. Lyle said that at this time, the borderline causes an alter-ego, if you will, to attack *me*!

The self-hate is still too strong. He suggested that I start scheduling in activities that are just for *me!* (To reinforce my self-worth.) I told Lyle that I'm afraid to call him when I feel like cutting, because the "reasons" for cutting are so stupid! He promised that he will *never* belittle me, and that I am *safe* with him.

I told Lyle that I'm beginning to contemplate the different types of *beauty.* He was pleased that I was able to say the "B" word! I told him that I'm suddenly aware of men, now that I've started looking around me. (Without fear.) I've stopped thinking that they're all perverts. That was the unhealthy "conditioning" that happened in the early years with my husband. Bill's repeated comments about women and their sexual body parts, and what he'd like to do to them, caused considerable damage in the way I viewed both men and women!

When Bill agreed to marry me, it was because he was ready to start a family. In his mind, that was the *only* reason you got married. So now that our daughter is grown, I'm wondering "what now?" Is there any reason to stay together?

I was tempted to decrease my meds, but voices from both Lyle and my former boss popped into my head! I heard, "It takes a *strong* person to admit she needs help and/or medication." (Dr. Stoune had repeated something along those lines as well.) In the last few days on the job, my boss told me several times that I was going to be okay. Maybe he's right! I know that as time goes by, it *will* get easier to do what's in my best interest. I'm gaining insight all the time and I believe that *eventually* I will be whole. Thank God for Lyle! He's truly been one of my angels! I know he's a human being like everyone else, but he truly has a gift. I pray that someday I will be well enough to help people who are hurting, just as Lyle has helped me. Maybe not in the exact same way of course, but the idea *is* that a time will come when I will find *my* gift and God will show me *how* to use it... to help others!

End of another journal. Lots of setbacks, but so much healthier than last year! When Lyle pointed out that I could have inadvertently *killed* myself, by cutting an artery, it opened my eyes to the fact that I don't want to die! I want to live! I *do!*

6

April 2007

I know I'm not done yet, with my journey to mental health, but I *am* getting closer and stronger each and every day! The goal of *wellness* is within my reach! Our last session woke me up to the fact that I *want* to live! For most of my life, I've held suicide in the back of my mind as a *way out;* an escape. The mental struggle to be normal has plagued me for so long that I *needed* to know that I had an escape! (Just in case I couldn't stand it anymore.) *Now* those suicidal feelings are all but gone! I can't promise that I'll never cut again, but I am *aware* of how dangerous it can be! I really do want to stop, but it's a habit that I've had for three *decades*, so it won't be easy. It's my hope, that as I learn to implement new and better ways of coping with difficult feelings, I will do it less and less. And someday I hope to stop altogether. I *am* getting better!

Bill and I had a serious talk. I'm not sure that I want to be married anymore. Bill's not a bad guy and we've had a lot of good times, but I've never felt loved by him, or even liked! He stated that he couldn't be *emotionally* intimate with me over the years, because he didn't want to get hurt. In trying to protect himself, he ended up hurting us both!

Even if he *could* learn to love me, I wonder if it's too late for me to reclaim the feelings I once had for him? As we talked of divorce, we held each other and cried. Maybe love *is* alive?

Bill and I agreed that we never meant to hurt one another. We've decided to start fresh. Bill really is trying. He's stopped being crude around me and I know that's a real sacrifice for him. I need to be more supportive of him. He needs validation too. I think that communication is key and with it there is hope.

I've been thinking about how "cutting" to me has been like a drug. And just like the *addict,* I've needed more and more to get my *fix.* I know that I need to put this behavior behind me because, just like a "low" number on the scale, it will never be *enough*.

I told Lyle about my revelation: I *want* to live! We also talked about my marriage and after a few minutes, he asked, "Why the tears?" I hadn't been feeling sad at all, but as soon as Lyle said the words, I burst into tears! *How* does he *do* that? How can *he* know that I'm sad when *I* don't even know it?

Lyle wasn't at all pleased about how eager I was to start over on my marriage. He doesn't think Bill will change in the long run. He said, "Either he can't or he *won't.*" How can Lyle know if that's true? But it did get me thinking. Maybe the tears came because I already knew, in my heart, what Lyle ended up putting into words. When I told Lyle that I *want* to believe that my marriage can work, he just warned me to be cautious. I'm so confused!

My daughter told me that I was too thin and it's gross to hug me! *Everyone* has an opinion! I don't know *what* I want regarding me. What should I look like? What should I do? Who the hell am I?

I was really frustrated at work today. I wanted to punch something, but I reminded myself that the anxiety would pass and *it did!* Choosing my thoughts *is* making a difference! Tonight, my husband brought up a lot of the "borderline" crap that I've pulled over the years. He's having trouble forgiving me, but I don't know what he expects me to say or do about it. I was just starting to feel good about myself and now I've been handed a crap-load of guilt! I got the same thing from my daughter a little earlier when I tried to apologize for everything I've screwed up on, including the suicide attempt. In a very matter-of-fact way she told me *not* to mess with my meds, even if I *feel* normal, because *the meds* are what *keep* me normal. She sounds like a *shrink*, instead of a kid! What have I done to her? I feel like I've messed up everyone's life!

I really hope I'm done with the cutting. Therapy has helped me in so many ways, even though Bill can't see it. I find myself wondering if *all* of our problems really are my fault. I know that's the black and white thinking, so typical of borderlines, but maybe it *was* me? Bill has stated that he's tried to get close to me over the years, but he claims that I've always put up a *wall*. Maybe he's right? I've caused so much trouble without ever meaning to. I guess all I can do now, is stay on my meds, try to get better, and hope for the best.

I'm back to seeing Lyle every two weeks instead of weekly, so I must be doing better. Bill and I talked about the day I overdosed. He told me about the fear he had that I was going to die or end up brain dead. Apparently the Dr. had told him that he didn't know *why* I was still alive. The drugs I took *should* have killed me! Bill said that a little later, when he returned to the E.R. with our daughter, I was no longer there! He was thinking the worst until he was told that I had been transferred to the Critical Care Unit, and *then* he thought the *next* worse! To have me *alive* as a "vegetable" would be worse than losing me altogether.

I told Bill that I had never meant to hurt him or Rachel! I'd only been trying to get away from my *own* private hell. I began to cry as I told him that I knew I had ruined our family. His response was very kind. He reminded me that *all* families have their demons. I said I knew that, but knowing that it was *me, personally,* who was responsible for our problems, made it exceptionally painful. He acknowledged how hard it's been for me trying to get better, and how difficult it must be to know that it could take *years* of therapy to undo the damage of border-line. I felt validated when he talked of the overwhelming task ahead of me. After Bill went to bed, I made a monumental decision! I gathered up all of my cutting supplies and threw them away! Being able to talk to my husband about my pain, and *his*, is a step in the right direction. It's these kinds of breakthroughs that can free me from the bondage of borderline.

I've been too afraid to weigh myself today. I've been such a glutton! I've got to get a grip on this bingeing! Am I substituting food for self-injury? I don't know. I've thought a lot about wanting to cut and *not* having the straight edge razor to do it with! I wish I hadn't thrown them out! Maybe I'm not ready after all? I have to be strong! I can do this! I *don't* need to cut!

Everyone, but Bill, keeps telling me I'm too skinny. Maybe that's why I keep pigging out? Do I secretly *want* to gain weight? My perception is wildly warped on this issue. I have no idea of what weight is truly best for me. When I told Bill that people keep telling me I'm too thin, he said that they're just jealous. I don't know *what* to think. Maybe he's right. Maybe they *are* jealous!

I've been thinking *a lot* about suicide *and* cutting! It's probably a good thing that I threw out the straight-edge razors. I'm feeling down and hopeless. Do I even *want* to get better? Is being *sick* too much a part of me? I don't know what to do about my marriage. I told Bill I was getting better, and most of the time I think I am, but I know that Bill only wants the "well" me. I honestly can't promise anything! I can't promise that I'll never cut. I can't promise that I'll never mess with my meds. I can't promise that I'll reach out for help when I need it. I can't promise that I won't ever kill myself. And most of all, I can't promise that I will *ever* be well.

I told my husband, that without emotional intimacy, I'm just going through the motions of being a wife; especially in the bedroom. I tried to tell him that I *need* to feel close to him. I *need* to feel loved! He wants everything to be porn-like; without tenderness or love. He didn't seem to listen to a single word I said! Our conversation left me feeling very sad and empty.

I couldn't stand *not* having my cutting supplies so I went out and bought more! I don't plan to use them. I just needed to *quiet* the anxiety of not having my ritual to fall back on. Just *knowing* that I have them, in case I need them, fills me with a calmness. The razors provide me with a sense of security. I know it's not rational, but...

Bill and I talked about what had first attracted us to each other. It was his confidence and my naivety. We also talked about the ways that we have unintentionally hurt the other. We've taken each other for granted for a very long time. Neither one of us realized how *alone* we both felt.

I'm back on the correct dose of my *atypical* anti-psychotic. (So does that mean I'm *not* your "typical" psychotic?) I decreased my meds for awhile, for various reasons, but within a few days, the symptoms started sneaking back in! I got shaky and agitated and jumpy. I had that awful feeling of *needing* to somehow jump out of my skin! When I started "seeing things," I knew it was time to "up the dose" again. Why can't my body manage without drugs? I'm not sure if I will *ever* get used to *having* to take medication just to be "normal."

I'm feeling very annoyed with people who harp on me to eat more! *I* don't harp on anybody about what *they* eat! Rachel was insisting that I eat dinner tonight (even though I wasn't hungry) and *then,* when I finally gave in and ate, Bill gleefully exclaimed, "You caved!" Talk about getting mixed messages! It seems that Bill and I are the *only* ones who think my weight is fine.

Bill got angry at me regarding sex. He thought that since he treated me so lovingly the last time, then it should be pornographic this time. When I told him that I had felt *valued* and *loved* when he treated me like a lady and that I wanted him to treat me that way again, he retorted with, "It's always about *you!*" I am so hurt! I was *finally* starting to feel safe with my own husband and then he pulls the rug out from under me!

Now I'm just plain pissed! I've been trying to be a better wife! I've been busting my butt trying to get healthy! Now I just feel like giving up! Fuck it all! Bill always turns the blame on me! No matter what it is, he finds a way to point to *me* as the entire problem! God, I'm angry! Why can't he accept, at least a part of, the blame? Neither one of us is completely innocent!

Lyle lectured me about weight. If he thinks 102 is low, what will he say to 92?

I'm *still* angry at Bill! It's all about sex and crudeness with him! There is *no* "depth" in our relationship; none whatsoever! There is no such thing as "making love!" Not in his mind! I feel like cutting, but why should I hurt myself? That's stupid. I'm not pissed at me! Bill makes me feel like *I'm* the entire problem. Maybe I am? Maybe I *should* hurt myself? I'm *done* with relationship books and all the other bullshit! *He's* not trying, so why should I?

I called Lyle and asked him to move my session up sooner. I'm feeling too panicky to wait. He said to call him if I need him. I'm really upset about the other night and the way Bill made it sound like *everything* is my fault! I've lost any ground I may have gained! I thought he and I were *finally* connecting! *Now* I find that it's all a lie!

I haven't been eating. I'm lightheaded and my mind is mush, but I've just got to lose weight! I have to! It's the only thing I have any control over! I modeled a new dress for Bill. I thought it made me look too thin, but Bill disagreed. He didn't think I looked skinny. Maybe Bill's right! Maybe people *are* jealous! I really wanted a hug tonight, but I decided to stay away from my goal-driven husband. Up goes the wall. I'm still floundering after Bill's harsh words Tuesday night. I'm truly devastated at his reaction to my request! I was only asking to be treated with respect, to be loved like a lady! I'm his *wife*! Why must he treat me like a whore?

I talked to Lyle about how upset I was with Bill. He said that Bill is afraid of true intimacy and that's why "it" has to be porn-like. And for me, without genuine intimacy, sex just leaves me feeling *used*. Bill's already told me that he views "intimacy" as a weakness, so I don't think there are any easy answers concerning this issue.

Bill said I was controlling because I asked him to turn the TV down when he was talking to me! I couldn't hear over the TV, so how was I supposed to hear what he was saying? *How* is that controlling? I was trying to hear *him*! I don't get it! I told Bill that I'm *gun shy* about feeling safe with him, because it always backfires! If I state a need, or something that's important to me, Bill turns it *against* me! He uses it as ammunition to hurt me. I've been trying to *own up* to *my* contributions to our problems, but if Bill isn't willing to do the same, then maybe this isn't going to work.

Bill and I talked about a lot of things tonight and I realized that he's *still* trying. He acknowledged how difficult the borderline issues have been for me. He *seems* to understand that it wasn't a matter of me not trying hard enough. As we were talking, Bill touched on one of the biggest roadblocks to me feeling loved by anyone: My childhood. (It definitely has a lot to do with my twisted perception of life.) He was right when he said that I don't feel loved by anyone in the *present,* because I never felt loved in the past, as a child. It's true! After Bill went to bed, I cried my heart out for the lost little girl I was. I'm *still* crying. I wish I could take the little girl I was and hold her in my arms and tell her that I love her more than anything in the world; that I will *always* love her! Here I am, a 44 year old woman crying her eyes out for the little girl I was and still *am!* The little girl who desperately wants to be loved.

Tonight, I had to draw blood from a 2 yr old. His mom sat in the recliner next to his crib and when her child started to cry, she did nothing to comfort him! He cried and cried and his mom ignored him! Even when I was done, and giving him stickers, she paid no attention to him. As I turned to leave, the little boy started to cry again. When I looked back, he was reaching through the crib slats... *for me*! I had just poked him with a needle, and he didn't want *me* to leave! He was starved for attention! He was starved for *love*! I couldn't believe that his mom could so blatantly ignore him! The whole scenario bothered me a lot more than I realized, until just now. Tonight's experience makes me even more aware of the little girl residing within. I need to *heal* that little girl. I think the only way to do that is to start by loving her, right now, with all of my heart!

I told Bill that he was right about my difficulty in feeling loved by anyone. It *does* stem from my childhood! I wanted him to know that I was going to *try* to love the little girl I *was*, now in the present. If I can heal *her,* then perhaps I can heal *me?* Then I began to share the story of the little boy I had drawn blood from the night before. As I started to explain what had happened, I began to cry. I couldn't hold back the tears! I literally *sobbed* through the entire story! (I'm not usually one to cry in front of *anyone.*) I had no idea that I was that shaken up! When I was finally able to compose myself, enough to get the words out, Bill stated simply, "That little boy was *you.*" He's right! Bill held me tight as I continued to cry. (I didn't know I had that many tears in me!) We talked about how I had never wanted more kids; how I had never even *liked* them. I told him, that when I hurt for that little boy, it was the first time I can ever remember *hurting* for a child. Ever! I don't know *why* I was so affected by this experience! Maybe it was the fact that his mother ignored his cries or that he looked like a *caged* animal or that even after I'd drawn his blood, he didn't want me to leave! It's not that *my* childhood was bad. My parents didn't abuse me or leave me wanting for anything. There were just too many kids! And, because I wasn't loud or bad, I faded into the background. I became *lost in the herd.*

I can't stop thinking about the child I was! She's in my thoughts constantly. I *need* to find a way to love *her*, so that I can love the *adult* I've become. Only then, will I be able to love the people around me and receive the love they give me.

I just bought a journal titled, "It's never too late to be what you might have been." I'm choosing to *love* that hurt little girl. To embrace her. To cherish her. I don't ever want to hurt that precious child again! How could I have hit her? And burned her? And cut her? And starved her? How could I have *hated* her? But I did.

April 2007- July 3rd 2007

I'm still amazed at my reaction regarding the little boy in the hospital! And I'm touched by Bill's response. I am awed by his insight! Hopefully, he'll continue to be more understanding as I navigate this path to wellness. It's been quite the struggle! (An arduous journey at best!) I've had many days where I've just wanted to throw in the towel, give up, and stop trying. But, if my own husband is willing to work with me, and I'm willing to work with *him*, then I think there's a fighting chance for *us*!

My goal, in recent days, has been to love the little girl within. In the last week or so, I've gained some valuable insight about myself and the child I was. I've known for a long time that I've hated myself, but what I didn't realize, was that I *also* hated the little girl I was! The innocent child, who never felt loved or valued or worth the space she took up, is still there, inside, waiting…

As I got ready for work this morning, I noticed that I felt neither up or down. There was no crisis to ruminate over. My marriage seems to be going well. (At the moment.) I'm working on loving the child I was. My job is going well. At first I felt *anxious* about the stability I was feeling! But then I realized that the "even keel" I was experiencing wasn't cause for alarm. It's what "normal" is *supposed* to feel like! The anxiety wasn't quick to leave and a part of me wanted to *cut,* but an even bigger part said, "No." And I listened! I *am* getting better!

Yesterday I talked to Bill about my share of the responsibilities regarding our marriage and the problems we've had through the years. I told him that Lyle has probably put *more* than a *fair share* of the blame on Bill; but only because he wanted to protect *me,* his patient. I know that Lyle wants what's best for me and because I haven't painted a totally accurate picture of Bill, I've unintentionally made him look like a bad guy. He's actually a good guy with *bad habits.* He treated me the way that *he* was taught *and* the way that I *allowed* him to. Now that we both want to save our marriage, he has become a willing student and I've become more aware of my own contributions to our struggles. I told Bill that I know I can continue to *heal,* by going to counseling, taking my meds, gaining insight and applying what I've learned. Bill said he's learned a lot too. He recognizes how he has hurt me, without meaning to, and he realizes that I didn't *choose* to be unhealthy. He's agreed to join me on this road to recovery.

I've been feeling very protective of the little girl within! I'm embracing her and loving her. No one had better say anything to hurt her, because I do believe I will speak up! This makes perfect sense since one of the goals of counseling, is to help me to find my own voice! (And then to use it!) I've also caught myself smiling at my reflection whenever I pass a mirror! In fact, I've been smiling quite a bit lately. It's as if I'm looking at myself, through the eyes of a *loving parent*. I'm beginning to see the inner and outer beauty of this person I'm just now getting to know.

I talked with Lyle today. I've been feeling panicky about my weight gain. Lyle finally agreed that we could "compromise" on what constitutes a healthy weight. We decided on a range of 102 lbs to 107 lbs. I still think it's too much!

Lyle said that I need to let people take care of me, but I'm not comfortable letting anyone take care of me. Heck, I *barely* allow myself to take care of me! I told Lyle that this "stupid borderline crap" is annoying and for some reason it made him chuckle, which in turn made *me* laugh! Being able to laugh at ourselves is a sign of healing, so maybe this therapy thing *is* working?

Before going to my session this morning, I styled my hair really curly, with the hope that it would make my face look less thin and then maybe Lyle wouldn't notice that I had gone below our agreed weight range. But he's no fool! He noticed right away! How can he do that? It was only a couple of pounds! Anyway, other than that, I enjoyed our visit. We talked of how we have the choice to "paint the day" any color, or in any*way*, we'd like. He even admitted that he was having a kind of *gray* day and that he had decided to just leave it gray! He said it's okay to do that once in awhile. Sometimes you just don't have the energy or strength it takes, to paint that particular day any other color but gray. I told him that I'm choosing to paint the day *sunny*! I felt bad later on when I realized that I could have stopped thinking about myself for two seconds, and paid attention to the fact that *Lyle* was having a bad day. He's human too! He probably could have used a genuine compliment and I *had* noticed that he was wearing, what appeared to be new clothes, and that he looked very nice! But I was so wrapped up in myself, as usual, that I didn't even comment on his new attire! I really need to start thinking of others!

How will I be able to drop my weight to 92 lbs without Lyle noticing? No matter how I try to hide it, he just seems to *know*! I have so much anxiety over this whole weight issue! I don't know how to stop it. Sigh.

I treated myself to a day in the big city! Just me, myself and I! Lyle tells me often, that I really need to do things that *I* enjoy and that I need to learn how to spend money on myself *without* feeling guilty! I don't know why it's so difficult for me. I bring home a paycheck. My husband has no trouble doing what *he* wants and spending as much money as it takes! Well... I listened to my therapist and I had a wonderful day! All told, I spent about $50.00 and it felt pretty darn good! That might represent pocket-change to some people, but for me, it was a huge deal! I purchased a set of coffee cups, complete with a special stand, that I'd been wanting for a couple of months. I also bought two bookmarks while I was at my favorite bookstore. They both say the same thing, "It's never too late to be what you might have been." How appropriate, since that's the quote by George Eliot written on the cover of my current journal. I bought one for Lyle, and one for me, so that we'll both have one to help us remember each other after therapy has concluded.

I sent Lyle a card today. It said, "Dear Lyle, Thank you for <u>never</u> giving up on me. I truly appreciate *you,* and all that you've done for me. I *am* getting stronger day by day and what *seems* like a set-back now, and again, is really just a stepping stone on this path to wellness. I continue to thank God for allowing this journey to unfold with you as my trusted mentor. I will do my best to *pay it forward."*

I think 102 lbs is about 10 lbs too much. I've been trying to cut back on calories, but I get so weak! I think some of the anxiety attacks might be related to my diet. But it doesn't matter *what* causes them, because I've learned that when I'm feeling panicky, the discomfort *will* pass and it always does! I told Lyle that I'm not happy with weighing this much, but I know it's "healthier." (I don't really believe that, but I figured it was what *he* wanted to hear.)

Lyle insists that I need to "let people in." I don't know about that. I still don't trust anyone, except maybe Lyle. I *wish* I could trust my husband. Although I *do* know he's trying because he's started giving me the non-sexual affection that I've asked for. He probably doesn't know it, because I've held him at arms length for so long, but I've been *craving affection* my entire life! There's a lot he doesn't know about me. He and I are both guilty of keeping our relationship superficial. It's not that either one of us is a bad person. We just haven't known any better. It's my hope, that if the little girl in me can feel loved and *safe,* then perhaps Bill and I can connect *emotionally.* And if *that* happens, then perhaps the *big* girl will feel a little freer to enjoy life as an *adult.*

I'm feeling a real change in me. I'm beginning to think of others *more* and myself less. I'm not sure *why*, but this frightens me! It's new territory and although I'm excited, I'm also *unnerved*! I find myself completely out of my element!

Why does my husband have to be "on" 24/7? He's *constantly* socializing! He finds it stimulating. I find it suffocating! He spends 5 mornings a week at the gym with a group of his friends and then they go out for coffee afterwards. They also get together several evenings a week! He wants me to be with him at these social engagements, but I find these events to be absolutely *draining* for me! I am truly a loner at heart. We just spent yesterday evening with the guys and their wives and now, less than 24 hours later, we're getting ready to go out again! In a few minutes, we're heading over to the house of one of his buddy's to "start drinking" before a wedding that we're all going to. It irritates me to no end that my husband and his friends drink so much! It seems as if they can't have fun without alcohol. I have no desire to drink, or to socialize, every flipping day! Is something wrong with me? Or with them? Or neither? I'm looking at the next 10 hours and dreading it with every fiber of my being!

Instead of jumping to conclusions with Bill, I've started asking him what he meant whenever I'm not sure. Apparently, asking questions to avoid misunderstandings is confusing to Bill. He gets irritated with me when I do! He'll say something like, "You know better than that!" And then I patiently tell him that I *don't* know and that's *why* I'm asking. He thinks that I should always *just know* what he means! Sigh

Rachel's graduation is approaching and we've been getting on each other's nerves. Lyle reminded me that this is a *normal* phase that children and their parents go through as the child moves on to adulthood. It's *especially* true with the mother/daughter relationship. It's as if the daughter is *competing* with the mother and therefore, the daughter cannot agree with anything that the mother says! (Or something like that.) When I complained to Bill about our daughter "suddenly becoming difficult," he said that she takes after *him* in the "lack of empathy" department. Maybe he's right.

The stress of Rachel's impending graduation is causing me to fall back a bit, into the self-injury mode of dealing with, or perhaps *not* dealing with, unpleasant emotions. I'm frustrated that I can't talk to Rachel about anything, without her having a condescending attitude. I'm finding this stage of her life to be quite painful. She's always been so agreeable and fun, but *now* she's like a stranger; someone I no longer know.

Thankfully I was able to refrain from cutting myself, but as I drove to town today, I felt anger rising up within me. Unable to diffuse it by thought alone, I pounded on my sternum repeatedly while screaming at the top of my lungs! Although tears welled up in my eyes, I refused to cry. Sounding like the stereotypical white-trash momma, I shouted obscenities at myself. "Knock it off you fucking loser! Don't you *dare* cry or I'll *give* you something to cry about!" I looked at my reflection in the rearview mirror and *hatred* for that person looking back, filled my empty heart. Maybe I never will be well. The self-hate is rearing its ugly head, once again, and I'm just too tired to fight it. Thoughts of suicide are back.

Bill is still trying to help me, and in turn, salvage our marriage. The fact that he's *willing,* makes me think that maybe I *should* give life a fighting chance. But... do I have the energy? I don't know about *anything* anymore. Maybe I never did. The tension of Rachel pulling on the apron strings is really dragging me down. Maybe it's time for a fresh start on both the mother/daughter relationship, as well as the husband/wife.

I sent Bill a card, to his work address, for no special reason. I just thought that since he's been trying so hard to be nice to me, that maybe he'd appreciate a card for no particular reason.

I'm learning to set boundaries! My dad called to invite himself over. I told him that he could come on Sunday and spend the night, but that *Saturday* would not be a good day to have company. In the past, whenever I referred to him as "company," he'd say he was family and *not* company. (He thought he should be allowed to drop in anytime, without notice.) I was really surprised when he actually respected my wishes this time.

There's a new girl at work and she is so hyper! She drives me crazy! I find myself wondering if I might have annoyed people like that, before I was diagnosed. (And subsequently put on medication that reined in my hyper behavior.) Maybe my "new normal" isn't so bad. I'm beginning to realize that "bouncing off the walls" probably wasn't that wonderful after all.

I was looking for some misplaced invitations and instead of getting pissed and irritated, I managed to stay calm by telling myself that there was no good reason to get upset. The invitations would show up eventually and they did! Wow! Changing my thoughts *can* change my behavior. Instead of re-acting, I can *choose* which *act*ion to take. Cool.

This "choose your thoughts" way of thinking worked really well for me on the job today. One of my superiors falsely accused me of something and instead of re-acting with anger, I chose to think through the situation and *then* I went to this person with the facts in hand and calmly explained what I had done. She realized that she had misinterpreted the earlier situation and, after thinking it through, she actually apologized to *me*!

My husband wanted me to go to yet another party with him, but I decided it wouldn't be in my best interest, so I told him that I needed some down time and wanted to stay home. He seemed fine with that.

I've been fighting a cold and one of the hospital employees told me that I was sick because I was too thin. How stupid is that? What is it with people anyway? I don't go around commenting on anyone's weight. Why in the hell does everyone have to harp on *me* about my weight? It really pisses me off! If they all think I'm too thin now...

I'm beginning to see what true beauty is. I was talking recently with a friend at the hospital and I asked her if she had ever worked with my mom, who had been a nurse there before she died. My friend said that yes, she had known her and that my mom was a beautiful lady! The reason this is significant for me, is because my mom wasn't beautiful by *movie star* standards, but she *was* a beautiful *person*! This encounter also reminded me of how my mom used to tell me that my smile was my best feature. That statement always bugged me because I never believed it was true! How could it be? I had crooked teeth! (I still do!) But *now*, I finally understand what my mom meant. When I'm happy, my smile lights up my whole face. So how can it *not* be my best feature?

Only 4 days until Rachel's graduation. I'm trying to be mature and bite my tongue whenever she pulls on the apron strings. *I'm* the grown up and I need to act like one!

I've been thinking about how I want to reach out to help others. I even prayed to God to help me to be a conduit of sorts. I want Him to show me *how* to use *His* love to love others; especially those who make it difficult to love them; myself included. I want to purposely love everyone I come into contact with. I no longer want to "pick and choose" who I'm going to give my love to. I want to learn how to think of my fellow human beings in a more loving way. I can start by *not* taking things so personally at work! I need to remember that most people are lost in their own little worlds and probably aren't even thinking of me or anyone else when they're rude. They're caught up in their only little dramas that only *they* can see.

I thought I would burst with pride and joy when Rachel received a plaque, at the awards ceremony tonight, for graduating from both High School and the Community College at the *same* time! She knew, since the 9th grade, that she wanted to enter the dual-study program so that she could get both diplomas at once! I have to admit that she gets her drive and ambition from her father. I'd like to think that I had a hand in her academic achievement as well, by exposing her to a large variety of experiences from the time she was an infant. (I wanted her to have the best possible start on life.)

I've been on a bit of an emotional rollercoaster lately with all of the graduation festivities. We had a graduation party for Rachel and I could see that my husband was having a ball playing host. He seems to be loved and respected by many.

I did the check-out for Bill, at the store, because he's on vacation. Last year I was a nervous wreck when I did it because he's never happy with the work I do! However, I didn't stress *at all* this year! I was also worried, last year that his employee might get sick and then I'd have to run the store! This year, whenever I would start to worry, I'd consciously shut the worry off by changing my thoughts! What a difference a year can make!

Well, I did something totally out of character for me. I bought form-fitting designer scrubs! The style doesn't hide my figure like the old unisex scrubs did. I'm a little nervous though, because you can tell I have boobs *and* a butt; unlike the baggy scrubs that hid both. I feel like this move has made the statement that not only am I done hiding, but I'm also worth the space I take up *and* I'm going to make that space beautiful!

I realized something today. I'm going to be fine with, or without, my husband. I'm *choosing* to have him in my life and knowing this has made a huge difference. I'm not stuck in some loveless marriage. I am choosing to work on this marriage, and hopefully make it a good one, but my self-worth is not dependent on being someone's *wife*. The power of choice is within me!

❧

Wow! I've been in therapy for 16 months already! This journey continues to lead me out of the darkness one step at a time. I thought for sure that I'd be done by now; either with therapy *or* with life. Lyle has truly been a gift from God.

❧

I wore the designer scrubs and got tons of compliments and I *hated* every minute of it! I'm not sure whether or not I can continue to wear them. They make me stand out, in a good way I guess, but it's too hard having that kind of attention all day! I was definitely out of my comfort zone!

❧

I had a strange dream last night. I had died and I was looking at the refrigerator in my house. There was a note attached to the door; simply stating, "Please don't leave." In the dream, I was aware that it was a message from my daughter in regards to my suicide attempt. As to the meaning of this dream, I suppose it would be my subconscious at work; still processing how my overdose may have impacted my daughter. I may never know the answer.

I've been thinking a lot about how we can change our lives, for the better, by first changing our thoughts. So whenever I begin to feel bad, about what I've put my family through, I need to change my thoughts. If I can remember that we're all here on this earth to learn lessons, then maybe I can see that my illness, and the actions it caused, are for the greater good. They are a part of the bigger picture: *The Master Plan.*

I wore the coral-colored scrubs today, and all I wanted to do was *cry*! I was completely out of my element! The other new scrubs made me uncomfortable, but this brightly colored combo *ruined* my entire day! Other people wear bright colors *and* fitted clothing all the time; people of all sizes, and yet I'm falling apart because of it! Lyle thinks that I should continue to wear these attention-grabbing scrubs, but I'm truly miserable! I don't think I can, or *should,* keep trying. Not at this time. Not on this issue. Not yet.

Why can't I be "well" and *still* wear baggy clothes? Why is it *not* ok, to *not* want to be noticed? The attention has been flattering, but I'm falling apart because of it! I've been told, over and over, how cute I look in these new scrubs and I just want to hide! My husband is irritated with me for not being thrilled with the attention these "cute scrubs" are causing. He can't understand how I could *not* like the attention. I'm feeling very angry and very frustrated with this whole issue. I've started up with the self-injury again; mostly hitting at this point.

This morning, as I tried to make my hair look nice, the inner critic taunted, "You're *not* kidding anyone! You're a middle-aged *has been.*" I wish I could quiet that voice. Permanently. A friend of mine told me that I look *older,* haggard even, since losing weight. Another friend said that I looked younger! So many mixed messages!

My husband just pointed out a woman on the TV that he thought looked fat, but I didn't think she was fat at all. I'm feeling out of control about so many things right now. The binge eating is running rampant and I'm feeling puffy and achy and chubby. I decided to wear the baggy scrubs today and I felt so comfortable! Fuck the critics!

One of the girls at work was being really pushy and I wanted to either blow up at her or hurt myself. But I chose neither! Instead, I took a walk and it worked! I calmed right down. The anger rapidly dissipated! I was able to recall what Lyle had once said about my self-injury, "So you were angry at _____ and to feel better, you hurt *yourself*?" Because I was able to remember his words, I could look at the current situation and realize how silly it would be to hurt *myself* when I was angry at someone else! Of course I would never injure another person, but learning to *not* injure myself as well, is a big step for me. The other thing that comes to mind, is the fact that I was *able* to draw upon the *past,* to help me with the present!

For so long, I was like a small child in the sense that I could *not* draw upon the past *or* visualize a future. The painful present was all there ever would be. I knew only what I was feeling, precisely at that moment. I didn't know that the pain would pass, or that I could draw upon memories or lessons to help me through it. I only knew that it hurt immensely and I wanted it to stop *at any cost*! And for me, that usually meant hurting myself physically. The pain of self-injury is very effective at numbing the pain of emotional discord.

I tried wearing the fitted scrubs again. I can't believe how much it seems, that people feel the need to comment on my size! They're bordering on *rude*! Even though each comment is actually a compliment, it bothers me that they have to say anything at all! I feel so chubby when I wear anything *fitted.* I weigh 20 lbs less than last year and yet I feel downright fat! I'm going to go back to the baggy, shapeless scrubs.

It's getting easier to state my needs or wants to my husband, in every aspect of our lives together. I don't think he always likes it, but I can no longer be his *puppet.* Lyle was right when he said that it's *draining* to always wear a *mask;* always trying to *be* what someone else wants. I'm learning to set boundaries with those around me. I'm no longer going to be at my family's beck and call. I inadvertently taught them to treat me as their servant, so I need to re-teach them. The unhealthy me allowed myself to be *used* without any thought of my own well-being. The healthy me says, "Enough!"

One day I feel great, full of life and then *wham*! The light and the energy are *gone*! Just *gone*! Where are you God?

Bill told me awhile back that he'd *never* leave me. Since then, I've quit pushing him away! That is, until yesterday, when I told Bill how much his "I'll never leave you statement" meant to me. His reply hurt deeply! He said that there are some things that I could do that would make him leave me, such as attempting suicide again. The *little girl* in me thought that his earlier comment had meant that he would stay with me no matter what! I'm heartbroken and disillusioned.

Lyle gave me an assignment today. He wants me to wear the new scrubs at least once a week. Why is it so fucking important? What's *wrong* with being comfortable?

I recently recalled a childhood memory. In it, I was locked in the basement. (That's where my bedroom was.) I had awakened from a nightmare and I was terrified, but I couldn't get to my parents because of the lock on the door. So instead, I woke my little brother and asked him if I could crawl into bed with him. I must have been about 3 or 4 at the time, so my brother would have only been about 2 years old. I thought he could protect me because he was a boy! (It didn't matter that he was probably *still* in diapers at the time!)

I weigh 102 lbs. It's enough to give me curves. I don't want curves!

I feel like I have *never* fit in with anyone, *especially* my own family. On the few occasions when I've tried to *act* like them, to *fit in,* I was belittled! I'm not sure *why* I even try? And this whole therapy process is downright draining! I'm so tired of trying to get better; trying to find a new and healthy *normal.* I've started skipping my meds with the hope of gaining some energy. (And losing a few pounds.)

I'm tired of being chubby! Less than 1,000 calories a day for last few days. Just do it! Are people actually concerned about my weight, or are they just jealous like my husband thinks they are? I looked in the mirror today and I *didn't* see a chubby person! (I wish I could see that reflection every time.)

Fat phobia intensifies! What if I gain weight due to an illness or a medication? I need to be *under*weight now! (Just in case.) Why on earth do I eat so much? Especially when I want to *lose* weight. I just downed nine granola bars and three full-sized candy bars in less than 20 minutes! *Why* do I do it? *Why? Why? Why?*

The CCU staff paid me a nice compliment today: They said that *they* love me, the *patients* love me, and that I do a great job! No wonder I like being at *work* rather than being at home! I get to feel appreciated when I'm working! I've decided to increase my meds to the proper dose, because I've started noticing the return of symptoms. I don't want to do anything that will jeopardize my job! Too much of my self-esteem is still tied up in what I do for a living.

Well… it's been two weeks and I still haven't worn the designer scrubs. I just can't do it! I'm so angry at being pressured, by both Bill and Lyle, to wear fitted, attractive clothing! I shouldn't care what they think! And yet, at the same time, I do wonder *why* I'm resisting so much on this issue?

Y

I finally caved and wore the new scrubs again. I was uncomfortable ALL day and very, very body-aware! When I got home tonight, I decided to try on clothes. I spent nearly two hours trying on practically everything in my closet and drawers! It's weird, but I didn't see a fat person when I was looking in the mirror. And the journey continues…

I've been trying to come up with a list of ways to enjoy life. My entire *sense of self* is tied up in work, so I've been racking my brain for ideas on how to enjoy life *outside* of work. At times it seems that my progress is excruciatingly slow, but I'm continuing to gain insight. And *sometimes,* I even *apply* that insight! The pieces are coming together and I know that, *eventually,* I will be whole!

I'm slowly, but surely, becoming less afraid to be with people, includ-ing my own family. When I talked with Bill this morning, I told him about my fear to be around anyone, even my loved ones, for more than 2 minutes. At that point, he got up from his chair and came and sat next to me on the couch. My first impulse was to pull away, but I resisted and then Bill sat even closer! I felt panicky at having someone, *anyone,* in my safe little "bubble." *Then,* Bill cradled my face in his hands and each time I turned away, he gently brought me back to face him. In a sense, he was helping *me* to face *my* fear of intimacy! I've been saying for months now, maybe longer, that I want *true* intimacy; *real* intimacy! But, if I'm honest with myself, I'm holding back as much as Bill; maybe *more*! Apparently my motto, "Reject them, before they can reject me!" is still very much a part of my makeup! Is there no end to this battle with myself?

One of the girls at work betrayed my trust and I called her on it. This tells me that I'm beginning to stand up for myself! I'm also trying to figure out *how* to accept myself, right now, just the way that I am. Recently, I've been bothered a lot about the signs of *aging* on my body. I think it's because my skin is looser at this lower weight. If I can learn to accept myself, my whole self, inside and out, mentally and physically, then maybe those signs of aging won't be so difficult to accept?

I believe, in my heart, that God will never leave any one of us unless we *ask* Him to leave. And even then, He will still be near, waiting for us to change our minds; to ask Him back into our lives. As a small child, I learned that *God is Love.* But that same church *also* told me that I would be damned to Hell, for all eternity, if I didn't do exactly what they said! Even as a *child*, I didn't want God to burn *anyone* for all eternity; no matter how bad that person was! And besides, he was *still* someone's child! And even if God wouldn't spare the *sinner*, how could He hurt the *family* like that? Wouldn't the knowledge that your loved one was doomed for all eternity, to burn forever in the lake of fire, cause you and your family a most horrible pain? Why would God devastate a family like that? In my heart, I don't believe He would.

I had to be around 5 or 6 when I was thinking those thoughts about God and Heaven and Hell. I sure as heck didn't want to be damned to Hell. But at the same time, I just couldn't see how this Father-figure, God, could punish anyone that harshly! If He truly loves us as a father loves his own children, then why on earth would He give us free-will and then wait for us to fail, so that He could render us sinners to be burned for all eternity. As a child, and even more as an adult, I believe that God loves each and every one of us. And I bet He probably gets downright pissed at us sometimes, and the choices we make, but that wouldn't make a Father *stop* loving His children. Years ago, I remember hearing the words, "…and a child shall lead them." I don't know *what* those words were referring to, but it makes me think that maybe *children* have the most accurate image of God. (Before they are *trained* in the ways of their church.) Just a thought.

I only ate 430 calories yesterday and I'm holding steady at 97 lbs! I do feel a little weak and spacey, but I'm happy with this weight. (*Today* anyway!) I went clothes shopping, but the only clothes that fit, looked *way too young* for someone my age! Seeing myself in the department store mirrors, under the florescent lighting, didn't help my self-image much! Parts of me are too skinny and yet other parts are too fat.

I read some passages, to Bill, from Rachel Reiland's book, "Get Me Out Of Here." Some of them are so powerful that I can't help but cry whenever I read them! Bill sat close to me as I read. His nearness made me anxious and nervous, but I *didn't* pull away! I know that he never meant to hurt me. His comments of "suck it up" or "let it go" were *not* born of malice. He truly thought he was helping! My perception of everything was colored by the borderline and, to some extent, the bipolar. I *saw* through a distorted lens. And for a long time, *nobody* (including myself) was aware of the faulty filter.

It's the 4th of July and I've been in therapy for a year and a half. I'm celebrating a personal sort of Independence Day; one just for *me*! I'm celebrating *freedom* from the borderline personality disorder, *freedom* from the hell it caused, and *freedom* from self-injury. It's not entirely gone yet, but recovery is so close. I know it's only a matter of time. My suicide attempt was 18 months ago today and I can't help but reflect back on this amazing journey!

My session today was awesome! I realized, for the first time, that when someone disagrees with me, they're *not* rejecting *me*! I've always tried to keep the peace, at all costs, because if I didn't and then someone disagreed, I thought they would abandon me. Then *who* would I be? I don't need those unhealthy attachments anymore; to *anyone*! I am a *whole* person just as I am! Lyle said that it's time to let the little kid in me play without caring about what other people think! *I* get to decide what I like and what I want!

I feel like I've reached a real milestone. I can tell that I am getting healthier all the time. I am no longer that little two year old trapped in the body of a full-grown woman. Am I ready to fly sole? Not quite. However, I know that with each passing day, I *am* getting closer to leaving the safety of the Lyle's "nest." I feel a little sad though, at the thought of ending therapy, because at one time I needed Lyle so much that it scared me! But *now*, as I become an adult *emotionally*, I will soon *want* to cut the apron strings. It's what healthy people do.

A few days ago I was thinking back over this journey. I thought about how I had felt that day, when I tried to end my life. I can still remember *begging* God to end my suffering. "Please take me home!" was my repeated and desperate cry. I wanted to be in His Presence, to feel His Love. But instead of taking me home, He brought His love to me! I recently came across some writings; all within the space of about 48 hours. They included: The Lord's Prayer, Footprints, The Serenity Prayer, and Amazing Grace! I think God wanted to remind me of His love in a very real and tangible way! I've seen all of these writings before, but *now* they all have *new* meaning for me! I'm beginning to see what God sees when He looks at *me*, His child. I'm beginning to see, through *His* eyes, a beautiful, wonderful woman!

July 4th 2007 thru July 31st 2007

Today is the first day of the rest of my life. Throughout this journey, God has placed people exactly where I needed them *when* I needed them. I call them my "Earth Angels." The *Earth Angel* I am most grateful for is Lyle… my therapist, my mentor, my friend. He's seen me through many dark and desperate days.

When I first met Lyle, I had absolutely no faith in myself and no love for myself. None! Nada! Zero! I was filled with self-hate, self-loathing and *rage*; *so much rage*! Because it had never been safe for me to *vent* unpleasant feelings, I held them all inside until I could stand it no longer! It was then that I would slip away from everyone, to diffuse the rage and the overwhelming anxiety it caused. I did this in the only way I knew how; by hurting myself.

Now I'm beginning to be able to draw upon what Lyle has taught me; even in the midst of a developing rage! I'm gaining ground in this new way of thinking. My perception is changing in ways I never thought possible. If someone had told me, a year ago, that I could "lose the rage" by changing my thoughts, I would not have believed them! Lyle told me, early in therapy, that these things would happen. He promised that new and healthy ways of thinking would become second nature; if only I would practice what he was teaching me.

Throughout my journals, I have penned the words, "Practice, practice, practice." They are there to remind me to *never* give up! The rage *within* threatened to kill me for so long, that I assumed it would *eventually*! Whether it was on the surface, just beneath, or buried so deep that I couldn't find its source, *it* was always there; this *rage*! But *now* it's finally receding! Perhaps someday it will dissipate all together.

My second earth angel is Dr. Stoune. He has battled his own demons and has *emerged* stronger and wiser. I know that I can go to him for advice, whether it's medical or spiritual, and he won't sit in judgment. I always enjoy our visits! I try to remember him in my prayers each day as I thank God for blessing me and those I serve.

I was at a party recently when a male friend of mine voiced his concern about my thinness, while another male friend said I looked *sexy*. (More mixed messages!) The words from the *first* friend made me feel safe and protected, but the "sexy" comment from the other friend made me feel dirty! I'm writing about this because I *know* that one of the reasons for wanting to be thin, is to be as *small* as possible; *childlike*. Inside, I'm *still* the little girl who craves to be taken care of; who wants to be protected; who *needs* to be loved! (Not as an adult, but as a *child*!) Maybe this has something to do with my failure to grow up *emotionally* at the proper chronological time?

Earlier today I felt like a 2 yr old ready for a meltdown, but I didn't *react* to the feelings. Instead, I made the conscious choice to *choose* my thoughts; thoughts that would be *helpful*. I was able to remind

myself that *feelings*, no matter *how* intense, will always pass! *Always!*
And because I was able to remember this, I calmed down without
incident!

I've been on a bender of sorts, but not with alcohol. My drug of choice
is sugar! I don't know what showed up first; this latest depression or the
binge eating? I just know that I'm feeling very *slowed down*. The symptoms of depression are back, including isolating behavior. With the
borderline nearly gone, I need to remember that I'm *still* bipolar and
probably always will be. I pulled out one of my books on bipolar disorder, so that I could refresh my memory about what to do when I'm
on a downswing. The self-help strategies included: Increasing meds,
regular wake/sleep cycles, taking it easy, not forcing interaction with
the environment, etc. I *had* been thinking about cutting down on my
meds, without my Doctor's approval, but now I think I'd better stay
on the higher dose. According to the self-help manual, just *recognizing*
your symptoms can help to *stop* the downward spiral.

After reading the symptoms for depression, I noticed that some of my
symptoms could only be found under the *mania* check-off list. That
would point to a *mixed* episode. Lyle tells me that "Drugs are good!"
(When he's trying to convince me to stay on them.) It sounds ironic,
since most mentors would tell you, "Drugs are bad! Don't do them!"
But, for people like me… Bill said he's worried about me because I've
withdrawn so much, but I can't help it. I just don't have the energy it
takes to converse.

I was down to 97 lbs at my last session with Lyle and he didn't seem
to notice. I don't know why I'm disappointed, since it just pisses me
off when he brings up the subject. Sometimes I think that maybe I

actually *want* the "weight lecture!" How messed up is that? It makes me realize that I'm *impossible* to please! I feel sorry for anyone who tries.

I wish I knew how to make myself eat like a normal person. I'm either "stuffing" or "starving." It's got to be hard on my body. I'd like to ask Lyle for help with my binge eating, but at this point in time, he'd probably be thrilled to know that I routinely scarf down 5,000 calories in a single evening! *Why* do I do it? *Why? Why? Why?*

My husband invited me to sit outside on the bench swing with him. I resisted at first because it wasn't a part of my regular routine. I felt extremely panicked! Hopefully, Bill didn't notice the internal struggle I was having. I don't know *why* it's so hard for me to be spontaneous! We're talking about a sitting on a bench, enjoying the outdoors with your spouse and all I can do is panic? I did the very same thing when Bill asked me to go to town with him for the afternoon. I'm sure I must be a thorn in his side.

I am so torn about needing Lyle and *not* needing him! I'm feeling really angry with him, but I'm not sure why? I've convinced myself that he's tired of me, and that he wishes I'd just go away. I don't know where these thoughts come from. Maybe it's just me. Maybe I'm pulling away from Lyle the same way that a daughter pulls away from her parents; the way that my own daughter is pulling away from me!

I might cancel my appt with Lyle because I'm embarrassed by how fat I've gotten! I'm up to 104 lbs. I have to lose this weight. I threw out all of my junk food! I even unwrapped it first, and ran water over it, so I wouldn't be tempted to dig through the trash later! Do I have any shred of dignity?

I am so disgusted with myself! How can I be such a glutton? What was I thinking? *Now*, instead of losing 5 lbs, I need to lose 10 lbs! How can I be so stupid? What an idiot! 10 lbs isn't enough. Who am I kidding? What a pig! I told my husband that I was disgusted at myself for gaining weight. I really wanted him to say that I looked good, but it'll be a cold day in hell before he thinks *any* fat is okay. What the fuck is my problem anyway? Am I trying to fill a void of some sort? My new wt goal is 89 lbs. I'm still feeling really angry with Lyle! Just when I'm getting my shit together, I blow it! Why is weight such an issue? How sad that this life was wasted on me! I'm so tired of trying to get better. It's too much work! I wish that I didn't exist at all. If I were to succeed in killing myself, it would hurt my family. I don't want to hurt anyone. I just wish that I *wanted* to live! Sigh.

I need to get my weight under control! I'm up to 105 lbs!!!!!!! Lyle claims to be worried about my health. Whatever. We talked about endocrinology and the effects of a poor diet on blood sugar. Blah, blah, blah. I know that I should, at the very least, take vitamin supplements, but when I'm depressed, even *that* seems like too much work. I'm running on empty. I would cut if I could get away with it *and* if I had the energy.

Yeah! Energy returning! Am I getting manic? Total obsession with weight! It's all I seem to think about. I'm so afraid of getting fat again! I don't want to be noticed and yet I *am* noticed! (Because of my thinness.) It's so confusing. A part of me is panicking at the thought of ending therapy. I get to choose when it's time, but I'm not ready yet. I still *need* Lyle! He's been like a loving parent to me.

I have to admit that I have *toyed* with the idea of holding onto the anorexia because "it" could keep Lyle and me together! I wonder if *that's* where part of my anger is coming from; knowing that the time is fast approaching for me to grow up and move on? The good news is that I don't feel any rage or self-hate; just anger and maybe some sadness. I decided that Lyle was right when he said that I should let my inner kid have some fun, so I bought a couple of easy puzzles and some sidewalk chalk. I had the afternoon to myself, so I put one of the puzzles together and found that I enjoyed it immensely, because I did it alone! There wasn't anyone there; trying to compete and making me feel rushed!

I'm still having trouble wearing the new scrubs. I have too much anxiety with being noticed. Might try again. Someday.

I sent Lyle a letter today:

Dear Lyle, I don't know what challenges you face personally, but thank you for helping me to face mine. The enclosed bookmark is one of two that I bought for us. The quote, "It's never too late to be what you might have been." makes me think of you and how your guidance has made it possible to believe those words. I'm a work in progress; as we all are I suppose and I'll do my best to keep working towards *wellness*. After reading through some of my more recent journal entries, I've come to the conclusion that one of my biggest fears right now is *leaving the nest.* (Therapy) Whenever I begin to feel healed and whole and ready to strike out on my own, I seem to panic on some level. A part of me wants nothing more than to be "grown up" and "ready to fly," but another part of me is <u>absolutely terrified</u>! I'll work on it, but I think I'm still going to need your help for awhile. Thank you for everything! I'll see you on the 31st."

I feel small and unimportant when I'm in a group. No one listens. (Went out with Bill and his friends.)

I still fight myself on the medication issue. I constantly doubt my need for it, but every time I try to decrease the dose, or even stop it altogether, the only thing I *prove* is that I do need it! I hope there will come a day when I can truly accept medication as a life-long treatment. On a happier note, I'm learning to trust my judgment about a lot of other things. For years I allowed myself to be practically groped by a dirty old man, who works at the hospital, because I couldn't let myself seem disrespectful. This man goes around the work place, at least once a day, and grabs each female employee in a bear hug; which in itself isn't bad. It's the fact that his hands always wander south! I've learned to be "unavailable" whenever he heads my way. I'm working on setting up those healthy boundaries!

I just woke from a terrifying nightmare! I was walking with a group of people, and we were all having a good time, when I happened to look down and saw that we were on a narrow beam, hundreds of feet above the ground! I came to a screeching halt and flattened myself to the beam. No amount of coaxing by anyone would make me budge. At one point, someone tried to move me just a little and I screamed for them to leave me where I was. None of the other people, I had been walking with, seemed the least bit concerned about the dangerous height we were at. In fact, everyone else seemed to be thriving somehow! I tried to formulate a plan for my rescue, but I found that not only was my body paralyzed by fear, so was my mind! I could feel the beam begin to collapse beneath me! First it fell just an inch, then a couple more, and then it completely gave way and I woke up! When I talked to Lyle about the dream, he reminded me that change is hard and that's what this dream represents. He said that the beam itself represents my old life, the one with the borderline personality disorder, and that even when change is for the better, it's still very difficult! That certainly makes sense.

I watched a couple of movies that helped me to see people, of all shapes and sizes, as being beautiful! For so long, beauty to me... was being what I *wasn't*! I thought that I had to be tall, busty, and blond, in order to be beautiful. I'm beginning to see that "beauty" truly does come in all shapes and sizes! Both movies also stressed the importance of being *yourself*. I'm trying, but it's still not easy.

I felt the familiar pangs of anxiety rising up within me and, without even thinking, my inner voice came through loud and clear, "I love you and I'm not going to let you hurt yourself." Wow! Maybe Lyle was right about how, "practice, practice, practice" could actually change my thoughts and behavior! My response to the anxiety was positive *and* more importantly, it was *automatic*; without conscious thought! Talking nicely to myself is becoming "second nature!"

Bill was pleased that I was wearing the size 0 pants when we went out. He said that I was getting skinny. (Does that mean I'm *not* skinny?) I've noticed that he contradicts himself quite a bit. He told a female friend of ours to finish our nachos because she was too skinny, but behind her back, he told me that she'd *never* be skinny! When I called him on it, he accused me of belittling him. How is that belittling? I'm just trying to figure out, whether or not, his opinion about *my* weight should matter to me. I'm learning to be true to myself.

Trouble with blood sugar again. Sigh. It was 49 this afternoon and I felt confused and disoriented, but *not* hungry. Weird. Lyle thinks I'm going to wear out my pancreas with my horrible eating habits. He thinks I could end up with diabetes someday. Whatever.

We've got company coming with us on our camping trip. They'll be in the motor home with us on the way up *and* throughout the entire trip! I'm already feeling suffocated! I need to work on changing my thoughts because I can't very well tell them that they can't stay with us, since my husband has already invited them! I have a hard enough time being with my own family in such cramped quarters. I'm not sure *how* I'm going to be able to get through these next few days. I'll try really hard to direct my thoughts in a more positive light.

Well, the camping trip was ok, even fun at times. It did feel too crowded and I actually sent people out of the motor home when I was cooking, so that I could concentrate better and have some quiet time. I did get super irritated with *myself,* once during the trip, when I got lost on the four-wheeler. But I recited the serenity prayer and was able to calm myself without resorting to unhealthy behavior. I have no sense of direction and the prayer helped me to remember that I wasn't born with "a sense of direction" and that it's something that I can't change no matter how hard I try. Normally I would not have gotten lost when we're four-wheeling, because at every fork in the road, the person riding the 4-wheeler in front is suppose to wait for the next rider, but *my* person didn't wait! I didn't know which way to go, so I guessed, but I guessed wrong. After awhile, someone had to go and find me! I was really embarrassed *and* angry, but I didn't show it. And I didn't take it out on myself either! I just recited the prayer and then I "let it go!"

I felt bad about several things I said on the camping trip. At one point, Bill tried to sit closer to me and I told him that he was in my "bubble." The real reason was because we were eating and I'm always self-conscious about chewing too loud, so I didn't want to be close to *anyone.* The reason for this issue goes back to when I first met Bill and he told me that I chewed too loud! I must have been eating chips or something else crunchy, because I always chew with my mouth *closed,* so I don't know *why* he made that comment. It's silly that it would *still* bother me after 24 years!

Another thing that I feel bad about, was what I said when my husband was trying to race someone on the freeway. (While we were all in the motor home.) I *yelled* at him, from the back of the RV, to stop it! His friends looked at me like I was a crazy! Normally I don't yell, but his driving was scaring me! It was downright dangerous as far as I was concerned! It also sets a really bad example for our child. It's not that Bill's a bad guy. He just makes some bad choices!

This morning I told Lyle about my camping trip and how I had felt when it seemed like one of the guys, who was staying with us, had leered at me all weekend! I hated it! I told my husband that the guy was "creeping me out" but Bill couldn't understand *why* it would bother me! He thought that I should be happy that someone found me attractive. I wanted Bill to somehow protect me from what I perceived as a threat, but instead he made me feel stupid! (Someday I'll be able to protect myself!) I also told Lyle that several of the guys complimented me on my thinness and downright praised me for weighing 96 lbs! I started to think that maybe I really was skinny, but when I got home and looked into the mirror, I once again saw a chubby person looking back!

Lyle tried to help me to understand *why* I see a fat person one day and a skinny person the next. (Without any change in weight.) It has to do with how I'm feeling about myself. Before and during the trip, I felt okay about both my weight and myself. However, by the end of the trip, after feeling like I had been *leered* at all weekend, and with no support from my husband, I started to feel like nothing more than a piece of meat! I became upset at being made to feel like a sex object and somehow that caused me to see an "untruth" when I looked into the mirror. I find it so bizarre, but it's true! Lyle has instructed me to say "That's a lie!" whenever I see a fat, or chubby, person looking back at me. My brain distorts what it sees and it's up to *me* to re-train it.

Lyle doesn't want me to wait two weeks before our next session. I got really teary-eyed today because I know, intellectually, that I'm very thin, but I'm having a hard time reconciling what's real with what's not. Lyle wants me to pay more attention to the *truly concerned* people in my life, regarding my weight. He said that he's very worried about how thin I've gotten. I feel like he really cares about me. I know that Lyle is right, but I don't know *how* to stop the dieting. It's taken on a life of its own! I can't believe I once thought that I looked good at 110 lbs. That sounds unbelievably *huge* to me now!

I told Bill about the nightmare of being "trapped" high in the air, on a narrow beam, and how Lyle said that the dream represents "change." I told him that I *do* want his help; but that I'm afraid he'll give up on me before I can get well. I've been thinking about how we are all here, on earth, to learn lessons. Perhaps Bill and I can learn from each other. Bill told me that a lot of the time, I reject him when he's trying to give me non-sexual attention. I thought about it and realized that he's right! It's true! It's a knee-jerk reaction! Am I still afraid of being groped? And why is that a fear anyway? I asked him to please keep trying and he said that he would. I told him that I *need* to know that I'm more than just a "body." His response was kind as he listed some nice qualities that had nothing to do with my appearance. He's learning! We both are!

My reflection is still distorted despite saying, "That's a lie!" I don't want to worry anyone with my weight issues, so I'm keeping quiet about what I continue to see in the mirror. I know that I've come too far to give up now, but I'm feeling hopeless about this body image problem! And I *still* wish that Bill would say, "Don't lose anymore weight!" I wonder if I'm substituting *starving* for cutting? Maybe I should ask Lyle; not that it will make any difference in how I feel or what I think. I've been entertaining thoughts of suicide again and I'm listening to sad music with lyrics about ending it all. What is going on? I thought I was done with that line of thinking!

I can't sleep and it's really pissing me off! I took my meds an hour ago and I'm still wide awake! It's so frustrating to not know *when* the damn pills will kick in! It could be 20 minutes or 3 hours! My fricking mind won't stop racing!!! I have that dreaded "jumping out of my skin" feeling and I can't sit still or think clearly! I want to physically explode! Maybe pacing for awhile will help. At least it'll burn calories! Why is "embracing wellness" so flipping hard for me? Racing mind, pacing body, nothing helps!!!!! Why is being "normal" so damn difficult? I'm so sick and tired of trying, day after day, with no end in sight.

Lyle and I talked about the anorexia again. I got teary-eyed as I told him that I don't know how to stop seeing a fat person whenever I look at myself. Lyle asked me to promise him that I'd eat more, but he and I both know that I can't promise anything. Not yet.

I felt very agitated tonight. I told Bill that I didn't want to be hugged, or even touched. I confessed that I didn't have a reason, except that my skin feels prickly; like it's on fire and I *need* to burst out of it somehow! I feel restless, on edge, and wired! Rachel will be leaving for college soon. Was I a good enough mom? Did the "good" outweigh the "bad?" I wish I could die, but without hurting anyone. Since that's not possible, I'm *stuck*! I feel bad for Bill. He deserves a wife who can be there for him in *all* ways.

During a code in the ER, the Dr. in charge asked me if I needed help getting blood from the patient. I told him that I was ok and I went ahead and drew blood from the patient *while* CPR was being performed! I feel very competent at work. I wish I felt that way at home.

I've been good about taking my drugs for 15 days now. I thought a lower dose would be okay, but it wasn't, so now I'm back on the correct dose. I wish I wasn't so thick-skulled on this matter! I did a lot of reading on diabetes today and the literature points to me being pre-diabetic! I find that hard to believe!

I recently re-read a book about borderline personality disorder called, "I hate you! Don't leave me." After reading it again, I can see that despite setbacks, I've come a very long way! I truly am beginning to form my *own* identity! I'm still taking baby steps, but I *am* learning to stand on my own two feet. I'm getting more assertive as well. I've come to realize that people routinely speak their minds, get on each others nerves, fight even, and yet they *still* like each other! This is a *huge* eye-opener for me! I thought I had to be nice *all the time*, and *not* speak my mind, in order to be accepted! I've discovered that people will either like me or they won't. But I only need to be true to myself! It's *my* acceptance of me that matters! One of my co-workers is always asking me to do stuff for her, but today I told her, "No" on two separate occasions! And the world didn't come crashing in! I'm finally setting boundaries with people because I'm realizing that I am *not* worthless. And I *don't* have to be "nice" all of the time!

I've noticed that my hatred of everything "female" is fading away. I'm becoming more comfortable with my gender. Just because there are men who treat women as nothing more than sex objects, doesn't mean that I have to share that narrow-minded view. I do *not* have to accept such prejudice as a reflection of *my* own beliefs!

I'm learning to control my anxiety and subsequent self-injury, by saying to myself, "I love you and I'm not going to let you hurt yourself." Sometimes it works and sometimes it doesn't. I've also been practicing what Lyle taught me about challenging the "distorted image" I see in the mirror. I'm suppose to say, "That's a lie!" whenever I see a chubby person looking back at me, but it's not as easy as Lyle makes it sound. I've also been trying to eat like a *normal* person, but that too, isn't easy!

My fear of getting fat is overwhelming at times. I feel panicky just *thinking* about gaining weight! If I can just lose a few more pounds, maybe the fear will let up. I've tried telling myself that it's okay to *not* lose any more weight, but it feels like a *lie*! Why can't I be normal? What would it be like, to *eat* like a normal person? And to *not* weigh or measure myself *every* hour of *every* day! My mind plays such tricks on me! How can I see something totally different from one day to the next? (Although… I *do* find it fascinating in a strange and morbid way.) Will I ever be thin enough, so that when I see my reflection, I'll say, "Gee, you need to *gain* a few pounds?" How thin do I have to *be* in order to *see* thin? It's probably not even about weight! I told Lyle that if I can just get past this so-called anorexia, then I'll be home free! Of course, in the very next breath, I acknowledged that it wasn't true. I'm aware that I still have a long way to go.

I've been such a whining ingrate when it comes to my meds! Instead of complaining about needing meds for the bipolar disorder, I should be thanking God that they exist! I see people every day that need a handful of meds, morning, noon and night; just to stay alive! And I'm bitching about one little pill? Enough of the pity party already!

I'm becoming more and more aware of this process of learning to trust people. It began with Lyle and, eventually, it will extend to include myself. And hopefully, with time, I will be able to trust other people as well. This applies also to *love*. Choosing to love people, with all of their imperfections, is a powerful choice. I read in a book, by Neal Donald Walsch, that we are all, "perfectly imperfect" and that we are also, "as beautiful and as individual as a snowflake." Good words to remember!

Two of my sisters are flying in today. Neither one of them knows about my suicide attempt. I'm feeling really stressed about seeing them and going to a family reunion together. I'm hiding this big dark secret and I don't know if I should share it with them. My relationships, with *everyone*, have been superficial. I don't know *how* to approach this is-sue. Maybe I should keep quiet. Bill could tell that I was struggling last night and he asked me if he could help. I was touched by his concern. He proved to be very supportive as he gathered me into a hug. He held me in his arms, as a father would hold his child, and we stayed that way for a long time.

I feel completely drained after the weekend with the extended family. I told my sisters about the OD and they didn't appear to be very affected by the news. Maybe it didn't have time to sink in. I just feel numb.

I was stuck behind a slow driver today on my way back from the air-port. As I relayed the incident and my frustration to my husband, *he sided with the driver*! Rage instantly boiled up inside of me and the numbness that I'd been feeling for the last few days quickly vanished! How can something, seemingly *benign,* unleash the monster of border-line in nothing but a heartbeat? My husband said I was overreacting and maybe I was, but *why* can't he ever side with *me?* I tried to stay calm, on the outside, as I kissed my husband and went out the door to "run errands." What I *really* wanted… was the privacy I needed, in order to beat the living shit out of myself! And for what? I don't have an answer! I'm such a fuck up!

I talked to Lyle about the family reunion and my numbness following it. He reminded me that "numbness" is covering up the *real* emotion, which could be anger. We talked about how superficial my relation-ships are with almost everyone. I told him about Bill siding with the driver when I first got back into town, and how I had really just needed to feel connected to someone. Instead, I felt betrayed. Poor Bill! He doesn't have a chance with this crazy woman!

Lyle and I talked about my discomfort with accepting compliments. It stems from the "conditioning" I received over the years from my husband. His vulgar comments about women, and who he would or wouldn't "*do,*" have tainted my views on the true value of women. My vision of real beauty has been warped in the process. I know he didn't mean to hurt me, but the incessant comments about sex, and the vul-gar delivery of these comments, did in fact hurt me. *A lot.*

The self-injury and the self-hate that began in childhood, was rein-forced and cemented in adulthood. Lyle's always telling me that I need to direct my anger to *where it belongs*! I need to stop blaming *myself* for everything. It's okay to accept blame if it truly belongs to me. But don't accept, as my own, the sins of another. He makes everything sound so easy! It's not that simple. I've accepted the blame for everything for as long as I can remember. I don't know *how* to stop. I'm feeling disconnected from everything. Anxiety has its claws in me again. (Or still!) Suicide floats around in my brain as a viable option to living with a madness that never truly goes away. But that's part of the problem also! If I choose to end my life, who's to say that I'll be *free* from *my mind?* Perhaps *it* will follow me forever? I feel completely overwhelmed at the depth, in which the borderline personality *resides* in my *psyche.* I can't get away from the *grip* that it has on *every* facet of my brain, of my mind, of my *life.* I want it *out!* I want it out *now!*

I called Lyle for a sooner appointment. I don't know what's wrong with me, but I'm scaring myself with constant thoughts of suicide.

Lyle thinks that I'm using the anorexia to hurt myself. He said that it's a slow form of suicide. Whatever. I just know that I'm feeling mentally fragile. Bill has been trying to offer me support and affection, but I always pull away! *Why* do I do that? Lyle said it's because of past conditioning, when a "hug" was never just a hug. Lyle is still the only person I trust. He asked me to promise him that I'd eat regular meals and, once again, I told him I can't.

A while back I told my husband that my cutting days were over and I truly meant it! (At the time.) I am such a liar! I don't mean to be a liar, but my promises mean nothing when they involve my health.

Bill and I had a long talk tonight. He thinks the only way for me to get better, is to live alone. He thinks that I would do a lot better without him; than he would without me! I feel like we keep having the same old argument: Life's too short. I don't spend enough time with him. He wants someone to party with… But I just don't see the point. Drinking and making small talk doesn't interest me. I'm never going to be the wife he needs. He wants to socialize constantly and I find it extremely draining. Maybe we *should* split up. It would take the pressure off both of us. Bill's not a bad person, and I'm beginning to believe that maybe I'm not so bad either. But it *is* painfully obvious, now that I don't automatically do what he wants, that we are completely mismatched!

Bill doesn't understand why I need so much downtime. Neither do I! Is it the borderline? Do I still wear too many masks? I don't know! However, I did do something just for *me* today! It may seem like a small thing, but for me it was huge! I wore my hair up! It was the first time in over 20 years! I stopped wearing it that way when Bill told me, back in our early years together, that he didn't like it up. And because of the disorder, I had to make sure he was happy because *he* was my identity! In my mind, if he left me, I would be nobody! These might be *small* steps, but they're in the *right* direction. I'm learning to think about what it is that *I* want. It's always been about what I *think* other people want from me. Now it's my turn, to figure out what makes *me* happy!

Bill and I had a long talk tonight. He thinks the only way for me to get

I'm so glad my vacation is over! I *need* the structure of a work week! I don't know if it's the bipolar or the borderline that's responsible for that little quirk! (Bill thinks I'm crazy for *wanting* to get back to the job!)

I've been thinking about how Bill and I have *always* been vastly different. We didn't grow apart exactly. It's just that, in our early days together, I *molded* to *his* identity rather than developing my own! He had no idea, and frankly neither did I, that I was doing everything in my power to *be* whatever he wanted! And in the process, I *lost* whoever it was that I had started to become. Now that I'm gaining an identity of my own, we're finding that we have absolutely *nothing* in common!

I was so naïve when Bill and I first met. Until I met my husband-to-be, I had *not* been around pornography, cussing, or any kind of vulgar talk. It never crossed my mind that men might be having lustful thoughts when they looked at women; when they looked at *me*! I never thought that men wanted to "*do*" every attractive woman they saw! But after being around certain people, I became influenced by their comments. Eventually *their* beliefs, about women being nothing more than sex partners, became my own.

Lyle is trying to help me develop healthy views about my gender, but I still can't make eye contact with men that I don't know (for fear that they will think I want them to "*do*" me.) Lyle has told me that this is a form of conditioning that I need to *un*learn.

I've decided to do what's in my best interest; stay the course if you will, to achieve wellness. It's not my husband's fault that I was damaged goods when we met and it's *not* his fault that he inadvertently made the damage worse. He was just being himself and if I had been a healthy person at the time, things would have been different. But I will never regret our union; after all, it gave us our wonderful daughter!

No more "living a lie" to please everyone else! (And I probably wasn't pleasing everyone anyway!) I need to figure out what my beliefs are and what makes *me* happy. I often find myself wondering how many people I've *snubbed*, unintentionally, by not making eye contact with anyone! Whenever I went shopping, I made it a point to *not* look around me; for fear that I might give a man the wrong impression! How warped is that?

I'm trying to recapture my innocence, by *not* weighing everything I say, when talking to my husband. He has a way of turning *anything* I say into something sexual. And because of it, I've limited my vocabulary! I quit saying peanuts for instance, because he would come back with "penis." He thinks it's funny and maybe it is, but not to me.

Lyle gave me an assignment. I'm supposed to make eye contact with men! He assured me that *not* all men are perverts! (He could probably see the panic in my eyes!) Lyle said that if I'm willing to make eye-contact and say, "good morning," it might be just what the other person needed! If the person turns out to be a creep, Lyle reminded me that I'm strong enough to ignore them! I'm beginning to realize, that by putting *all* men into the "pervert" category, I was being totally unfair to the innocents!

Gotta get my wt under control! Up to 101 lbs! Measurements indicate 98.5 lbs. I only lasted, at the reduced dose of my meds, for 5 days this time. I know I could lose weight if I could just stay on the lower dose (or stop the damn drug altogether!)

I had an interesting dream last night. In it, the kitchen was a mess and as I walked in, I saw that a male coworker of mine was washing a stack of dishes. In the dream, I wasn't embarrassed by the mess or the fact that I had just awakened and hadn't brushed my teeth or gotten dressed yet. The really odd thing for me about this dream was how *comfortable* I was in the presence of another person! I was totally at ease! Then the co-worker said in a very matter-of-fact way, "You are an attractive woman." The compliment was sincere and I accepted it easily. The dream ended as this man began to cook my favorite breakfast. What I took away from this dream, was that I was perfectly content and accepting of *myself*, even in the presence of another person! I'm not that way yet, but this dream gives me hope that it is possible.

Bill asked me about my latest visit with Lyle. While I was telling him about the session, per his request, he had no expression on his face and he made no comments; not even a grunt. I stopped mid-sentence and asked him what was wrong. He said, "Nothing, what else?" So I finished telling him what I could remember and then he proceeded to tear Lyle apart! Sometimes I feel like my husband doesn't want me to get well. I don't understand this hatred that he has for the man who has, without a doubt, saved my life! I feel like Bill is always trying to twist whatever Lyle says, into something bad. Maybe Bill's "ways of thinking" are just as distorted as mine?

I'm starting to feel more sure of myself. I'm excited at the idea of getting to know *me*! I no longer feel the *need* to justify my every move. I'm learning to be true to myself without worrying about what other people will think. I don't have to be defensive anymore. I know that I'm choosing to do what's in my best interest and that's okay! I can disagree with people. I can even get mad at them. (It doesn't mean I have to be rude about it.) It just feels so liberating to be free…to be *me*!

I plan to be a strong, independent woman who has a lot to offer. If my husband can accept that, then we have a fighting chance. I don't expect him to change altogether. I'm just asking for the respect and love I deserve. I'll give him the same in return, but I don't need to lose myself in another person ever again. I am an individual, a real person. I also need to remember that episodes of depression are *not* indicative of a person's true character.

I don't like the bar scene. From now on, I'm sending Bill without me and I will *not* feel guilty for not being at his side. Instead… I'll look for activities that we can enjoy together. Surely, we can find something that appeals to both of us. And when I mess up, I will forgive myself and move on.

I just realized that I can get mad at my husband *and* love him at the same time! In my distorted black and white thinking, I thought about divorce every time I was unhappy with him. Now that I'm getting healthier, I can see the whole picture! I really *was* like a child in the way I related, or didn't relate, to other people. If I was angry, then that was the *only* emotion I could feel, or remember, or imagine for the future. And that anger would drive me to believe that I *hated* the person who *caused* my pain! And then, because I *needed* that person so badly, I would turn the anger on myself so that I wouldn't be abandoned!

I'm going to stop telling Bill about my sessions. His stoic responses are hurtful. If something major comes up, I'll share it with him. Maybe.

I'm feeling such a sense of freedom! It's okay to be *me*! I don't have to justify my existence, or my actions, or my thoughts. It's okay to apologize if *I* screw up, and I *will* screw up from time to time, but that doesn't make me *bad*. It makes me *human*! I know that if someone is upset, it's not my job to fix it *or* to become immersed in their pain. I can *choose* to be helpful, and to have empathy, as long as I remember *not* to allow myself to drown in it.

Bill and I have a 24 year history together and I don't want to throw it away. I still have hope that we can make our marriage work, if we can learn to respect our differences and allow each other to blossom. We also need to find a way to connect, by finding some common ground.

I've always felt that Bill's love for me was conditional. In looking back, I can see that *I'm* just as guilty! I've been a hypocrite in so many ways. I *could* choose to ruminate, to have a lot of regrets *or* I can do as my step mom taught me. She once told me, "Don't have regrets. Learn from your mistakes. Seek forgiveness. And move on!"

9

August 2007 thru October 2007

And the journey continues...

In looking back over my journals, I can see that I've gone through a tremendous amount of growth. There is, indeed, *light* at the end of the tunnel! I am so thankful for this journey leading me to a *sound* mind. Just recently, I've started to pray for *my* health and *my* wellbeing. Until now, I never felt worthy. When I asked for blessings in the past, they were always for someone else. It's still difficult to ask God to bless me, but I'm realizing that He *wants* to bless me! This morning, as I prayed for both my husband and my daughter, an overwhelming sense of love seemed to emanate from somewhere deep within! I felt a genuine love for my family *and* for myself! It's happening! Lyle said that a day would come when I'd be able to love myself and, for a moment this morning, I felt it!

I grew up with The Ten Commandments like most of the kids I knew, but there was one commandment that had me terribly confused: To love my neighbor as *myself*. I didn't understand what the teacher was talking about and I was too embarrassed to ask! To the best of my knowledge, at the ripe old age of 6, I had never *known* love for *myself*. I had no point of reference in which to figure out *how* to love *anyone*! On the other hand... I knew what *hate* felt like, because I had an abundant supply of it for myself! I believed, early on, that I was completely worthless. I'm not sure where these feelings originated, but I do believe they were fostered, in part, by some of the church doctrine. I don't mean to bad-mouth organized religion, but some of the things that are taught to small children are horrible! I won't go into detail, because I truly believe that most churches are trying to be helpful. And perhaps I was more sensitive than the average child. Even with these less than desirable circumstances, I still had a personal relationship with God. Through the years I've managed to hang on to it; just barely at times. But there's always a part of me that knows, without a doubt, that He loves me. No matter what.

I've been thinking about Divine intervention and how it is everywhere, if we'll just open our eyes to it. I'd like to start focusing more on the spiritual part of my life. Years ago, I had an extraordinary experience. It was a visit from someone who had passed away. For a brief moment, I was allowed a glimpse into Heaven. I was given the chance to *feel*, on a spiritual level, *love* in its purest form. There are no words to describe what I felt. I can only say that the *love* was more real than the human mind can comprehend. It wasn't about words or physical touch; those are of this world. This was something far greater. The experience inspired the following poem:

Forever

Although he'd died
Just days before
He showed up in a dream
And as he gently touched my face
It was God that I did see
Emanating ecstasy
Nirvana here on earth
God came to me, through him
To guide me in my work
Such power in the moment
When he brought to me, His Grace
And a Love beyond description
Coursed through every vein
I never knew before
The Oneness that is He
My soul has felt its worth
Forever changed I'll be

I was truly blessed to have received that Heavenly visit. I wish that I could have held onto the intense joy and peace of that moment; but now, it's barely a memory. I only know that I'm changed forever *because* of it. To be surrounded and filled with the purest love; to have it emanate from somewhere deep within, made me acutely aware of how limited we are in our human form. But, at the same time, it gave me hope. It allowed me to know, for certain, that there is so much more to life than what we can see or feel on this plane. To know that we are connected *spiritually* to the *greatest love of all* is, in itself, a gift. For a long time, following this experience, I wanted to leave this world. Knowing that something so wonderful awaited me, made it difficult to *want* this life. So on January 4th 2006, I was ready to leave this world behind. I swallowed the pills, praying to God to take me home, but God said,

"No." Apparently... He needed me *here*! And now, after nearly two years, I'm ready to embrace *this* life; to accept my blessings and to *become* a blessing. I've been afraid of life, afraid of *living*, for long enough. I'm grateful for this second chance.

After the *visit,* I knew, without a doubt, that our souls move on to a place of love that we as human beings cannot begin to fathom! And because I *knew* of this heavenly love, I wasn't afraid to die; but I was still afraid to *live*! I knew in my heart, that my soul, once freed from this body, would be embraced by God's infinite love, if *only I* could leave this world! But God had other plans. He would bring His love to *me*!

I still couldn't love myself, but I knew that God *could* and would and *does* love me! No matter what I did or didn't do, or what I do or don't do, He loves me! Even suicide could not take His love away! Somehow I just knew that God's love was not going anywhere. It was, and is, here to stay. But even with this knowledge, I *still* hated myself deeply! Until recently. Now the self-hate is quickly receding. Suddenly, I feel as if my eyes are open, really open, for the first time! I'm beginning to see what God sees when He looks at me; what He has *always* seen... a completely lovable *me*! I *am* worthy. We are *all* worthy because God created us! That alone, makes our lives sacred! Lyle tried many times to convey that message to me, but I wouldn't (or *couldn't*) believe him. Thankfully my dear mentor was right! Again.

I'm choosing to be fully present with each person I encounter. I'm trying to focus on each individual; to truly *listen* with an open heart and an open mind. To be fully present is a true gift; one that we can give to each other!

I made it 7 days at the lower dose this time, which was 2 days longer than the last time I tried. I started feeling jumpy and shaky and *startled* by "things" that weren't really there! I feel like a new person now, with more medication on board, so *why* do I mess with the dose? *Why? Why? Why?* Is it because the borderline is nearly resolved and, on some level, I want the *bipolar* to be resolved as well? *Intellectually,* I know that the bipolar doesn't work that way, but *emotionally* I continue to struggle with this fact.

I found myself getting angry, about trivial stuff, when suddenly it dawned on me! I'm *not* angry. I'm *sad!* My daughter's childhood is *over.* A part of me is excited for her, but I can't stop the tears! I feel like a part of my heart is being ripped out! My little girl is leaving home and I worry that maybe I wasn't a good enough mom. I worry that my suicide attempt might have harmed her for life. It doesn't *seem* like she's been affected, but I don't know what's going on inside her mind and her heart. I worry that my overdose will haunt all of us forever. Rachel is so bright and popular! I would feel horrible if she was harboring pain from something *I* did. The disheartening thing is that not only is it *possible,* it's *likely!* I hope and pray that she can forgive me and somehow *know* that I did the best that I could. I'm feeling a bit apprehensive about this next chapter in our lives.

Rachel was late getting home from work last night and I started to worry. I thought she'd be home by midnight. When 12:30 rolled around and she still hadn't arrived, I tried calling her, but she didn't answer. When no one answered the work phone, I really got worried, so I headed to town to make sure she was ok. I drove up to the gas station where she was employed and saw her visiting with friends outside. Once I saw that she was safe, I headed home. (I didn't want to embarrass her in front of her friends.)

As the relief I had felt began to fade, it was replaced by feelings of rage. But why? The anger bubbling up inside of me was completely unwarranted! Rachel hadn't done anything wrong! I had just *assumed* something and I assumed wrong! The desire to injure myself was quickly building. The *blade* seductively beckoned... but I resisted! When Rachel came home, I appeared calm (which I was grateful for because Rachel was innocent!) It wasn't her fault that I had *assumed* she'd be home at a certain time. Normally I'm in bed when Rachel gets home, so even if she *had* been late, she wouldn't have called and risked waking me up. Although I was tempted to self-injure, I didn't! I'm still on the path to wellness.

Bill was talking about a friend of ours, and the weight she had gained while she was recovering from an illness, and I instantly thought, "I'd rather be dead!" (I *definitely* have issues!) My weight is hovering at 94 lbs and all I can think of, is losing more! I am aware, however, that *no* weight will ever be low enough! Knowing that I'd rather be *dead* than fat is troubling, but I don't know *how* I can change my thoughts on this matter! My identity is completely wrapped up in what I weigh! How do I separate myself from a number on the scale? *Can* I separate myself? I don't know. It might be too deeply ingrained in my brain.

I spent my free time visiting with my husband this morning. (Instead of having my alone time to read.) It was out of my usual routine, but I seemed to do okay. I did another thing, this week that was out of my comfort zone. I wore the new scrubs a couple of times. It's another one of those "practice, practice, practice" things. I did pretty well this time around. I've also been working on my assignment to make eye-contact with men, and even *that* is getting more comfortable! It turns out that it's not so scary after all. I really *was* being prejudice against *all* men; and all because of the *sins* of a few.

When I told Lyle about telling Bill that he was in my "bubble" on our recent camping trip, Lyle said that it wasn't actually a "chewing" issue. It's a "proximity" issue. I still haven't allowed anyone into my inner circle, not even my own husband.

I'm still terrified of gaining weight! These thoughts consume much of my energy. I've been trying to keep my calories below 800 a day, but it leaves me feeling weak and lightheaded. I'm so afraid of losing control and getting fat. If I start eating, *will* I be able to stop? So much for the target weight range that Lyle and I agreed on.

I stopped by to visit my daughter for a few minutes this morning and she wanted *us* to go shopping, but I already had plans for a *me* day, so I told her that I needed a day to myself. (I'm learning that it's okay to say, "No.") While I was shopping, I had trouble finding age-appropriate clothes to fit. The children's section had stuff that fit, but all of it looked way too young. I'm down to 93 lbs, but I'd really like to weigh 89 lbs.

I had a dream that Lyle's life was being threatened and I was too afraid to help him! When I woke up, I realized, maybe for the first time, that Lyle is a real person! He's not just my parent figure waiting at my beck and call. I've been like a self-absorbed little kid who knows that her parent is always nearby, but fails to recognize her parent as a separate entity; with his or her own problems, interests, likes, dislikes, etc. I often include Lyle in my prayers, but it's always to thank God for bringing Lyle into *my* life. This time I prayed *for* Lyle. I'm beginning to let go of my needy-attachment. Just one more step in growing up.

I JUST BEAT THE HOLY CRAP OUT OF MYSELF! I FEEL SO MUCH ANGER INSIDE!!! I AM SO FUCKED UP!!! I HAVE A SHITLOAD OF CHORES TO DO AND WE HAVE TO GO TO ANOTHER GOD DAMNED PARTY! I REALLY REALLY JUST WANTED SOME *DOWNTIME* AND I'M NOT GOING TO GET IT AND NOBODY GIVES A SHIT!!! WHY SHOULD THEY? *I'M* THE FUCKED UP ONE!!! *I'M* THE ONE THAT DOESN'T WANT TO SOCIALIZE ALL THE TIME!!! *I'M* THE FUCKING LONER WHO CAN'T STAND TO BE AROUND PEOPLE FOR ANY LENGTH OF TIME WHATSOEVER!!! WHAT THE FUCK IS MY GODDAMN PROBLEM ANYWAY? I'M NOT WORTH THE FUCKING AIR I BREATH!

By the time the rage receded, I had bruised my thigh so bad that my pant leg was tight! I had struck myself repeatedly with my bare fist and was amazed, once I'd calmed down, at the size and swelling of the bruises I had left behind! It baffles me to think that I could do that much *damage* with my *bare* hands, and yet I would *never* strike another person. Whenever the rage is gone, and I look at what I've done, it's as though I am someone else looking on. I'm a stranger! I'm *detached* somehow from everything, and everyone, including myself. I'm so far removed, emotionally, that my *memory* of the event is barely a memory at all. Why is this *still* happening? I thought I was better. Do I need another med? It feels like I'm escalating and I don't know how to stop it! Even though I desperately try to hide my outrageous behavior, from my family, I know that they suspect that something isn't right.

Thoughts of suicide are back. I'm afraid of *myself.* I should call Lyle, but I don't want to disappoint him. I don't deserve to live. How can I make it look like an accident? My family doesn't deserve this. They shouldn't have to walk on eggshells. I'm losing control, and I feel powerless to stop it! *Why* is it so hard for me to be around people? Why is it so hard to be *normal?* With any luck, the severity of the bruises I left behind will cause blood clots to form and then maybe, if I'm lucky, one will dislodge and end up in my heart. It'd be my ticket out of here.

It's been a week since I beat the crap out of myself and I *still* ache all over from the bruises *and* from the muscles involved with inflicting the injuries. I don't know *where* the agitation comes from! What the fuck does it matter anyway? I am *never* going to be a normal person. It's not in the cards for me. I'll always be unstable.

I've fallen into a big black bottomless hole and I can't seem to get out. There is no light, no joy, no hope. I felt the familiar agitation boiling up inside of me; a restlessness I can't explain. I was home alone and I couldn't stand it for one more second. In a manic rage, I flipped the coffee table over; its contents flying across the room. (Now I'm trying to figure out *where* everything went and what "survived" the attack.) I thought I was done with these mood swings!

Bill lives and breathes sex. If he'd leave me alone for awhile, then maybe my sex drive would come back. In fact I had a rather disturbing thought recently which made me realize; that maybe, with the *right* man, I could indeed have a healthy sex drive! For 19 months I've thought of Lyle as a loving *father* figure. I was so desperate for love! I latched onto him as a child would a parent. But suddenly, I saw him as a sexual being! What the hell? I know that patients can, and often do, develop sexual feelings for their therapist, but I thought I was somehow exempt! After all, I loved Lyle as a *child loves her father*. Even though these thoughts are considered normal during the therapy process, they *feel* inappropriate. However, they do lead me to believe, that under the *right* circumstances, I will *want* the physical expression of love with the right person. For me, sex is sacred; for my husband, it is not. Of course I would never act on these feelings I've developed for Lyle, just as he would never abuse our patient/therapist relationship by acting on any feelings *he* may have. What I've learned from this is that if I *feel* loved by my partner, then I will *want* to express it in a physical way. I hope that someday, my husband will be able to sincerely love me. And that I, in turn, will be able love him back.

I feel so dumb when I'm around my family. I know I'm intelligent in my own way, but I feel stupid in comparison with my husband and daughter. Of course I have Lyle's voice in my head, challenging every negative thought that crosses my mind! Down the road, when therapy has ended, I think I will still have Lyle with me because his words of wisdom will always be in my mind and in my heart. I know there will still be times when I will shut his voice out, but eventually I *will* listen and hopefully, at some point, his voice will become my own.

Now that Rachel is off to college, it really *can* be about *me*! I don't want to feel responsible for anyone else. Maybe Bill was right when he stated that the only way for me to get well, is to live alone. It's true! I don't even want the responsibility of being someone's wife! I want freedom from the worry and stress that goes along with taking care of other people. After all, I'm quite a handful all by myself!

Depression lifted suddenly and now I'm downright chipper! *What* were the stressors, and where did they go? I'm glad that I didn't call Lyle, although the fading bruises *are* a reminder that I'm not entirely well yet.

I enjoy my work and the short interactions with a variety of people, but I still can't spend any *length* of time with any one person. With the exception of Lyle and my best friend Debbie, I feel very anxious spending more than a few minutes with anyone. (And even with Lyle and Deb, I tire out after an hour!) When I spend time with my own family, I feel defensive and on edge the whole time! Why is it so hard to be with them; the very people I claim to love the most? Is it just *me*; or is it one of the disorders that makes it so difficult to be with people? Am I just a recluse by nature? Lyle says that we're not meant to live alone. But it's the only way I know of, to truly feel at peace.

Tonight I've been thinking about what it would be like to live alone and I'm not so sure it's something I want to try. I *thought* I did, but Bill's been gone less than 2 days and it already feels lonely around here. What's with that? I don't remember *ever* feeling lonely before! I'm more confused than ever!

I only made it 5 days at a lower dose this time. I was feeling too jumpy and irritable and I started *seeing* things again. I knew it was time to increase the meds when I braked for a car....that wasn't there! So *why* do I do it? *Why* do I mess with my meds?

I told Bill that while he was gone, I'd read through my journals from the past year and a half. He asked what I'd learned and I told him that I could see how far I've come. I told him that his opinion, as well as everyone else's, used to matter way too much! It's not that his opinion isn't important. It's just that it mattered more than it should have. I lost *myself* along the way. Now, I'm learning to value my own opinion. I told him that I've learned that I don't always have to agree (or be nice) to be liked. I've discovered that people can argue and fight and *still* like or love each other! I've learned to stand up for myself, even if it means saying *no*! Whether it's someone at work trying to pawn off a task, or Bill wanting me to hang out with him in the bar, it's ok to be true to *me*! I also told Bill that I actually felt lonely while he was gone. We both agreed that it's nice to have someone to come home to.

I dreamed that I was in some kind of a rehab center and Dr. Stoune was there to see me. I have no idea of what this dream might mean. Maybe it has something to do with the help I'm getting through therapy? And maybe it's implying that I'm *not* done yet?

I tried to stop recording my wt and measurements and only lasted one day! I want to be normal, but.....

What do people see when they look at me? A lot of people say I'm too thin, but Bill never tells me that! I'm trying to form my *own* opinion about what I should weigh, or what I should look like, but I have no idea! Even though I'm still confused on this issue, I know that I *am* starting to heal from the borderline.

The flare ups of rage are lessening, although I still have various cuts and bruises in different stages of healing. I believe that I'm becoming less re-active, and more in control of my actions, when I'm feeling upset or anxious or agitated. *Most* of the time I'm able to stop, and think through what I'm feeling, and then select the appropriate action (rather than just re-acting to intense feelings.)

I'm getting better at being proactive. I'm learning to halt "automatic" negative *re*-actions. The other day, as I was running to answer the phone, I tripped and fell. Normally my day would be ruined from what I felt to be a personal failure on my part. *Instead,* I chose *how* to think about the situation. I realized that I'm *human* and it's ok to make mistakes, to *not* be perfect! I'm *not* defective because I fell. Another example, of how choosing appropriate thoughts can help us through what we perceive to be difficult situations, was when I got stuck in traffic the other day on my way to visit Rachel. I knew I was going to be late, but instead of getting angry, I chose to turn on the radio and relax to some music! I knew that it wouldn't be the end of the world to be a few minutes late. The 3rd example, and it probably seems minor, concerns an incident that happened in the kitchen. I had accidentally spilled coffee grounds and it seemed that they had ended up everywhere! I felt the familiar stirrings of rage, building up inside of me, but I told myself to calm down and just clean it up. And I did! None of these incidents *seem* major, but to a recovering borderline, they can spell disaster!

I've started spending money on myself. This is big for me because I've never felt worthy of buying things for myself. Even though I bring home a decent paycheck, I still couldn't spend anything on *me* without a terrible sense of guilt! I've always felt the need to justify, or explain, *every* purchase I made!

I heard an advertisement for the Women's Fitness Run and I didn't think any negative thoughts about females at all! That's a far cry from last year! Back then I believed that we were somehow *less than* by being women. I've since decided that being a woman is a good thing. We tend to be more nurturing and sensitive than men in general and these are wonderful qualities!

I've started making eye contact with men on a regular basis now. It's helped me to appreciate people more and to realize that everyone struggles in some area. As I'm getting more comfortable in my own skin, I've noticed that I'm trying to spend more time with friends and family. I've even enjoyed the attention I've been getting whenever I wear the new figure-hugging scrubs. I'm *not* hiding anymore!

Happy birthday Mom. You would have been 70 today. I still miss you. I will always love you.

I did some reading last night out of *The Angry Heart*. It's a self-help book for people with borderline personality disorder. When I first perused the pages, about 18 months ago, I had to stop because it was too overwhelming! The road it painted seemed hopelessly uphill. I couldn't begin to apply the information to my life. I was too deeply into the mindset of a borderline. I would need Lyle's help. I knew, without a doubt, that I wasn't strong enough to do it on my own. And even *with* help, I wasn't holding out for a full recovery. *Now* I'm so close to being well, that I can't help but feel joyful! There's a line in *The Angry Heart* that states, "The power of *choice* frees me from life in the Borderline Zone." It's a line worth remembering and a lesson worth learning.

For a long time I insisted on choosing the borderline behavior, even though it was painful, because it was a *comfortable pain*. I was familiar with it. Now, as I'm beginning to let go of the unhealthy behavior, I am choosing to forgive anyone who ever hurt me; whether it was intentional or not (and that includes myself!) For nearly two years I've been plugging along in therapy, hoping it would heal me and at the same time, clinging to the Borderline Personality with a death grip! I wanted to be well, but I was afraid. I was afraid of holding myself accountable for my actions; afraid of developing new and healthy ways of dealing with stress. The old ways were so much a part of me that I didn't know *who* I was without them! I was still a child in my thinking. My world was black and white, good or bad. I've since learned, that there's room for in-between and that the world can be full of color! The choice is mine.

I'm excited about discovering my *voice*! The smallest things *now* hold power for me! It's getting easier, with every passing day, to express my opinion about anything and everything! There's no stopping me now.

I wrote a poem for Lyle and when I gave it to him, he noted that it didn't have a title. After he read it, he offered to name it for me. When

I accepted, he titled it: *Joyful Heart.*

Joyful Heart

My heart is overflowing
With the joy of being loved
At last the fog has lifted
There is light where darkness was

I saw the world in black and white
A choice I never knew
To see beyond the borderline
I didn't have a clue

My hate for me was more than strong
And love I pushed away
My will to live was all but gone
Until you came my way

At last I felt a glimpse of hope
For the first time in my life
Someone listened to my words
And saw the pain inside

Perhaps there was a chance for me
Perhaps I could be loved
But first it had to start with me
This foreign thing called love

And so with fear, the work began
The journey seemed too long
Without you holding steady
I believe I'd long be gone

But steadfast and true, you never wavered
Your guidance always there
My trust in you began to grow
I had someone to care

And step by step, I've come this far
To a place where I can see
That to truly love another
Begins with love for me

Because of all I've learned
And with the insight I have gained
My heart is truly bursting
With love instead of pain

My love for me is growing
Getting stronger day by day
I never thought it'd happen
But then you came my way

Now here I am with a joyful heart
Glad to be alive
Giving thanks to God and you
For standing by my side

Lyle thanked me profusely for the poem! Lyle means the world to me! I would not be here today, if it weren't for his dedication. I will *always* be grateful.

Why am I sabotaging myself? I ate over 5,000 calories yesterday! And all because of the turbulence within! An unquiet agitation threatened my wellbeing, so to pacify it; to calm it; to *medicate* it, I stuffed it down with food! What I had *really* wanted to do was to *punch* something! A wall? A door? *Myself?* I've damaged enough property over the years, so I chose to sedate the beast within by feeding it! I said, "No" to self-injury, but doesn't the very act of "binge-eating" cause damage in its own right? Doesn't the binge leave destruction in its wake? The *hangover* the next morning, from the excessive sugar intake, riddles my body with pain and puffiness and muddled thinking. So *why* do I do it? Do I *want* to feel like I've been hit by a truck? Do I think that's all I'm worth? Abusing my body with food is just another way to hurt myself! I *know* this, so *why* do I do it? It's a never ending battle! I *know* this to be true. I'm *aware* of what I'm doing and yet I continue!

I stopped by the store to see Bill. I visited with his employee for a few minutes while Bill was in the backroom. When I went back to talk with him, he proudly showed me that he'd been watching me and the clerk on a new surveillance camera system. When he told me that I had just been *videotaped*, I became instantly enraged! I was able to hide my true feelings. I didn't let on to Bill how upset I was. Instead, I just said that I had to go somewhere and I left abruptly. I felt, and *still* feel, totally *violated!* Bill videotaped me once before, without my prior knowledge, and that incident left me feeling vaguely uncomfortable, but *not* enraged; not that time. I'm not sure *why* this bothers me so much? I should probably talk to him about it, but I'm afraid that he'll twist it around to make *me* the bad guy!

I asked Lyle if we should go to 3 weeks between visits, but he wanted to keep it at 2 weeks. He didn't say why and I didn't ask. I trust him to know what's best for me. He always has my best interest at heart.

When reading my old journals recently, I laughed at some of the things I said or did! (Stuff that I certainly didn't think was funny at the time I wrote it down!) I know, from reading about mental illness, that it's a sign of *healing* when we can learn to laugh at ourselves! Another thing I realized, from reading the previous journals, is that when I wrote about my *rage*, my words didn't do it justice! I *knew* what I had felt, but my words fell short. They couldn't begin to describe the emotional turbulence or the mental unrest. I don't think there *are* any words! When *reading* about my painful feelings, I couldn't completely *feel* the intensity of my emotions through the words I used! I could feel it, to some extent, from my own memory. But *no one* can ever know how bad it really was, or is, when the pain and the struggle are *hidden* within one's mind. No one, except *maybe* another who suffers from their own mental hell; but even then, their experience may be completely different, yet just as painful.

Bill called me at home, on my day off, to tell me to bring some insurance papers to him *right now*. I used to jump when he said jump, but I'm not doing that anymore. I have a voice, and a mind, and I'm choosing to exercise both! I know darn well that he doesn't *need* the papers right this second. He just wants what he wants, when he wants it! I stood my ground and told him that he'd have to wait a few hours, because I had other plans for the morning and *then* an amazing thing happened! He called me back to say that what he *actually* needed was just some numbers off of the papers! The world didn't come to an end just because I said no! Imagine that!

Speaking my mind allows me to be an equal partner in this marriage. I'm *never* going back to being a silent partner again. Standing up to my husband, and not feeling guilty about it, was empowering! I'm not going to "jump" for *anyone* anymore.

☙❧

I was stuck in another boring meeting that went into "overtime" because of a longwinded speaker, so I decided to tell the committee that I needed to leave because I had a prior commitment. No one batted an eye when I stood up and left. The other appointment was really a coffee date with my friend Debbie, but no one needed to know that. My plans are important to *me* and I'm finally treating myself with the respect I deserve!

☙❧

I showed Debbie *Joyful heart*. She said that I should write a book about my experiences in therapy *and* about this journey that I'm on. She thinks that my story could help others, but I don't know. Can it really help? And if it *can*, am I *brave* enough (or strong enough) to share my story? It's so personal!

☙❧

I'm beginning to notice the people around me. I'm finally thinking of others and not about how they can help me, but how can I help them? What is *their* story? It's not just about me anymore! I'm finally waking up to the fact, that *everyone* has a story to tell. *Everyone* has heartache, disappointments *and* joy! While I sat in my car at a red light, I found myself looking around at the other drivers and wondering what was going on in their lives. For so long, I kept my world as small as possible and I kept *everyone out* of it! It was my way of controlling the chaos in my *head*! Now that I'm thinking *outside* of myself for a change, I'm seeing that it might be a part of the answer! (In overcoming some of *my* problems.) Perhaps, by getting *out* of my head, I can free up my heart.

Took my meds but not getting tired. Earlier tonight, I told Bill that Deb had lost weight and looked great. He said that she should watch *The Biggest Loser* for inspiration. I hate that show! It fills me with fear! (Fear that I could end up huge like the contestants.)

I'M FEELING AGITATED. HAVE ALL DAY! SOOOOO AGITATED! NO REASON! I'VE HAD THAT RESTLESS IRRITATED JUMPING OUT OF MY SKIN FEELING. SORTA, KINDA, I DON'T KNOW! HAD TO GO TO TOWN TODAY AND EVERYONE WAS SOOOOO SLOW!!! I WANTED TO DRIVE *FAST*, BUT CARS WERE IN THE WAY!! AT THE STORE, SOUNDS WERE TOO LOUD AND IT SEEMED LIKE THE CLERK WHO SAID HI, WAS YELLING AT ME AND THE MUSIC WAS BLASTING AND PEOPLE WERE IN MY WAY!!! WHAT THE HELL IS WRONG WITH ME? IF THE MEDS AREN'T WORKING, WHY TAKE THEM AT ALL? FEELING HOPELESS. THOUGHT I WAS BETTER. MAYBE EVEN READY TO DISCONTINUE MEDS AND NOW THIS? WILL I EVER BE COMPLETELY WELL? WHY BOTHER AT ALL? I'M SICK OF ENDLESS UPS AND DOWNS. SICK OF IT!!! WHEN WILL IT ALL BE OVER? DEATH? CUTTING? NO! NO! NO! I'M NOT GIVING UP ON ME! DAMN IT!!! STOP IT!!! HURTING MYSELF IS SOMETHING I *USED* TO DO!!! I HAVE THIS CLIMBING THE WALLS, PHYSICALLY RESTLESS, TOTALLY AGITATED THING GOING ON!!! HOW THE FUCK DO I STOP IT? HOW DO I SURVIVE IT? IT'S AS THOUGH EVERY CELL IN MY BODY IS BURSTING AT THE SEAMS, NEEDING TO EXPLODE!!!

I get it! I get it! I finally get it! The bipolar disorder might make me agitated, irritable, physically uncomfortable, too energetic or whatever, but *because* of what I've learned, by dealing with the borderline personality disorder in therapy, I *still* have a choice in what I choose to do! When my thoughts are racing and my skin is crawling and I can't settle down, I *still* have the power of *choice*! "The power of choice frees me from life in the Borderline Zone."

A video I watched recently, said that we should focus on what we *want* and we shall have it! Is it really that simple? Well, I want a life without meds!!! Is *that* possible? Can I do it? All the literature I've read says absolutely *not*; that I will *always* need bipolar meds. But *maybe,* if I just concentrate hard enough and really focus.....

After a couple of days without meds, I scribbled (in barely legible handwriting) the following journal entry:

"I want to be well totally well; no borderline, no bipolar! it just takes focus I want stability I want freedom from drugs! want to be well and free I want life without meds! if I focus on being positive and being calm I can do anything! I can sleep as much as I need or as little as I need I can be cheerful and focused I can do my job well I can be comfortable in my own skin and stop my cells from feeling prickly smooth them around the edges I can live on air and water..."

I appreciate that Bill's been nice day after day, but I'm still uneasy about whether or not it will last. I'm afraid to trust him and a part of me still doesn't feel worthy of being treated kindly. Sigh.

I'm so afraid of gaining weight, but I'm still eating like a pig! God, what if my metabolism slows down and I do get fat, really fat, like the people on The Biggest Loser? I know *intellectually* that my identity is too wrapped up in my size, but I don't know how to stop it!

I'm setting boundaries at work now. I'm no longer expecting myself to do the job of 3 people! If my employers refuse to hire enough staff, then that's their problem! I will no longer make it *mine*.

The neighbor's dog was in our yard barking incessantly at *our* house! After 10 minutes of listening to the canine assault, I went outside and chased the dog back into his yard, yelling at him the whole way! I was embarrassed when I realized that I had been "caught" by the neighbor who had finally ventured outside to collect her dog. Before I could beat myself up about it, I remembered what Lyle had said about *anger*. He had told me that it's a *necessary* emotion and that it's perfectly okay to get angry. It's what we *choose* to do *about* that anger that can sometimes get us into trouble!

I'm beginning to see Bill in a good light, regarding his need for socializing. He's very popular and I know that he actually gains energy from these interactions. I, on the other hand, do not. He and I are separate entities and complete opposites. We're not bad people; just *different* people. I told him that I do appreciate him, even though I don't always act like it!

I'm a work in progress. I am healing and I'm beginning to trust myself and others. I've come too far to ever go back! I'll still have my dark days, to some degree, but I have insight now! Insight that can help me to weather the storms of life. I'm choosing to *embrace* life. It's *not* always easy for me, to make that choice, but I *am* trying!

One of the nurses in the CCU gave me a huge compliment. She was referring to a recent crisis, in which I had helped. She told me that I had, "Lent stability in a stressful situation!" *Me*! I didn't think I had any "stability" to lend! She has no idea of how big an impact she made on me, with her sincere compliment. Her words touched me deeply. They remind me of the fact that I *am* growing and healing and becoming whole! Her words *also* remind me that we have the power to impact people's lives by what words we "choose to use" in our interactions with others. I will do my best, to impart goodwill, by choosing my words thoughtfully.

My husband doesn't like it when I stand up for myself. Lyle warned me that as I get stronger, Bill may not like the new me. And even if he *does* like the person I am, he may not like the change in the "status quo." Earlier tonight, I was looking for the *written* instructions for my new phone. Bill was irritated with me because he wanted to *tell* me how to use it, but I insisted on finding the instructions. He was mad because he thought that I didn't want to learn from *him*. It wasn't that I didn't want him to teach me, it's just that I learn by *reading*. I tried to explain to him that I need to *see* the instructions written down because that's the way my brain works! He couldn't, or wouldn't, understand!

Anything that is different from *his way* is wrong in his mind. Well I refuse to let *him,* or anyone else, bully me! I am *not* going to blame myself anymore for things that I have no control over! I'm done beating myself up just because I am *different* from the "norm." I learn in different ways than some people, but that doesn't make me bad or wrong. *My* normal is fine! I don't *need* to be someone I'm not!

Thoughts are so powerful! Does that mean that mind-over-matter can work for bipolar? Can I stop my meds? I *know* the answer, so why do I entertain such thoughts?

I will *not* give others the power to bring me down! I was angry at work, and I *wanted* to self-injure, but I resisted! I am gaining control in the impulse department! Intense feelings pass! Always. If *only* I can be patient. Sometimes it only takes a few minutes for the fury to fizzle. Even if I can't control the agitation, I can *choose* which behavior to call upon in response to it.

I felt agitated at work today. Everything seemed so loud and irritating! How can the voices of 5 people sound like 100? And the humming of a few machines sound like 1,000? It's hard to explain the noise and the commotion and the confusion that goes on inside my head. It takes every ounce of strength I have to *appear* normal! The outside world sometimes appears to me as a disconnected, rambling, disordered mass of confusion! When this happens, my coherence is greatly lacking in this foreign, yet oddly familiar, home away from home.

I'm down to 92 lbs and when I look into the mirror, I still see fat. Sigh. No weight will ever be low enough, so *why* do I continue on this path? I *know* it's not healthy! Even my bones are beginning to look too big for my body and yet I stay on this road to disaster. Lyle's voice is constantly in my head, challenging what I see in the mirror, but I still can't seem stop what I see! I don't like my reflection at all. Perhaps I don't like *me* at all?

Lyle seems worried about my weight. And yet, one of the nurses at work *complimented* me on my weight! So many *mixed* messages! The battle continues.....

Very hyper at work lately. Sometimes I'm embarrassed by my behavior when I'm "up!" I cut back on my meds 11 days ago. I know I should increase them again, but I have to lose weight!

Lost 5 lbs in 16 days. Tried on clothes. Still have love handles. So grossed out. Couldn't eat. Got on the scale while still wearing clothes. The number I saw has me *completely* freaked out!!! Confessed to Lyle that I'm having a hard time with food and weight issues. Maybe getting better isn't in the cards for me. Feeling agitated. Had to increase the meds. Damn.

I went to a party with Bill and while I was there, I noticed a young woman that was very attractive. The thing that surprised me was that she was rather "hippy" and yet I thought she was beautiful! Maybe someday I'll be able to accept curves on me! Maybe.

My thighs won't get smaller than 18 inches! Maybe I've gained muscle from the stairs at work? I'm still addicted to weighing *and* measuring myself several times a day, and also to recording the numbers! It's a compulsion I can't seem to control. I even have to line the scale up on the tile before I step onto it. I hope that a day will come when I can let go of this obsession! I hate being tied to the scale and the tape measure. I hate counting every calorie and thinking nonstop about diets and binges and numbers! I pretend not to care about what I weigh, but in reality I never stop thinking about it. I pretend to eat when others are around and then I hide the food in the garbage. For every day that I overeat, I starve myself for the next 2 or 3.

I went shopping for clothes today. Reflection looked chubby. No point of reference for me. Is Lyle lying when he says I'm too thin? I don't think 92 lbs is quite low enough. Bill seems very pleased with my new low weight. Sometimes I feel too bony for comfort reasons. I've had a lot of muscle spasms lately and my body hurts everywhere. But I don't want to take any pain meds because they might make my stomach hurt if I don't eat and I don't want any extra calories right now. My mind is fuzzy and I have a vague sense of unease, but I can't really explain it.

Went to comedy show with Bill and friends. Laughed a lot. Clean humor. Loved it!

I have finally learned to take breaks at work! I'm learning to value myself enough to take a break when I need one. I know that doesn't sound like much, but for me...

Deb and I had a great visit this morning! I told her, that even though my goal is to embrace wellness, I'd been holding onto the *borderline behavior* with a "death grip!" But *now,* "I'm letting go... one finger at a time!"

I had a conversation with a prisoner today that really touched me. When I was drawing his blood, he told me about his choice to be "joyful" because that's what God wants for us. He told me that he tries to get up early every morning, so that he has time to read from his book of Daily Devotions, before he's called to breakfast. It's moments like these that make me especially glad to be doing what I do for a living! My five minutes with each patient is priceless! If I did what others have advised me to do, which is to further my education so that I can make more money, I wouldn't get to interact with nearly as many people as I do now. I love what I do! *More money* isn't a motivator for me. Making a *difference* is!

As my confidence has risen, so have my positive interactions with doctors and nurses. Once I realized that I didn't *need* anyone's approval, I got it! Interesting.

Because of the darkness and despair I have experienced, I hope that once I am healed (and with God's help) that I can reach out to those who are suffering. I want to make a difference! To give back. To pay it forward. I know that I'm responsible for *causing* some of the past hurts in my life; both to me and to my loved ones. Knowing this is painful, but it is also *empowering*! If I can *cause* pain, then perhaps I can also cause *joy*?

It's my day off and I had planned to spend it at home alone, so when Bill announced that we were going to have company, I felt like someone had punched me in the stomach! He was leaving for work, so it would be up to me to entertain. The joy I had felt this morning quickly dissipated and was replaced by anxiety, quickly followed by anger. My entire day was ruined before it had even begun!

The company that I had fretted all day about never showed up! I wasted my entire day off for nothing! The whole fucking day! I am in such a pissy-don't-give-a-shit mood!! I keep walking around the house aimlessly, pacing without a purpose! I'm so agitated! What the fuck is wrong with me? I woke this morning feeling grateful and then, within minutes, I turned into a raving lunatic! Just because my plans were altered! How selfish is that? I'm supposed to be well now, or close to it, so what the fuck is my problem? I spiraled down and out of control and before I knew it, I was cutting! Again. So much for recovery!

I paced the house like a wild animal last night! I awoke already feeling *defeated*. I'm pissed at the world! I'm pissed at God! I'm pissed at life! I want off the fucking ride! I have that dreaded feeling of *needing* to somehow jump out of my skin! It's like every cell in my body is prickly and bursting with nervous, agitated energy! My body wants to explode, at the cellular level, into a million little pieces... scattered across the world!

Coming to terms with my need for medication hasn't been easy. It's an ongoing battle with myself. I feel like I should be able to control my symptoms with willpower, even after reading again and again that bipolar disorder *cannot* be controlled by sheer willpower. (Nor can other biologically-based illnesses.) I feel somehow defective because of my need for medication, so I continue to resist them. It feels like a personal weakness on my part. I told Lyle that I feel like I'm giving up control by taking meds, but he pointed out that it's actually the opposite. By taking my meds, I will *gain* control in the long run. Achieving continued mood stability means that it's more likely that I will become a more productive member of society, and that my relationships will improve tremendously. And one of the *best* rewards will be the ability to *plan ahead* for things I want to do, without fear that it will be a *bad day* when it arrives. It seems like a no-brainer to stay on meds (at the correct dose) so why do I continue to fight it?

Okay, I'm ready to take care of me. I've been doing a lot of soul searching regarding this whole medication issue. I'm not ready to promise *myself* anything, but I *am* ready to promise Lyle, so I wrote him the following letter:

Dear Lyle,

I've thought a lot about what you've said regarding medications. I *know* that the Seroquel works for me and I *will* get it out of my head that I can stop taking it. If this is the only medication I need, then instead of complaining, I should be counting my blessings!

Everyday, I see patients *my* age who are on medications for *blood pressure, diabetes, cholesterol, seizures, ulcers, blood clots, cancer, rejection drugs, thyroid problems, drug addiction, autoimmune disorders, pain management, chronic infections, hepatitis,* and the list goes on! You have helped me to realize that taking *one* medication everyday, is a very small price to pay for wellness!

I really do want to be healthy! That's why I'm writing to you. To make a promise to *you*, and to myself, to take the prescribed dose of Seroquel *every*day until our next session. I *could* promise just myself, but I need someone to hold me accountable. (At least for now.)

Thank you, once again, for not giving up on me!

Sincerely,
Terresa ☺

✒ ⌒

I sent the letter after much hesitation. It's a very big step for me to promise *anything*, especially when it concerns my health! The most I was able to do, in the past, was to promise Lyle that I'd *try*. And I certainly would *not* have signed any kind of contract concerning my wellbeing! So today, when I was willing to put my promise into *writing*, I *knew* that I was getting better. I *am* truly overcoming the borderline and, at the same time, accepting the bipolar disorder. I know that it will still be difficult, mentally, to take the pills from time to time. After all, the child in me wants to stay up all night! But, thankfully, I'm also in touch with the loving parent *within* and *she* has the strength to say, "No." I still can't believe I had the courage to do it! For me, making this promise is HUGE!!! In doing so, I'm making a statement to myself. I'm saying that I'm worth the time, and the effort, to make myself completely well. I'm finally ready to *embrace wellness!* I'm very much aware, that by taking this step, I am indeed *choosing life!*

❦

I've been on the proper dose for a week now. It's amazing how it softens the prickly edges somehow. If I hadn't sent the letter to Lyle, I would have already started cutting the dose again. But I did, and I didn't.

10

October 27th, 2007 thru December 24th, 2007

I am choosing life!

My death-grip on the borderline is finally loosening! I am consciously letting go of it. (Although, I do feel a little lost without it.) My world is no longer black and white, all or nothing, good or bad. There is room for in-between, good enough, and *love*! In learning to love myself, I am building a foundation that will not only allow me to love myself, but will also allow me to love others; to *truly* love them, *without* condition.

Lyle has been a Godsend. I am incredibly grateful for his continued guidance. With the insight and knowledge I've gained through therapy, going back to old beliefs and behavior is *not* an option. As this road to recovery continues, I'm aware that I will still have shifts in mood, but doesn't everybody to some degree? I've learned through therapy, and with a daily dose of Seroquel, that I can and will manage the bipolar symptoms and enjoy a normal life. I've come to accept that the borderline can be healed, but the *bipolar* cannot. It can, however, be controlled by a combination of meds, life style and choosing my thoughts wisely. I am blessed beyond measure and I've come to terms with the continued use of medication. I'm letting go of the *victim mentality*. The *pity party* is over. I'm choosing to enjoy the good health I've been blessed with. I'm choosing to take care of me. I'm choosing *life*!

I've noticed that Bill's been treating me with respect. He hugs me now, without groping, and he refrains from lewd comments in my presence. He's really making the effort, and that helps me to see him in a better light.

I was in a really good mood yesterday and last evening. I was tempted to skip my meds, so I could stay up all night and enjoy the *high*, but I couldn't stop thinking about the promise I had made to Lyle! I'm proud to say that I kept my promise! The "grown-up" in me is finally in charge!

I offered to host thanksgiving this year. Wow! I *must* be getting better! Normally, hosting *anything* would stress me to no end!

I've been a little worried about some "contract negotiations" between the hospital and the lab, but I've decided to "let go and let God." While I was at work today, I had to draw blood from a cancer patient. She was just a little girl! It made me ashamed of myself and my petty problems.

I've stayed on my meds for two weeks now! (Just like I promised I would.) I don't know *why* I fight this so much; especially when I'm back on the therapeutic dose and the "hypersensitivity" recedes, allowing a calmness to move in. I feel so much better! It's as if every cell in my body has had the rough, irritated, prickly edges smoothed out. So why do I fight this? Why do I fight this calm? Do I really prefer chaos?

I've been feeling kind of down lately. I'm not sure why. I really don't want to socialize with anyone. I don't even want to keep my coffee date with Debbie this morning, but I know that it's in my best interest *not* to isolate myself. And besides, maybe Deb *needs me?*

Overstaffed at work. Almost as stressful as when we were understaffed. Too much visiting. I know the meds took away the irritable, edgy, restless feelings, but now I feel blah. I don't know whether it's the Rx or just the depressive part of the bipolar cycling. I just know that I don't want to do *anything* at all. It's an effort to make conversation for any length of time. And to make matters worse, we have to go to a party tonight! I shopped this morning for pants, but everything I tried on was too big. And yet I still want to lose more! I weigh 93 lbs. All of my clothes are too big and I *still* want to lose weight. Sigh. I feel like I'm letting Lyle down by not being better. I do so well for awhile and then I crash. I feel sad and empty. I don't know *why* exactly. Am I missing Rachel? Is the boredom at work getting to me? I'm *not* looking forward to *anything* except the peace of nothingness; the peace of *death*. Maybe if I don't eat for a few days, it'll trigger an upswing. I *would* cut my meds, but I promised Lyle…

I felt bad for a patient that I drew today. She was in tears as she described to me, the chronic physical pain she suffers from. I really hurt for her, in my heart. I'm once again reminded of how good I have it!

I wore form-fitting clothes when I went out with Bill last night. And, without any crudeness, he told me that I looked nice! I felt a little uncomfortable in the tighter style of clothing, but at least I did it!

I need to stop thinking of myself 24/7! It's time that I started noticing and complimenting other people, including my husband! I've been extremely self-centered for years! My lack of self-esteem and self-worth has put all of the focus on *me*! (And my perceived imperfections.) It's time to stop!

Well I just got the lecture of how "dangerous" anorexia is! I went to my session with Lyle this morning. We talked about all of the topics on my list and *then*, when we had 10 minutes left, he brought up the one subject I hadn't planned on discussing! My weight. I told him that I was only planning to lose 3 or 4 more pounds and then I'd stop when I reached the upper 80's. I even mentioned that I planned on gaining a few pounds back once I reached my goal. Lyle instructed me to ask Dr. Stoune if it would be healthy for me to lose a few more pounds. I told Lyle that I would *not* ask! (I already know what the answer would be.) I also reminded Lyle that he's *not at liberty* to say anything to Dr. Stoune about my weight, because of privacy laws. At that point, he tried a different approach. He wanted me to list the pros and cons of losing more weight. The only *pro* was proving that I could do it! On the *con* side, I listed that I'd be even more bony and uncomfortable than I already am!

And also, there'd be no *reserve* in case of an illness. I admitted that I'd already lost the "radiance" I had begun to notice at a higher weight. I acknowledged my lack of stamina and problems with blood sugar. Lyle seemed genuinely concerned about me. He commented 4 or 5 times on the fact that he was worried about me! Maybe this issue is the last stumbling block of overcoming the borderline personality disorder. If we can get past this, then perhaps I *will* be healed?

Still keeping track of calories, weight and measurements. I am *obsessed* with weighing myself *any*where, and *every*where, there is a scale: at home, in the lab, in the hospital gym, in dietary, on the scales in the hallways throughout the hospital, in the E.R., etc. It's a compulsion that has turned into a full blown obsession! Lyle's brought up "OCD and me" in the past, but I wouldn't admit that I was compulsive or obsessive. How could I be so blind?

Working with a new *eager to please* employee, has reminded me of how I *used* to be! My unhealthy motto was "please and agree." I'm glad I'm not that person anymore! I get to be *real* now! A real person with likes and dislikes, opinions and feelings, and a voice I'm not afraid to use!

I've put down some of the masks that I used to hide behind, and Lyle was right… it *does* free up energy! However, I'm still hiding behind one mask. It's the one that says I don't care about how much I weigh. It's the mask that doesn't let anyone know that I am completely obsessed with the scale *and* recording my weight and measurements *and* counting calories! Lyle is the *only* person who has any inkling as to how bad it is. I've told him more about me, and my hang ups, than any other person on earth. And yet, I've still held back on telling him *everything*. When it comes to my disordered way of eating, and not eating, I can't seem to open up completely.

91 lbs. Yeah!!! I'm soooooo close to my goal!!!

Bill told me that one of the girls he hired is hot and the other girl is homely. *Why* must he always comment on a woman's appearance? It's as if the *only* thing that a woman could possibly have to offer, is her *looks*! I find it to be *demeaning*! His comments about women bother me, but how much can I ask for, and expect, without sounding demanding? I just wish that he could, for once, describe a woman in some other way than, "She's hot!" or "She's homely." Is it one of the disorders that makes me so angry on this issue? Or is it just me? Am I being too sensitive? Or is it just a "husband" thing? How can I insist on him changing certain behaviors, when my own ideas are constantly changing?

I dressed nicely for a grocery shopping trip, but I felt uncomfortable because of the form-fitting outfit I wore. But at least I did it! (I even exchanged greetings with several men!) I'm still moving forward! I told Bill that I'm down to 91 lbs and he said that I looked great! I told him that the pants I was wearing actually fit better when I'm 3 or 4 pounds *heavier*, but he said that they looked fine just the way they were. I really wish he'd tell me to *gain* weight, or at least to not lose anymore!

I didn't get any alone time this morning and it left me feeling out of sorts all day. The scales at work indicated that I weigh 92 lbs. What the heck happened to 91 lbs? I told Bill that it was too hot in the house and he replied that I could wear a "thong." I laughed it off, but it put me in a bad mood because I started thinking of how ugly my body is! I could *never* prance around the house in something skimpy! I don't think he has any idea of how bad my body looks, because I never allow myself to be unclothed around him (unless it's night time and the lights are turned off.)

Rachel called and wanted to know if I was busy. I was in the middle of cleaning house, but decided a visit would be nice. (Even if it hadn't been a part of my plans for the afternoon.) That's big for me, because I'm not a spontaneous person at all; even if it is just my daughter coming by for a visit! I'm learning to let go of the *need* to plan everything in advance. It's done nothing but make me miserable. Being able to *adjust* to a change in plans is one more step in the right direction!

When I start to get upset about something, and I want to react in an unhealthy manner, I can stop myself now! I just say, "That's the borderline!" It helps me to put my problems into a proper perspective. It also allows me the opportunity to think through the situation and ultimately choose a healthy behavior! (At least most of the time!)

Each person I work with brings something different and good to my life; as I probably do for them. No one has to be perfect! It's okay to make mistakes. People will still like me, just as I will still like them! I used to think that I had to be perfect before anyone would accept me. And I also expected the people around me to be perfect! What a stressful way to go through life; as we are all imperfect. It's part of the *human*

condition and that's okay! Accepting that none of us is perfect, is key in learning to enjoy life fully; *now* in the present. We *don't* have to wait until we can get it right!

Until recently, I never really thought about having dreams for myself and my life. Now I find myself thinking about *who* I am and *what* I want. As the truth of *who Terresa really is* becomes clear, I've begun to entertain thoughts of what my dreams might actually be! At the top of the list, is to have an inner peace that stays with me consistently no matter what I'm going through. And *with* this inner peace, God's love can flow *through* me, so that those I meet might also feel His love. To be able to spread joy and love and grace, would indeed be a gift. It's my dream to be that instrument.

I've been such a glutton! I was so close to my goal and now I've sabotaged myself once again! I felt like crying when I realized how much I'd eaten in the past 48 hours. I have to get back on track right. *Now.* I'm terrified of being fat again! I've been thinking about the "cons" that Lyle had me list concerning my drive to lose more weight. He insists that this is *borderline behavior* and that it's up to me to change it. He's absolutely right! I haven't been thinking of anyone but myself regarding this issue. Starving myself down to the eighties could put my patients at risk! What if I passed out while I had a needle in their arm? And do I really want to scare my family by ending up in the hospital again? No, I don't. As far as "proving" that I can do it, I could also "prove" that I could jump off a bridge, dart out in front of traffic, or carry out any other reckless behavior. The adult in me is taking a step back and looking at the whole picture. She sees that dieting down to eighty-something only proves that I'm still refusing to take care of myself. My all-time goal, from my teens, was to weigh

92 lbs. Well I've done that, so why am I continuing to try for 88 or 89 lbs? I've said all year that my goal is to "Embrace Wellness." If that's true, then the dieting has to *stop*! As well as the binge-eating. Neither is good for me.

I started out taking only half a dose of my meds last night. But as I lay in bed, the "mommy" voice in me wouldn't let up! It kept stating, "You *know* better!" I finally got up and took the other half. And what do you know? The "mommy" voice went away and I slept great!

I wish I could eat like a normal person. I'm still bingeing on junk food some of the time and *not* eating at all at other times. Why is this so hard for me? I really want to eat like normal people, but I can't! Not yet.

The song, *You are Beautiful* is stuck in my head. I used to get really upset when Lyle used the "B" word. I still don't believe it, but it doesn't bother me like it used to.

My boss asked me about something I sent to client services. At first he was angry, but I stood by my decision. Eventually he realized that I'd done the right thing after all! It feels so good to have enough self-confidence to stand my ground at work *and* at home. Another thing that I've gotten better at is to *not* take "cranky people" personally! That one step has helped me tremendously! Sometimes, when the cranky person wants to go off on a tangent, I just let them. I remain as respectful as

I can and let them have their say and then I very calmly try to validate their feelings and engage them in finding a solution.

John from ER noticed my new tailored scrubs and the bright colors. He's been encouraging me, for years, to wear brighter clothing. He's another one of my earth angels!

I went to the CCU today to draw a patient. When I had to poke him twice, I said that my "pride" could take it, but I still feel bad for *the patient* when this happens! He said, "It's nice to know that there is still compassion in the world." I agreed and he said that some of the people who had "worked on him" didn't seem to have any empathy at all. Of all workers, *healthcare* workers should probably have the most! Sadly, that's not always so.

At my session with Lyle today, I told him that I've accepted that Bill will always describe people by their looks, and that he isn't always kind in what he says, but I'm okay with it. It doesn't make *him* wrong. Lyle warned me about falling back into an unhealthy attachment to my husband. He said that it's *not* okay for Bill to describe women as "hot" or "homely" when he's talking to me. Apparently it's not respectful.

Lyle is pleased with the awareness I've gained regarding the borderline personality disorder and how I'm better able to manage it now. It's especially evident since I've been compliant with my meds and the bipolar symptoms are under control. However, he did warn me about the weight loss and how it's related to *both* the borderline personality disorder *and* the OCD. As soon as I get my weight up, we will move the sessions to every three weeks, but for now, they will stand at every two; more often if the need arises.

I was going along just fine this morning, cleaning house and getting ready to host Thanksgiving, when Bill called to tell me that one of his employees had called in sick and that Rachel had called him to say she had a flat tire! She still had to get back to school for her finals and there was no way Bill could leave the store and drive the 25 miles to where she was, so I instantly became stressed at the thought of dropping everything and rushing to get Rachel to her finals. In hindsight, I can see that I offered no support whatsoever to Bill. I can't believe how selfish I can be! All I could think of was myself and how I didn't want *any* interruptions in my day. As soon as I realized that my plans were probably going to be screwed up, just 24 hours before having company, I had that horrible sinking feeling! I impulsively punched the frig to calm myself down and left not only a huge bruise on my fist, but also a huge dent in the side of the frig! (I tried to hide it with magnets.) Rachel ended up getting help from someone who worked at the college, but by then my mood was already shot. It's not her fault and it's not Bill's. It's just me and that damn *borderline*!

It was a battle all day not to hurt myself anymore than I already had. I even dropped to my knees at one point and begged God for self-love! I had so much anger and self-hate swirling around in my veins, that I could hardly focus. All I wanted to do… was to beat the holy crap out of myself! I thought I was done with those kinds of thoughts and behavior. Maybe I'm not meant to be well. Maybe I *should* give up.

In looking back over the events of yesterday, I've come to the conclusion that it's not a total loss or setback *if* I can learn from it! At first I had wished that Bill had never called me about his employee or about Rachel's tire, but then I realized that if I'm to continue getting better, then I need to face things as they happen and work through them. Protecting me, by remaining silent, is not helpful in the long run. I told Bill about what I had learned and instead of judgment or criticism, he gave me a hug!

Hosted thanksgiving. It went fine. Hoped no one noticed bruised hand!

Julie gave me a book called The Alchemist, by Paulo Coelho. There were so many references to being an *instrument of love* that it leads me to believe that I *am* on the right path!

My friend's dad isn't doing well. She called to tell me that they were considering taking him off life support, but she felt so guilty! I assured her that it was *not* a horrible thing to do. If anything, it would set his spirit free! That same spirit had been trapped for years in an alcoholic body, with all of its human limitations! She expressed her concern that, because of his sins, her dad's spirit would go to Hell once it was free from his body. I told her that he'd already lived his *Hell*, as an alcoholic. I told her that I didn't believe, for one second, that God would send her loved one to Hell. Why would God do that when it would devastate *her*? I told her that I knew, in my heart, that her father would be going to a place of perfect love. A *love* that is so pure and so complete, that it's beyond description. We cannot begin to fathom this love in our limited capacity. I told her that I believe that "Hell" is a self-imposed separation from God and that we can choose to be reunited at anytime. We are spiritual beings living as humans, and sometimes our weaknesses in the physical life can cause us to do hurtful things! We forget who we really are! I told her that the addiction her dad had, to alcohol, turned him into someone he really wasn't. Somewhere, underneath the addiction, was the real man; hidden from everyone including himself.

Talking with my friend about her Dad, reminded me once again of the *love* that waits for all of us! Two years ago I was ready to embrace, through death, this perfect love, but it wasn't my time. I wonder if the reason I'm still here, is because God wants me to share what I've learned; both about mental illness *and* to remind people that God's love is *infinite*! It's a love without boundaries.

One of the girls I work with needed someone to talk to. Normally I wouldn't want to visit with this person because she's very mean-spirited, but I knew she was sad, so I let her talk. I'm learning that it's *not* all about me and if I'm serious about being an instrument of God's love and grace, then I should be willing to start with my enemies.

Choosing to love people unconditionally can be an amazing experience! When love "hinges on certain requirements," then it really isn't *love* at all!

My supervisor needed someone to work graveyard and I told him that I couldn't because of the medication I take at night. I could tell that he was irritated with me, but I stood my ground! One of the other girl's had already offered to work the shift, so it wasn't a big deal anyway; he was just being a jerk. And besides, I'm on day 38 of taking my medication as prescribed! I don't want to mess that up by working all night!

The holidays are upon us and I'm feeling grateful for the love I've discovered; both for others and for myself. Embracing wellness has been my goal this year and I feel like it's finally within my grasp!

I've been thinking about *love's pure light.* I was listening to a Christmas song and when I heard those familiar words, they held *new* meaning for me! For the first time, the words "love's pure light" opened my eyes to the idea that if God *is* love and Jesus is God, then *Jesus* is *love*! To *me,* this is just one more way for God to reveal His *own* pure light! (Or love.) In my heart I don't believe that people who aren't *Christian* are doomed, although I *do* believe that Christianity is *one* of the paths that leads to *love's pure light* (or God.) There are many paths; be it one of the many religions around the globe and throughout time, or perhaps a direct path, as in the case of Spirituality. Some people, myself included, don't want the middle man or the church elders delving into their personal relationship with God. It's my belief that *love's pure light* is waiting to embrace each and every one of us *when* we are truly ready.

I watched an episode of *Law and Order* last night. I cried when the main character realized how much he loved his wife when he almost lost her. It makes me realize that, no matter what happens between my husband and me, I still care about him.

We found out that Bill's blood pressure is dangerously high! I've been on an emotional rollercoaster. I'm really worried about him. I guess I *do* love him! I sure wish that my mom was still alive. I need her words of wisdom and her calming ways, but *I'm* the grown up now and I need to be strong for my husband.

Day 42 of correct dose!

I read another book by Paulo Coelho. This one is titled, *Veronika Decides to Die.* It's about discovering the will to live! It also talked about living in the *present,* and how it's important to *not* be afraid of life's uncertainties; to *worry* about something *never* makes it better.

Glucose problems again. Maybe Lyle was right about the low weight causing blood sugar problems? But I don't want to eat! Am I afraid to gain? Do I want to lose? Is it a control issue? Sigh.

90 lbs! New all-time record! Average daily calorie count for last 8 days is 1,200. I should be basking in the glory of reaching this all-time low, but all I can think about is that I'm absolutely *TERRIFIED* of

gaining weight!!!!!!!! I'm just ounces away from my goal and I can't enjoy it because the fear of getting fat is far too great.

I ate 650 calories yesterday and now I feel extremely weak and light-headed. I had to leave the grocery store in the middle of shopping and force myself to eat! I ate an entire egg sandwich and I did feel better afterwards.

I purposely asked Lyle a lot of questions, about irrelevant things, so that he wouldn't have time to bring up my weight. I also told him that I was proud of myself for not cutting a week or two ago when I was upset. Lyle said that although it was good that I refrained from self-injury, I still let the *borderline* color my entire day. I felt let down by his comment, but I know that it's completely accurate. He said that I need to allow myself to get angry at other people, or even the situation itself. Apparently I'm still not comfortable enough to show anger and because I don't feel safe expressing that anger, I punish *myself.* This time I did it by ruining a perfectly good day! I'm still choosing to direct any anger that I feel, towards *myself!* I have enough awareness now, that I need to make the choice to *not* engage in borderline behavior. As I was leaving the session, Lyle asked me if I had noticed that he hadn't brought up my weight. I told him I had and I thanked him for it!

The rumor around work is that the hospital is *not* renewing the contract they have with the lab, which means that my job could be on the line. I'm not stressing about it though, because my self-worth is no longer tied up in my job! That's HUGE for me!

I say that I'll stop at 89 lbs, and then gain a few back, but I don't know if I can! Just the *thought* of gaining *any* weight fills me with an overwhelming and *crushing* anxiety!!!!

I saw a quote somewhere that said, "I can do anything I want, but what I *want* is determined by my awareness." I don't know who the author is, but I really like the saying! It's powerful! Maybe it's my *awareness* that has kept me faithful with my meds. I've taken the correct dose *everyday* for 46 days straight! Yay, I'm doing it! Perhaps I've finally made peace with my need for medication. Now it's time to work on the weight issue… I don't know if I can *ever* make peace with that!

I'm embarrassed by how thin I am, but I'm *terrified* of gaining! I am so panicky about my weight!!!!!!!!! Sometimes I still see a chubby reflection when I look in the mirror! Why is this so hard for me? It makes me want to cry! I *know* that I'm too thin, but there's something driving me to lose more! And seeing "chubby" in the mirror is just fuel for the fire! I feel nervous and anxious about my size. I know that I should weigh more, but there's a fear in me that I can't explain! One minute I think I'm too thin, and I'm desperately trying to hide it, and the next minute I'm fighting a rising panic about gaining! I'm addicted to the scale *and* the tape measure. I lie about what I've eaten to keep people off my back. I keep saying that I want to be well, and that includes fixing the distorted thoughts and images in my brain. So why am I hung up on this? Am I afraid of wellness? Am I'm afraid to be *fixed*? Why does this scare me so much? Is it because I fear, that once I start eating, I won't be able to stop and I'll start gaining? I feel *sick* about this! I'm doing so well in other areas, so why is this so difficult? It seems that my entire self-worth now hinges on my weight. My job no longer defines me, but a number on the scale still does. So *why* am I letting my weight affect, and completely control, my self-image and the worth I place upon myself?

Bill called me his "skinny mini." I wanted to ask him if he thought I was too thin, but I was afraid that his answer would fan the flame of anorexia (and the self-doubt that goes with it.) I suppose it's a step in the right direction, to *know* that it's in my best interest *not* to ask him. Baby steps are better than *no* steps.

I've been reflecting back on the first few months after my overdose. I've come a long way since then. I'm incredibly thankful to God for bringing Lyle into my life. I can't begin to describe or explain all that Lyle has done for me. I doubted so much of what he said in the beginning. I didn't have any hope for me; especially in those first few months! But Lyle never gave up on me. He had faith in me long before I could even imagine having faith in myself. I'm also thankful for Dr. Stoune and the fact that God put him in the right place at the right moment. Because he crossed paths with Bill that day, I not only received the diagnosis and proper medication, I was also blessed to have the most compassionate and caring MD I have ever known taking care of me! With Dr. Stoune taking care of my medical and spiritual needs and Lyle taking care of my psychological needs, I have been helped tremendously on this path to healing. As I was reflecting, I found myself talking to God. At first I asked Him to help me rise *above* the human condition, but then I changed my prayer to ask that He would help me to *embrace* the human condition, starting with the humanness of *me*! I prayed for Him to show me *how* to love and accept myself *just as I am*!

Bill's very discouraged right now. The problems with his blood pressure came out of nowhere! He's lean, and very fit from working out regularly and watching his diet, so this has really brought him down. On a selfish note, I'm discouraged too. Bill has always seemed invincible to both of us, and I didn't realize how much I've depended on his strength over the years; the physical as well as the mental. He's always been so tough and even though I've complained about that, I'm already missing it! I'm afraid that this health issue will take away his edge; his spark. I want him to be his loud, cheerful, outgoing self; the life of the party! I've never seen him so down before. I need to be the strong one right now, but I feel so helpless.

I decided to be spontaneous. I called Bill at work and asked him if he wanted to go to Jackpot tonight. It's a long drive and I knew it would be close to midnight before we could get there, but I overcame my aversion to spontaneity for one reason only; I wanted to help Bill. I thought that a little weekend trip might be just the ticket to pull him out of his depression. It was 6pm when I called, and he still had an hour left to work, but he's always been a *spur of the moment* kind of guy, so he said, "Yes!" He asked me to have everything ready by 7pm and we'd leave as soon as he got off work. Wow! I can't believe that I'm actually doing something at the last minute!

The trip ended up being a *turning point* for me in a way that I did *not* expect! First of all, the 4 hour drive was physically painful because of *less padding* on my frame. The second thing that happened was concerning my reflection in the hotel mirrors. Since we go to the resort at least once a year, I'm used to what my reflection looks like in the full length mirrors; especially the mirror adorning the closet door in the hotel room. What I saw, when I undressed, *shocked* me! I couldn't believe how far my bones stuck out! How grotesquely thin I was! I was appalled at the skeleton looking back at me! Every one of the vertebrae jutted out! My pelvis was clearly defined. My arms looked like toothpicks and my collarbone and shoulder blades protruded more than I had ever seen before! I was horrified at how emaciated I'd become! Suddenly I was *embarrassed* by the way that I looked! So embarrassed that I didn't want to leave the room; but my husband was waiting. So I dressed in bulky layers, trying desperately to hide the truth of what I had just witnessed! I felt like a walking advertisement for anorexia! The sheer horror, of what my eyes were finally opened to, helped me to eat *normally* while we were vacationing. But... once we got home, and I could look into my *own* mirror, the *roundness* was back! What the heck is going on?

I thought that I'd be ready to gain some weight after that trip to Jackpot, but it's not happening. I'm more obsessed than ever! I'm weighing and measuring myself dozens of times a day! If my measurements go up a fraction of an inch, or my weight a quarter of a pound, I freak out!

The stress of dealing with my continued "weight problem," and worrying about Bill's health, is taking its toll on my nerves. Because of my continued inability to express my concerns and fears, I constantly feel the familiar pangs of anxiety cropping up, followed closely by anger. The anger is at *myself* for being so weak! A few days ago, that same anger boiled into a full-blown rage. Once again, I quietly slipped away. As I pummeled my head with my fist, I couldn't seem to stop the hitting *or* the internal barrage of insults hurled my way... by yours truly. I struck myself repeatedly with the force that can only gain its strength from unbridled rage! I know that I'm hurting myself in two ways: One is the actual physical pain or injury, and the other is by not letting anyone in. By keeping everyone *out*, nobody can know how distressed I am. But it's the only way to be *safe*; the only way I know how. Aside from my sessions with Lyle, it's still too scary to trust *anyone* with my real feelings and fears, concerning this thing we call life.

I'm NOT ready!!!!!!!!!!!!!!! I'm having major second thoughts about gaining a couple of pounds! I convinced myself to eat more these last few days, especially protein, but now I'm panicking! I asked Bill if he'd still love me if I got fat and he answered that he loved me when I *was* fat! I felt like I'd been slapped in the face! I know that he's always been attracted to very thin women, but I hadn't realized that he actually thought of me as *fat* when I was heavier! I told him that people are always telling me that I need to gain weight. He looked at me in disbelief. I am so fucking confused! I thought for sure, that after what I saw in Jackpot, he'd finally think I was too thin. *Why* does his opinion matter so much? But it does and I can't help it. I know I'm in danger of falling back into the unhealthy attachment mode, but I feel powerless to stop myself. Screw any crazy ideas about gaining weight! I give up.

Blood sugar problems again. (2 hours after I ate, it was 53.) My irritability caused me to be short-tempered with a patient, which is so unlike me because the *patients* are my favorite part of the job!

I'm not looking forward to my visit with Lyle. How do I get better? Do I even want to get better? If we don't talk about my weight, I know it will feel like a giant elephant is sitting in the room with us. I just got an amusing mental image of a large elephant sitting on the coffee table between Lyle and me! I actually chuckled, as I thought of us *stretching* around the elephant to see each other!

Lyle made some valid points yesterday. He defended Bill when I complained about the way he answered my question regarding my weight. Lyle said that, in the past, Bill might have purposely or inadvertently said hurtful things, but *now* he's thinking about what he says to me before he says it. Lyle told me that because I'm more vocal about what I want, Bill's not sure of what the appropriate answer is. As I'm getting stronger and no longer accepting the family dynamics as they were, it's confusing to my husband.

In our early years together, I *internalized* every "mean" thing Bill said. (Even if it was said in "in fun.") I didn't speak up, but instead tried to conform to whatever it was that I thought Bill wanted me to be. I quit being *me* before I ever got the chance to know who I was! An example that comes to mind was my use of the word *wonderful.* Bill thought it was a silly word and teased me whenever I used it. I internalized his teasing as criticism, and quit using the word soon after we met. That's just *one* example of probably thousands! If I had been free from the *borderline* when we first met, I would have had a clear appreciation for who I was and Bill's teasing would have been exactly what it was suppose to be; simple teasing! (I am happy to report, that after a 25 year hiatus, the word *wonderful* is back in my vocabulary.)

I forgot to record what Lyle said about my weight at our last session. He was pleased that I'd finally seen the truth of my underweight status while I was in Jackpot. But... when I told him that my reflection had morphed back into the chubby version once I looked into my *own* mirror, he was blunt in his reply. He put the responsibility directly on my shoulders. *Because* I saw the truth, I am now *aware* of it! It's *my* responsibility to rectify this issue. He told me that I am in control of what I choose to eat or not to eat. I'm also in control of what I see, or don't see, when I look in the mirror. I have already proven that with my disorders either cured or controlled, I am now in the *driver's seat*. My fear of gaining is *left over* from years of being "at the mercy of my moods." Now that I'm healthy, it's time to give up that fear. I am in control and even though I can't control outside forces, I *can* control how I choose to react. For the first time in my life, I am truly in control. It sounds great in theory, but can it really be that simple?

A surgeon was rude to me on the phone at work and I called him on it! "*Expect* Respect!"

I'm learning to enjoy the journey! Yesterday, while I was grocery shopping, I made it a point to smile at everyone I saw. Yes, I was actually looking at people! I smiled at the old men sitting on the bench near the entrance. I smiled at the bell ringers for the Salvation Army. I smiled at the clerks and the customers. I struck up conversations with strangers. I didn't look away from people in wheelchairs; instead, I purposely made eye contact, smiled and said, "Hi." Most people smiled back and that felt good, but more importantly, I just wanted to spread a little good cheer. When I was in line to pay for my groceries, I looked at the people in front of me and realized that they were people I knew! The husband is always friendly, but his wife is usually cranky. I'm trying to accept individuals, just as they are, so I chose to be friendly with both the husband *and* his not-so-nice wife. Imagine my surprise, when she wished me a Merry Christmas and gave me a great big bear hug!

I need to keep in mind that most people are truly doing the best they can with what they know. *Awareness* is huge! As we become more aware, we can make better choices.

My Dad came through town tonight. When he got to my house, he hugged me really tight and for a long time! We had a very nice visit. I told him about the bipolar disorder and then anxiously waited for him to dismiss it as either unimportant or not real. But he did neither! Instead, he acknowledged *bipolar* as a very *real* disease that requires medication. I was shocked *and* thrilled! I was so sure that he would pass judgment on me, but he didn't! He did comment on how thin and bony I'd become, but it felt like genuine concern, not criticism. I wonder how much of our relationship was damaged over the years, because of *my* distorted perception? Now that I feel free to be *me*, and I don't have to wear any masks, I'm finally able to enjoy my loved ones!

Bill's doctor scheduled an appt for him with a specialist regarding his recent blood pressure problems. His appt is on the same day as my appt with Lyle! I want to be there for my husband, but I don't want to miss my appt either. I left a message for Lyle stating that I couldn't make the morning appt, but I could come in the afternoon if he had an opening; otherwise, I'd see him on Tuesday the 8th. I waited all day for him to call back. I even drove by his office and saw his parked car. I can't believe how abandoned I feel! Why didn't he call me back? (I suppose that would be the *borderline* rearing its ugly head again.)

One of my coworkers was in a very bad mood and she wouldn't say why. I finally went up to her and wrapped my arms around her in a big hug. I playfully told her that she needed a hug; at which point, she physically and forcefully pushed me away! I had never been so hurt by a friend before! My eyes instantly filled up with tears! I told the techs that I had to go upstairs to pick up a specimen. In reality, I just needed to compose myself! I left the lab and walked to one of the lesser-used hallways, where it was fairly dark. I was standing near the back entrance to the CCU, trying to stop my tears, when Dr. Stoune walked by. As soon as he realized that I'd been crying, he gave me a hug! If it had been anyone else, I would have been embarrassed, but with him I felt *safe*.

I was really feeling low last night. I felt that I'd been rejected twice in 24 hours! First by Lyle and then by my so-called friend at work. I tried not to cry, but I couldn't stop the tears! Do I *not* have fucking control over anything? I get so pissed at myself sometimes! I tried calling Lyle again last night and ended up leaving a message, telling him that I'd just see him on the 8th since he never called back. I know I sounded really down when I left the message, but I didn't care. I just wanted him to call me back! I felt like saying, "Fuck it all! Fuck it on gaining weight! Fuck it on getting better!" I knew it was the *borderline* talking, but I just didn't give a shit!!!!! I couldn't stop crying. I knew the only way to stop would be a straight-edge. I told myself that I wouldn't cut if Lyle returned my call by 10pm; but I didn't wait and he didn't call.

I'm feeling a lot of anger at Lyle for not returning my calls. I know he has a life, but it would have only taken a minute to leave me a message! I thought he cared about me! Now my head is filled with doubts! Maybe I'm too much of a burden for him. Has he lost faith in me? Is he annoyed with me? Maybe he's just plain sick of me? I know *I* am.

Bill called me into the family room to watch a segment on TV about anorexia in adult women. The painfully thin woman, who was being interviewed, admitted that she saw *roundness* whenever she looked at herself in the mirror. I wondered, for a moment, if maybe my husband was trying to tell me something.

I'm still angry at Lyle, but I don't feel like I have the right to be angry with him. He's done so much for me! Maybe he wants me to end therapy. Maybe I *should* end therapy. I might as well... since no weight will ever be thin enough for me anyway! *Any* fat is too much! So why continue? Isn't it ultimately *up to me* anyway? Lyle said as much the last time I saw him. Maybe I should just be grateful for how far I've come. It's not fair to Lyle if I'm not willing to do my part on this last hurdle, but maybe this *last issue* is just too deeply ingrained in my mind to fix; or maybe I don't want to be well after all. I can feel the tears welling up, but I don't want to cry! If I start crying... how will I ever stop?

Later—

I couldn't stand the tears, so I numbed myself with a straight-edge. Now I don't care enough to cry.

I'm up to 93 lbs! I can't believe that I almost let Lyle talk me into getting fat again! He was right when he said that *I'm* in control of what I do, or don't do! He said that it's up to me to make healthy choices! Well that means I can also make *un*healthy choices and that's what I intend to do! Fuck Lyle! He doesn't care about me, so why should I? It feels like dieting really *is* the only thing I have control over!

I know that I'm suppose to have control over more than just dieting, but the other stuff is just too hard; like trying to reconcile what I *see* in the mirror with what is real. I'm tired of fighting it, so I'm choosing to believe that the *thinness* I saw in Jackpot was an illusion… and that I am indeed, *round*.

JOURNAL

11

December 25th, 2007 thru February 13th, 2008

**Setbacks and tribulations...
The journey to wellness continues...**

I really thought I had the *borderline* licked. After nearly two years of therapy, I felt very confident in my ability to control my impulses. Doing what's in my best interest had become second nature, or so I thought. Now, once again, I'm covered in bruises and I have a deep gash on my leg. Most of my scars, from the earlier injuries, had faded enough that I barely noticed them anymore. Now it seems I'm starting over again. I thought I was done with self-destructive behavior. I'm ashamed and embarrassed at my regression; especially since I had been doing so well! I can't afford to be weak. Bill *needs* me right now!

I still see fat when I look into the mirror! I'm up to 93 lbs. The mirrors in Jackpot were *wrong*! I've got to lose this weight! It's disgusting and I can't live with it! I won't! And yet I still continue to binge. I'm such a glutton! I ate so much last night that my stomach was stretched to the limit! I felt nauseous, and I thought I was going to vomit a couple of times, but I was able to keep it down. Perhaps I *should* have allowed myself to throw up. If I was bulimic, I could binge and still lose weight.

I feel huge at 94 lbs! This binge eating has got to STOP! I feel so chubby and yet, when I went shopping for clothes today, the smallest sizes were too big! Everything points to me being too thin, but I can't (or won't) allow my mind to wrap around it.

I've been feeling lost at work lately. We've been through about 8 managers in the 5 years that I've been employed with the lab. I really liked the manager we had most recently, but he was transferred to another city. Once again we are *leaderless*. Not knowing if we'll lose our jobs, because of contract issues, leaves me feeling a little unsettled. It's hard to stay excited about a job, and coworkers you love, when you know that everything is about to be yanked apart and you have no idea of what (or who) will survive the restructuring.

I'm worried about my husband's health and who will work for him if he needs surgery. Fearing for his health, and maybe even his life, is always in the back of my mind. I've been thinking about how crappy of a wife I've been to him. I've held him back in so many areas! I'm dead weight to him. I no longer want to die, but I do think about setting *him* free by granting him a divorce. I know he wants one, but he would never leave me. To do that would make him feel as if he'd failed and he's far too competitive to fail at *anything*. I also know that if he left me, he'd feel guilty and he'd worry about me. As stoic and as strong as he seems, I know he does worry.

I had the worst muscle spasm of my life! I was at work and it hit without warning. It was in my upper back and neck. I couldn't turn my head without excruciating pain! Leaning over patients, to draw their blood, was impossible. One of my coworkers gave me a couple of muscle relaxants. Within an hour I was able to function, but the pain and tightness didn't go away completely.

I went to a friend's wedding recently and had a wonderful time. At the reception, the photographer was going to each table to take pictures of the guests. I actually posed for the photos! When I saw them later, I was dismayed at my *perceived* imperfections, but then I thought, "Hey, that's *me* and I'm having fun!"

I had a weird dream about my eye glasses melting on our woodstove. I'm wondering if it has something to do with how I *see* myself.

One of my coworkers thinks that the recent muscle spasm I had, was a result of the stress I've been feeling at having my daughter home for the holidays. I had gotten used to having my home neat and orderly and now it's a mess! I need to step up to the plate and *tell* Rachel what it is that I want! (She can't read my mind!) The residual pain and stiffness in my back and neck will serve as a reminder that I need to set some boundaries! I hated the dreaded chore list when I was a kid, but my childhood was so different than Rachel's. I'm not asking a lot; just that she clean up after *herself.*

I've been trying to assert myself by speaking up and it works well on the job, but not so much with my husband. No matter how I try to *word* things, he comes back with comments like, "Why are you being defiant?" On the other hand, when I'm at work, I gain respect each time I speak up. Just yesterday, a police officer told the patient that I was drawing that she was freaking *me* out by being unruly. It wasn't true, so I spoke up immediately! I told the cop that the patient's behavior wasn't bothering me at all.

It's becoming easier and easier to speak up and voice my thoughts; whether it's just an opinion, or a need, or even anger. I will not be silent anymore.

Good news! The specialist for Bill didn't seem too concerned about the test results or the blood pressure readings. Based on Bill's excellent fitness level, and his diet, the doctor said he was in better shape than some of the marines he has worked with! That definitely boosted Bill's frame of mind!

Yesterday morning I had something *odd* happen. I was getting ready for work and even though I'd just eaten, I thought to myself, "I'm hungry!" And *instantly*, a stern voice in my head said, "You DON'T need anymore food young lady! You've had enough!" Then a pitiful child's voice whimpered, "But I'm still hungry." I've never had this happen before and I'm not sure what to make of it. Was I *actually*

told that same thing at some point in my childhood? It left me feeling kind of sad.

Weight is back down to 90 lbs. (Just ounces away from the 80's!) I'm feeling really shaky and weak, but I'm so close to my goal that I can't stop now!

One of Bill's favorite shows is called, "The Biggest Loser." He's always asking me to watch it with him, but the show fills me with *fear*! Seeing those enormous plus-sized people scares me to death! They remind me that, if I'm not careful, I could get that huge! I told Bill that I can't watch the program because it creates more anxiety than I can handle at this point.

A few people, who think that my weight is fine, have asked me for diet tips. Whenever someone does that, I change the subject! I don't want to talk about my weight, or what I eat, with anyone!

I'm making sure that my friends and family *see* me eating. I don't want any lectures from them. It makes me uneasy though; to eat anything in front of other people. Recently, when I went to a party with my husband, I tried to hide my thinness by *not* tucking my shirt in. I also put food on my plate, and pretended to nibble on it, so that no one would tell me to eat. I tried to have fun, but I was physically uncomfortable throughout the party, because the chairs had no padding and it hurt to sit in them.

The needle on the scale won't budge! It's stuck at 90 lbs.

Bill told me that he really worries about me. He was very sweet and seemed genuinely concerned. He said that he's noticed that I've been down recently. I told him that I'm just burned out after another hectic holiday season and having to socialize too much for too long!

I want to be left alone! I'm so tired of having to be "on" all the time! I'm in desperate need of some down time. Alone time. Quiet time. No TV. No radio. No phones. Bill wants to know if it's one of the *disorders* that requires so much alone time. I honestly don't know.

I did it! 89 lbs! I had a session with Lyle this morning. I told him about the cutting episode that followed my feelings of rejection and abandonment. I told him about the coworker who forcefully pushed me away. (I didn't tell him that I'd also felt abandoned by *him*.) Apparently it still has to do with me not being able to express my anger. I told him that it wasn't anger I had felt, but sadness, when my friend at work hurt my feelings. He disagreed and then I suddenly remembered that my *first* reaction was to punch the frig! I'd completely forgotten about that! (Man, Lyle is good!) It was my *second* reaction to burst into tears! Near the end of our session, Lyle asked, "Why the sadness?" I told him that I was disappointed in myself for falling back. He asked me if I thought that I had disappointed *him* as well. I whispered, "Yes," and he assured me that I hadn't. He reminded me that it takes *practice* to adopt healthy habits. He used the analogy of a toddler who is learning to feed himself from a spoon. He keeps trying, or practicing, until he succeeds! It just takes, "Practice. Practice. Practice!" I can live with that motto! It's much better than what I've heard my entire life, which is… "You just need to try harder!" I was already trying harder than anyone I knew! Lyle reminded me of how far I've come and he reassured me that this was just a little hiccup; a last hurrah. Maybe he's right. Maybe this, along with the anorexia, *is* the last hurrah; the *final hurdle*.

Lyle wants to see me back in one week. Hopefully I'll be ready to go 3 weeks at that point. I know I'm getting better… one baby step at a time! (And aren't baby steps better than *no* steps?) Deep in my being, I know I'm getting healthier. Lyle knows it too; even when I was obviously down, he asked about my feelings regarding the approaching end of therapy. I know that I'm getting close to being ready for therapy to end and it no longer terrifies me. It does sadden me though. It's bittersweet to know that the *little girl is growing up.*

I had to work on my thought processes a bit today. I had a ton of chores to do and not enough hours to do them! Each time I felt the anxiety rising up, I redirected my thoughts and it worked! At one point I stepped outside to shovel the steps and the neighbor's dog was right *there,* in my way, trying to get petted. I was angry that she was on *my* turf, but I knew it wasn't her *fault* that she was starved for attention. (Since she doesn't get any at home.) So I quickly petted her and then retreated back into the house, without getting the shoveling done. Once I was back in the house, I felt anger welling up in me. I didn't want *anyone,* not even a dog, intruding on what was supposed to be *my* day! My day to be *alone*! Suddenly, I remembered Lyle saying to me, "You have the *right* to get angry." Since I was alone in the house, so I chose to yell that it was *my* day and I wasn't going to share it with anyone! (I even peppered it with some cuss words!) Knowing that it was okay to be mad, made it easier to get it out of my system with absolutely no harm to myself! I *am* still moving in the right direction!

I had an appt with Dr. Stoune today. As I talked to him about my recent muscle problems, I joked with him by saying, "Now that my *mental* health is good, my *physical* health is taking a nosedive!" Then, on a more serious note, I told him that I used to blame Bill for everything that was wrong in our marriage. I told him what Lyle had said to me, near the beginning of therapy, when I first told him that, in the weeks leading up to the OD, I couldn't imagine living with Bill for another 20 or 30 or 40 years! Lyle had replied that it was *me* I couldn't live with; *not* Bill! Dr. Stoune agreed with Lyle and said that we have to truly see ourselves, as we are, before we can get better. And sometimes that means hitting rock bottom first. He's right! I love talking to that man! He truly understands. He *knows* how difficult the journey can be!

I wonder if Lyle has ever hit rock bottom? Wow! I'm thinking of others! Has Lyle ever experienced profound low points in *his* life? Is *that* where he gets his empathy? I wonder if he understands me so well *because* of his *own* trials and tribulations? Or did he just learn it from school and books? I think this is only the second time that I've stopped to wonder about Lyle the *person*! Not just the man I see as *my* father figure, *my* therapist, *my* mentor. M*y, my, my*! Everything has been about *me*! But now that I'm growing up *emotionally*, I'm developing empathy for other people. Even with setbacks, I'm *still* moving forward, still embracing wellness... or *trying* to embrace it!

Down to 88 lbs!!!!! I should be thrilled, but I'm mentally and physically exhausted! I think I'm getting a cold. I took a higher dose of my meds, so that I could get some much needed sleep. Does that mean I'm taking care of me? I don't know. My Dad stayed with us for a couple of days and as soon as he was gone, Bill started complaining about him. It bothers me when he does that, because all of his complaints are about things that I do as well. I'm so much like my Dad, in some ways, that it hurts to hear how much Bill hates those traits

Dad's like the absentminded professor. He wanders off with things and then leaves them somewhere other than their rightful place. Tonight, I realized that he accidentally took my new pill splitter! It only cost a few dollars, but I feel like crying! I *just* bought it! It was the first one I had *ever* bought and he wandered off with it before I even had a chance to use it! Because I was upset, I asked God why I couldn't be normal like everyone else and then it hit me. I *am* normal! It's okay to feel sad or angry or whatever! The feelings are no longer too intense for me to deal with. I'm no longer that *emotional* hemophiliac! *I'm* in control! I have a wealth of knowledge and insight to draw upon. I don't have to hurt myself ever again! I know that my *feelings* will *not* kill me, but the self-injury could have!

My perception, when it comes to my weight, continues to be warped. I know it's up to me to fix this. Lyle has given me the tools. Deep down I still want to lose weight, but I know this isn't healthy! I *think* that I want to get better, but it's *still* an uphill battle at this time. I won't give up though! I *will* keep trying!

Tired but wired again. Constant motion. Increased meds. Doing what's in my best interest.

I'm beginning to think of the borderline as a *separate entity* from me! Just like John Nash in the movie, *A Beautiful Mind,* when he learns that some of the people in his life *aren't* real! He finally chooses to ignore them when he realizes that they are manifestations of his schizophrenia! For me, it's about letting go of, or *ignoring,* the borderline thoughts! (Thoughts that *lead* to borderline *behavior.*) As the *black and white* thinking recedes, self-injury and self-hate are becoming a distant memory!

Ate 5,000 calories yesterday!!! Wt up to 92 and one half pounds! Glutton. I say that I want to eat like a normal person and then I binge. So which is it? Do I want to be normal, or do I want to be miserable? The choice is mine!

I've decided that 94 lbs is a reasonable goal. I don't want to be a skeleton anymore. I have the awareness that I need in order to accomplish this. My weight is up to me. Thin, fat, or normal. *I'm* in control.

Appt with Lyle went well. The bipolar disorder is *controlled* and the borderline personality disorder is rapidly receding. I'm pretty much doing it on my own. Lyle confirmed what I already knew in my heart, I'm nearing the end of therapy. The next session will involve a review so that we'll know what issues we can put on the shelf and what problems still need to be worked on; before I'm considered "cured."

I am such a basket case! I know I'm getting better, but I can't imagine my life without Lyle in it! How do I say *good-bye* to the man who saved my *life*? He was with me every step of the way, guiding me to wellness, to wholeness; helping me to find the *real* Terresa; helping me to choose *life*! My heart is breaking. I can't stop crying!

I know that my feelings of sadness are normal. I wanted to call Lyle this morning to tell him how sad I am and to ask him if these feelings are normal, but I already know the answer. I need to work through this *on my own*. Lyle has given me the tools, through therapy, and I've gained a tremendous amount of insight during our two years together. I know that I have it within me to make good decisions. I am *able* to work through my painful feelings. It's okay to be sad or angry or afraid! It's what makes us human. It's what makes *me* the person I am! These painful feelings will pass and I will become stronger *because* of them. My feelings no longer terrify me. They won't kill me! I don't have to flee them anymore, through self-injury or any other unhealthy behavior; borderline or otherwise. *Feel* the feelings, *accept* the feelings, and then move on! The power of *choice* frees me! I can do this!

I sent Lyle a note:

Dear Lyle,

I knew in my heart that I was nearing the end of therapy. When you confirmed it today, I felt a sense of pride. But now, just hours later, I can't stop the tears. It's begun to sink in that along with wellness, comes the *end* of our patient/therapist relationship. I'm having a tough time with that. I suppose these feelings are normal, but WOW does it hurt! How do I say good-bye to the man who literally saved my life? I keep reflecting on these past two years. You were with me *every* step of the way, guiding me on this journey. You showed me how to not only *choose* life, but to *want* life! I know that our next session will be about reviewing my progress and working towards a conclusion. I just wanted to get this off chest.

Thank you for everything!

Sincerely
Terresa

I bought a new *2yr day planner* this afternoon. As I retired the old planner, I became extremely emotional. The old planner holds the last 2 *years* of my life in it! It's been a very difficult and painful journey and that *planner* holds so many memories in it! Good, bad, and bittersweet. It went from just days before my suicide attempt right up until today, when I purchased the new one. In the old one, *every* visit with Lyle has been recorded, along with so many other things. And tucked into the flaps at both ends, are dozens of scraps of paper containing messages of hope. It's more than a small notebook. It contains, within its pages, the two most difficult and rewarding years of my life!

I told my husband that I was having a very rough day. I told him about the 2yr planner and how it had affected me. He asked me how he could help. (He's really trying!) Once I opened up to him, my tears finally stopped. I know I need to let him in. His behavior is rarely judgmental anymore. He seems to understand that I wasn't *choosing* to be difficult all of those years. (Although "difficult" is exactly what I was!) He now knows that it was the *illness*. Perhaps the wall, which I've kept around me, is beginning to crumble.

I told Debbie that I had felt really emotional lately and she pointed out the obvious! It's the *transition* that's causing this cascade of emotions! I'm leaving behind the *borderline* way of thinking and behaving. No matter how tempting it might be to slip back into the comfortable *old shoe,* I've learned too much to ever go back! Lyle re-parented me in a sense and this little girl has finally grown up! Lyle did his job and he did it well! It's time for me to leave the *nest*, to spread my wings, and to not only fly… but soar!

I know that Lyle will be pleased that I've gained a few pounds. Of course I know that, ultimately, it's up to *me* to figure out what my healthiest weight is.

I've been thinking about the significance of my *retired* 2 year planner. It amazes me that the planner just happened to *catch* the two most important and pivotal points of my healing. The first being my surrender to the illness through my suicide attempt. The second, two years later, my willingness to *embrace wellness* after two years of therapy. I *could* think of it as two years *lost* forever, *or* I can choose to see it as two years of huge personal growth! The choice is mine!

I'm beginning to panic about my weight gain! 95 lbs is too much! I feel pudgy and fleshy and gross! I can't stay at this weight! Gaining was a mistake!!! I was healthy and energetic at 89 lbs!!! Why did I listen to Lyle? Why, why, why?

In looking back at yesterday's entry, and going back even further in the journal, I felt the need to comment. I was *not* energetic at 89 lbs. How quickly, and conveniently, I forget. Bill called me tonight because he needed a ride. (He'd been drinking.) Normally I would be upset with having to drop what I was doing, but I was actually *happy* that he'd called me! When I picked him up, he was complaining about something one of his employees had done. He had watched his in-store video and had seen that she had left the premises, for two minutes, to go across the street for a soda. (She didn't leave the store unmanned as there was a second employee.) I asked him whether, or not, he had ever *told* her that he didn't want her leaving the store on her break. He said, "She should know better." I called him on it! I told him that people can't read his mind. He expects everyone to think like *him*. I told him it's unfair. The reason I'm writing about this, is because I'm learning to stand my ground during a discussion or an argument. This is a big deal for me. I will no longer agree just to keep the peace. I've done that my whole life and I'm not going to do it anymore. I have a voice *and* an opinion and they *matter; m*aybe not to anyone else, but they matter to *me*!

There's no stopping me now! I'm getting good at asking for help, stating my needs, voicing concerns, etc. I'm also getting better at stopping the knee-jerk reaction of saying, "No," every time someone asks me to do something on the spur of the moment. I may *still* decline, but not until I've taken the time to think through the request. More often than not, I end up saying, "Yes."

The "blinders of borderline" are coming off! I'm beginning to see the big picture in all its beauty. I can honestly say that my soul has felt its worth. I'm routinely doing what's in my best interest which includes taking the proper amount of medication. (And I'm happy to report that I've been on the correct dose for 3 straight months now.)

One of my coworkers told me that she feels a "kind of peace" when I show up to work! *Me?* Either I'm a really good actress or God is beginning to work through me! Several people have told me that I should write my story, so that I can help others who struggle with mental illness, but it's such a *personal* journey! I'm not sure if I'm ready to share it with the *world*. If writing a book is meant to be, then God will show me the way.

"To be an instrument of God's love and grace." That's a request I've made from God, so maybe I'm *suppose* to have this illness. Maybe I'm supposed to share what I've learned. I don't know. Do I have the strength it would take? *Can* I share my *demons?* Am I *willing* to share them? I don't know. I just don't know.

The binge eating has to STOP! It's like a run away train! I'm up to 97 lbs and I want to cry! How could I have let myself go like this? I'm out of control! I'm losing my enthusiasm for life! My self-worth is *still* tied up with my weight and I don't know how to stop it. How do I separate *me* from "it?"

Why am I abusing my body with junk? I need to stop! No more excuses! It's time to take responsibility for my actions. No longer will I blame someone or some *thing* for my behavior. I'm *not* at the mercy of my moods and out-of-control whims! Not anymore. I am in control! No longer will I abuse my body. No more cutting, starving or bingeing!

I took a long hard look at myself in the mirror this morning. I looked slender and fit. The fat has added a softness. I can still see muscle, but there are also curves. Am I okay with that? I don't know. Do I *want* to look womanly? Curvy? Sexy? I honestly don't know.

I noticed that I was getting puffy. Too much salt? Too many calories? Even my fingers were swollen! I felt the panic rising! I found myself becoming withdrawn, distracted and distraught. To quell my growing anxiety, I snuck off to the bathroom to weigh myself. When the needle stopped at 98 lbs, I nearly cried out. I covered my mouth with my hand and sunk to the floor! What had I done to myself? I was *huge*! A full blown panic attack took hold. I shook with the intensity of it. *How* could I have let this happen? In 3 short weeks... I had gained *ten pounds!*

I was suppose to go out to dinner with my husband, but how could I now? As I looked at myself in the full length mirror, I saw rolls of fat hanging on my body! Lyle's voice was in my head, challenging what I saw, but I chose to ignore *it*! I didn't resort to any self-harm, but I *wanted* to! Boy did I want to! Finally I decided to let my husband in on what was going on. He was supportive and gently reminded me that what I was seeing in the mirror was mostly in my *mind*. When he asked me how much of it did I think was probably my distorted perception, I whispered, "half?" He shook his head and said that it was much more than that! I knew in my heart that he was right and I thanked him for his perspective. He hugged me and thanked me for letting him in.

I got mad at myself for being angry about something minor. Before I knew it, I was slamming my fist against the side of my head! Everything that Lyle had taught me suddenly seemed inaccessible. I didn't do much damage, but it bothers me that I did any at all. I thought I was done with that! After I had calmed down, Lyle's words of advice came back to me, "Practice, practice, practice." When it comes to *ending* border-line behavior, I'll still slip occasionally, but it will be less and less. I need only to remember, "Practice, practice, practice!"

I don't know *why*, but I've been so jumpy lately and downright shaky! I'm constantly hearing music that isn't playing and seeing things that aren't there! It's not that I actually *see* a person. It's more like I see, in my peripheral vision, a person running by! It definitely doesn't help with my anxiety level.

I shared with my husband the idea of writing a book. He was surprisingly supportive. I need to give him more credit! I was pleased to hear that he had been sharing some of the lessons or quotes that I've learned, through therapy, with his friends. One of the phrases was, "You're not that important." Taken out of context it sounds cruel, but it's not at all! It just means that when you've done something that you're embarrassed or ashamed about, *you* will remember it long after everyone else has forgotten! For the most part, people are so wrapped up in their own lives that the last thing they're probably doing is thinking about you and your perceived blunder. That quote has helped me immensely in putting things into a proper perspective. It's definitely worth sharing and I'm glad that my husband thought so too.

I thought that Lyle would be pleased with my recent weight gain, but he said it's *not enough*! Our session had started out great. I had been upbeat and quite talkative for the first half, and then Lyle said that he wanted to talk about something. He warned me that it would make me angry. He then told me that I need to *gain* at least 10 lbs! *GAIN 10 lbs?* The second he said, "Gain 10 lbs," I slipped into the familiar panic mode! I'm sure he could read it in my face and mannerisms. My good mood came to a screeching halt! He went on to give me an assignment. I am to ask friends and family how they think I would look, if I gained 10 lbs! I don't remember exactly what I said. I mumbled something about not knowing *if* I could ask that question. He reminded me that I *can* ask it *if I choose* to ask it. But it's *not* that simple! I honestly don't think I can do this.

I'm so ANGRY with Lyle regarding my weight!!!!!! I felt sheer panic when he first brought up the 10 lb idea, but *now*, after having time to think about it, I'm downright PISSED! I don't want to talk about this subject anymore!!!!!!!!

The wall is going back up! The one that separates me from Lyle! I'm so angry at him! He fucking wants me to *gain* weight? I'll show him! Not only am I *not* going to gain the 10 lbs that he thinks I need, but I'm going to *lose* the 10 lbs I've just gained! Fuck his fucking assignment!

I can't focus on a damn thing! This weight issue is driving a wedge between me and Lyle. It wasn't too long ago that we talked about the importance of setting boundaries instead of building walls. But right now… all I want is the biggest damn wall I can build! And I want it standing directly between Lyle and me!

I know that my thoughts and behavior, regarding Lyle and the weight issue, are a form of "twisting," but I can't seem to stop it. I'm still so angry with him! I thought he'd be pleased with my weight gain, but nooooo, he wants me fucking fat!!!!

I honestly thought I was well and now Lyle has ruined it! He had to go and throw the damn weight thing into the mix! I'm embarrassed at how big I've gotten! Maybe I should go ahead and quit therapy early. Besides, Lyle won't say I'm well until I'm fat and I don't want to be fat! *Ever*!

Why the hell does Lyle keep pushing me to gain? It pisses me off to no end!!!! I'm too restless to function! I can't focus on anything! I can't watch TV. I can't read! I wander around aimlessly, even at work! I'm a mess! Is that what Lyle wants? I was doing so well! Why the fuck did he have to go and ruin it? I am so fucking confused!!!!! I agreed with Lyle that "starving or stuffing" are unhealthy behaviors, and I agreed that I need to improve my diet, but I do *NOT* agree that I need to gain a single fucking pound! How would Lyle like it if I dropped to 80 lbs? That sure as hell would make my current weight look good!

Why can't I stop thinking about this damn weight issue? Why does Lyle's opinion matter so goddamned much? I'm up to 99 lbs! It's Lyle's fault that I'm getting fat!!!!!!! I feel sooooo chubby and sooooo gross! I can't stand it! It's totally unacceptable that I'm gaining and yet I can't seem to stop!!! I am sooooooo pissed at Lyle!!!!!

I thought I was ready to work with Lyle on an exit strategy for the conclusion of therapy, but now I'm not sure I even want to see him again! Before that last appointment, I'd been feeling very good about myself. I'd even looked into the mirror one day and saw a beautiful woman looking back! Now I only see fat! I've become standoffish with Bill, once again, because I'm embarrassed by my doughy body! It's Lyle's fault! My poor husband! He's seen me go through so many ups and downs over the years. It's not fair to him. If I thought that I could free him from me, by killing myself, I'd do it. But I know that my suicide would hurt him by haunting him forever. He would still be stuck with *me* in the form of the *memory* of me and the tragedy of my death. I can't do that to him or to our daughter. They don't deserve that kind of pain. At least I'm well enough to know *that*!

How can I go from being so up, and seeing beauty in the mirror, to a basket case who's thinking about suicide? What the heck? I nearly stopped breathing when Lyle suggested that I *gain ten pounds*! I am so angry with him!!!!! I'm deeply ashamed about the fat that I'm carrying. I tried so hard to get well and now this! Well, FUCK IT!!!! I don't give a shit about anything! FUCK LYLE!! He was right when he said that there would be days when I'd leave his office *hating* him! Well I fucking don't like him right now!!! FUCK HIM *AND* MY BEST INTEREST!!!!

I can't keep this weight!!! It's gross!!!! It's disgusting!!!! I'm aware that my obsession with this whole *issue* is not healthy, but I feel powerless to stop it. Even my husband is trying to help me accept this higher weight. He said that I look better than before. What the fuck? He's even trying to make me eat! He's always praised me for thinness. What the heck is going on? I'm more confused than ever!

Lyle's been a godsend in so many ways, so why do we butt heads on this issue? He won't budge and it's really pissing me off! My weight has taken center stage and I'm not liking it at all! I'm not liking *me* at all! I feel blah. I feel dead inside. Just going through the motions. It seems surreal that there was ever a time when I thought 98 or 99 lbs was thin. Now, it seems huge! I don't want to *let* Lyle bully me into gaining weight, but I feel myself wearing down on this issue.

I'm trying to communicate better with my husband, but sometimes he can be so condescending! I hated the belittlement I received from my Dad, and I sure as heck don't want it from my husband! Every time I try to speak up about something important to me, he shoots me down with an antagonizing retort. Lyle has told me time and again, that it's okay to get angry and it's okay to speak up! But every time I do, I end up feeling worse.

I was just beginning to figure out who I was. I was starting to be *real* more often. I had thrown out most of the *masks* that I used to hide behind. I thought I was *done* with the *borderline* crap. Now I'm just flat out discouraged about *everything*! Borderline has had its claws in me for 25 *years*! Maybe I can't overcome it after all? I'm wasting everyone's time! I feel hopeless, worthless, helpless. Do I have anything at all, that's worthwhile to offer? I doubt it. I am sure of one thing though. I'm growing weary of the battle.

Killing myself would hurt people. Staying alive hurts them too. I hurt everybody either way. Perhaps I should limit my contact with everyone, so that I don't bring them down. Isolating myself is in the *best interest* of anyone unlucky enough to know me. I need to separate myself from others, because I never know when the monster of *borderline* will be unleashed. What will trigger the next episode? What will cause sheer *joy* to turn into sheer *rage* in nothing more than the blink of an eye?

I've noticed over the years, at work, that I've gained the respect of quite a few doctors and nurses. The funny thing is that I no longer care! Respecting *myself* is what counts. So why am I *still* butting heads with Lyle?

The black and white thinking, so typical for *borderlines,* has been hard to let go of. But, with practice, I'm hoping that eventually I *will* succeed. I am in control of how I choose to live my life. Borderline does not have to control me. Not anymore. Black and white thinking is a knee-jerk reaction, but I know enough, now, that I can choose how to respond to a given situation. Same thing with my weight. I can choose *not* to panic as the number on the scale inches closer to 100 lbs. (Easier said than done.)

I visited with one of the employees in the CCU today. She has a lot of health problems, and I decided to be a friend and just *listen*! It seems that *listening* has become a lost art, but it's something that I *want* to get better at. I *want* to be a better person. I *want* to help others. (Even if it's just to listen for a few minutes.)

I had a good day at work. I felt energy flowing from me, to the patients, and back again. There was a cranky elderly man in the CCU who actually thanked me when I was done drawing his blood! No matter how cranky a patient is, I try to remember that they are *somebody's* loved one.

I'm beginning to see that Lyle truly does have my best interest at heart. My anger at him has slowly, but surely, dissolved. Beyond the weight issue, there is the even larger issue of taking care of myself. I know that my eating habits are not exactly healthy. I don't fit neatly into any of the *eating disorders* listed in the DSM, but I am aware that I have a very *disordered* way of eating. Learning to eat when I'm hungry is the next step to wellness. Binge eating and starving are *not* healthy!

I went to the ER to draw blood from an elderly lady. She was tiny and her two daughters, who had accompanied her, were average in size. They both mentioned something about being "huge." I could easily *see* what they could not! Because their mom was *little*, they grew up thinking that they were big! When in fact, they were neither big nor overweight. They were *normal*!

I felt it was noteworthy to say that I've been faithful with my meds for 114 days! I'm doing it! I'm choosing to do what's in my best interest. But, am I ready to tackle my bad eating habits? Am I willing to *gain* weight? *Courage* is moving forward, even when you're afraid. Well, I'm afraid, *very afraid*, but I'm going to give it a try.

I overheard a patient tell his nurse that he felt that God was punishing him, with an illness, because of his past sins. I could hardly believe my ears when the nurse *agreed* with him! I couldn't let it go! I spoke straight from my heart when I said that I didn't believe that God was punishing him. If that were true, how would you explain the *children* who are stricken with cancer or some other horrible disease? I saw something flash across the face of the RN, but I'm not sure whether she was angry or confused. I don't think that there were any hard feelings though, because she and I continue to be friendly when we work together. She's normally very outspoken, so if she *was* upset with me, she would probably say something. It's just that, in my heart, I believe that God *is* love. And reaching people *for God* should be done with *love*...not fear.

February 14th, 2008 thru April 10th, 2008

Thinking about cutting

The anxiety's rising

How could I have gained this weight

Too thin I was not

Though they all said I was

What do they know anyway

If I cut just a little

Enough to see blood

Have it bead up and trickle

Will that be enough

Or do I need more

Like a gash that will flow

Enough to pool up on the floor

Why did I listen, why did I gain

The terror is back with a vengeance

How could I have binge'd

All the days that I did

Gaining pound after pound of fat

What was I thinking

I should have gained muscle

If I had to gain something at all

The panic is rising, escape it, I can't

Or maybe I can with a cut

How deep should I go

But where can I hide it

I can't let my loved ones know

The fear that possessed me

Is starting to fade

My husband is on his way home

The window of freedom

To cut on myself

Has closed once again

For now

I don't know if the above poem captures my panic or not, but it's how I was feeling yesterday. I chose to write the poem *instead* of cutting. Despite the darkness of the poem, or maybe in spite of it, I continue to move forward!

I agree with Lyle that 88 lbs is too thin, but 98 lbs feels too heavy! I never did ask anyone to give me their opinion on what they thought I would look like *if* I gained 10 lbs. It still freaks me out to even *think* about it, let alone actually *gaining* it! Lyle must understand the difficulty in this assignment, since he was the one who told me that I was going to be angry! Before I felt the anger, I felt sheer panic! I'm afraid that the power of suggestion, regarding the 10 pounds, will cause the floodgates to open and I won't be able to stop eating! I'll be enormous in no time! Maybe I'll even be large enough to be on "The Biggest Loser." God, that isn't even funny!!! I have so much anxiety right now. I'm drowning in it! It's affecting every aspect of my life!!! I *want* to be able to separate my *worth* from my weight, but I can't! Why does Lyle insist on me getting fat? Couldn't he see that I was happy at 94 lbs?

Oh my God! I'm the heaviest I've been in 6 months! I reached the triple digits! I'm a disgusting 100 lbs! I've got to get my sweet tooth under control. This is just gross! I know, deep down, that Lyle does care for me, but I really don't understand *why* he thinks I need to gain!

If I'm to become completely healthy, I know that I need to take care of myself both physically and mentally. For two years I've been working on the *mental* part, so maybe it's time to take care of my body? It will take a lot of "Practice, practice, practice!" I know I can do it, but I'm scared! Of what?

Even though I was furious with Lyle, I still thank God for him and also for Dr. Stoune. Those two men have been *lifelines* for me. I know that this journey has been rough not only on me, but also on my husband. I'm glad that he hasn't given up on me. He and I have had our share of problems, but I still love him. We've been trying to focus on the good in each other. We're learning to respect our differences. Maybe there is hope for us.

My bones are no longer sticking out all over. I miss seeing my ribs. There's a softness, or roundness, to me now. I'm trying to appreciate it, but I still think that 94 lbs was better. I gathered my courage today and wore a brightly colored scrub top. And I didn't die.

I opened up to Lyle today about some of my food issues; things that I hadn't wanted him to know. I told him about the *hoarding* that started when I was barely out of diapers! My parents actually resorted to locking me in my room at night! Otherwise, I'd sneak into the kitchen and raid the cupboards. I hid food, not only under my bed and in my closet, but also in the backyard! (I *know* that this is *not* normal behavior for anyone.) Lyle told me that these were, and are, symptoms of anorexic behavior! He claims that I developed a disordered view of food, because I hadn't been allowed to feel good about myself as a child. I don't know if that's true or not. I do know that *thinness* is very important to my mom, but I don't know how that affected me as a child. I don't remember a lot from when I was little. Just a few snippets. I know that I liked and *needed* a lot of alone time from early on. I also know that when it came to sweets, I was always left wanting for more! Sharing with eight other people, definitely cuts into each person's serving size!

I shared with Lyle, the poem about wanting to cut. He said that *writing* was a good alternative to cutting, *but* I still need to deal with the underlying issues of self-directed anger. As a child, it wasn't safe to show anger. We had to be pleasant at all costs. The anger in me would grow so strong that I *had* to do something with it, so I learned to take it out on myself in private. Lyle thinks that I hold, somewhere deep inside me, anger for my parents. I don't agree. I might have been angry at one time, but I'm not now. I know that my parents did the best they could with so many kids! Lyle insists that I am still angry and that I need to deal with it, so he gave me an assignment. I'm to write a poem about the anger I "still harbor" for my parents.

Lyle told me that he's proud of me for *not* giving up, for sticking with therapy. No matter how hard it was, or how angry I've been, I kept coming back. He told me that a whopping 78% of *borderlines* will drop out of therapy during the first year! He told me that I should be proud of myself; that I had done a good job by *not* giving up! He told me that *borderline personality disorder* can be more difficult to treat than schizophrenia! I don't know about that, but I *am* pleased with myself for *not* giving up. God knows I've wanted to!

I don't know how people have healed from this disorder on their own. I suppose that there are a few individuals who have used the self-help books, and somehow managed to overcome this debilitating disorder, but I know in my heart that I couldn't have done it without Lyle! I needed him! I needed him to listen to me, to guide me, to teach me, to give me *hope*! He had faith in me long before I could even imagine it as a possibility.

I told Lyle that I wanted to go 4 weeks between sessions. He thinks we should keep them at two for now. He does know what's best. I felt so chubby during our visit today! He's tickled that I'm up to 100 lbs, but I just feel gross. How can he *not* see the fat? I told Lyle that I honestly think that a healthy weight range for me would be 92 lbs to 97 lbs. He calmly and firmly, said, "No."

123 days at the correct dose! I'm meeting a friend for lunch today. It was *my* idea! And tonight, Bill and I are going out. Also my idea! I'm choosing *life*!

Lyle gave me another assignment. I'm supposed to make a timeline, using childhood photos of me. I'm *glad*, because *now* he will see the truth; that I was a fat child!

Okay, now I'm *really* confused! I set out to make the timeline, but as I looked for the *fat* photos, I couldn't find any! What follows is an essay that I decided to write regarding this particular exercise:

False Memory

I grew up *knowing* that I was fat. It was drilled into my psyche from the day I took my first breath. When my twin sister and I were born, I weighed 2 lbs more than she did! Two *pounds*! From the very beginning, I was known as the "fat twin." I grew up hearing it over and over again. Most of it was just my siblings having fun, by saying things like the reason I was born first was because I couldn't wait to get out and start eating! Or that the reason my sister was so small, was because I hogged all the food *before* we were born! I joked about it too, never knowing the damage it was causing. In addition to the jokes, my perceived fatness was reinforced by comments from well meaning adults. At the dinner table, "Do you really think you *need* that second helping?" Or the sales lady in the clothing department, "Oh my, you need the half-sizes. They're for chubby girls like you."

By the time my twin and I entered our teens, I was convinced that not only was I fat, but I was also a loser! My dear sweet, skinny sis was so popular. She was a cheerleader and part of the "in crowd." All of the boys wanted to date her. I figured it was because she was so little and fragile. (In my mind, it was *all* about appearances.) I really believed that nobody liked me because I wasn't *thin*. But now, as an adult, I can see that her popularity might *not* have been entirely due to her petite cuteness. It's quite possible that her kind and gentle nature drew people to her as well. Even though I know that a lot of boys were attracted to her, I know now (as an adult) that some of them were actually attracted to *me*. (In fact, I've learned in recent years, that some men actually *prefer* a girl with a little meat on her bones.) I was hopelessly caught up in the physical presentation. I didn't understand that we are so much more than the body we live in.

Until I went through counseling, I didn't realize how disturbed my thinking was. I thought it was all about the *body*. I believed that my body was the *only* thing I had to offer to another human being! Talk about shallow! Or maybe I was just misguided. How could I think that I had nothing else to offer? Maybe back then, I didn't? I was too busy trying to be what everyone else wanted me to be, or what I thought they wanted. At the time, I didn't know any better. It wasn't until I mentioned to Lyle that I'd been the "fat twin" since birth, that I realized I might have it all wrong. He asked me how much I weighed when I was born. When I told him, he said, "Now let me get this straight. You weighed 7 lbs at birth, so you were an *overweight* baby?" He then asked me if the doctor had put me on a diet! As soon the words were out of his mouth, I realized how ridiculous they sounded! All this time, I had truly thought that I was an overweight baby! Even with this new insight, and realizing I hadn't been a fat baby after all, I *still* believed that I had been a fat child. Lyle didn't think that this was an accurate memory, so he asked me to go through my old pictures and put together a timeline from infancy to young adulthood. I told him that I would, and that he would then be able to see the truth; that I was fat!

I told Lyle about how my Dad used to poke at my belly and tease me about being chubby. I heard it from other people as well. I know it was never anyone's intention to hurt me, but they did! There are many stories to confirm my plump past. Lyle tried to convince me that I had been falsely labeled as fat, because my sister was skinny. He said that *I* was actually the "normal" twin and my sister was not, because of her underweight status. I told him he was wrong and that I would *prove* it! (Just as soon as I put my timeline together.)

As soon as I started to go through my childhood pictures, it quickly became clear that I wasn't the morbidly obese person I remembered!

And to think I honestly believed, without a doubt, that I'd been a fat child; because in all of my memories, I was! As I gathered the pictures to create an "accurate" glimpse into my youth, I became acutely aware of my distorted self-image. Where were the photos that would document my pudgy past? Where was the *proof?* Could I really be so wrong? I spent hours searching through boxes of old black and white photos, but every time I found what I *knew* would be *the* picture, I'd shake my head in disbelief. The image I thought I knew so well seemed to change right before my eyes into someone I didn't know at all. No matter how many photos I studied, the transformation remained. After exhausting every avenue, I had no other choice than to believe that Lyle was right! *Again.* The *fat child* was an illusion; a false memory.

I was looking through some old cards, when I came across one from my first mom. It was a beautiful card and she'd written a really nice letter in it. The troubling thing is that I have *no memory* of ever receiving it! How can I *not remember* such a nice card? Why is it so hard for me to "connect the dots" in my life? When I look back, my memories are distorted and disconnected! *How* can I hope to develop a stable sense of self, if my memory is completely fragmented, or worse yet, gone altogether?

I'm trying to dismantle the wall I've built around me. It was there to protect me, but it's only hurting me now. Lyle taught me how to set boundaries, so I no longer *need* the wall, but I'm finding it very difficult to tear it down and *leave* it that way. I want to let loved ones in, but I'm still having trouble with the trust issue. I feel panicky at the thought of letting *anyone* into my safe little circle. I didn't even want to commit to plans, for a *second* lunch date with my friend the other day! (And we had a great time!) I do have some serious intimacy issues!

What is wrong with me? Don't I *want* to be better? It seems that my greatest fear of all... is *people*.

❦

I'm finally admitting, to myself, that maybe 89 lbs wasn't so great after all. I'd forgotten how painful it was to sit for any length of time because I was so bony! And I was always cold! Always! But I still need to remember to eat healthy! I've been bingeing AGAIN! I ate 4,000 calories two days ago and 5,000 calories yesterday! I know it's not healthy to do that; especially with all the sugar I'm consuming! If I'm going to gain healthy pounds, then I need to be eating more protein and other nutrient-dense foods!

❦

The flood gates have opened! I'm out of control with the binge eating! I can't seem to stop! It's all or nothing, black or white. I know this is the *borderline* talking! I *need* to be strong! I can choose to ignore it! I can change my thoughts to healthy ones!

❦

This food problem is too hard to fix. It's too ingrained in my mind! My brain thinks it would rather be dead than fat, and yet it continues to demand excessive amounts of food! I wonder if the borderline can be healed *without* resolving the food issue? Because I honestly don't know if this can be fixed. And I don't want to see Lyle anymore if we have to talk about this issue! Heck, even if we didn't talk about *it,* we would still have that giant *elephant* hanging out in the office with us!

❦

Lyle asked me whether, or not, I had written the poem about my parents. I told him that I *don't* feel any anger towards them at all! In fact, I feel *compassion* for both of them. I know that they did the best they could, especially with so many kids! Lyle still insists that there is anger in me towards them, and that I *need* to address it. Blah! Blah! Blah! I guess I'll try to drum up something for him.

I'm trying to accept my weight of 100 lbs, but it's not going well. I told myself that I should be glad because now I can wear some of the clothes that had gotten too big for me. But I'm *not* glad! I'm pissed! I'd rather be anorexic than chubby. Heck, who am I kidding, I'd rather be *dead* than chubby!

I need to remember to *not* take my anger out on my husband. It's not his fault that I'm gaining weight. It's *Lyle's*! Bill has been nothing but supportive in this matter. He's also been supportive in other ways. In fact, he was very patient just this morning! We had plans for the day and I had accidentally overslept. Before I could panic, Bill assured me that there was *no* hurry! That's huge for him! Usually, he's *always* in a hurry and then he gets irritated with everyone when they're not ready 30 minutes *early*! (Like he is!) So I know that he really is trying to be a better husband. I wish that I could have been a better wife to him all of these years, but I can't change the past. I'll just try to do better from here on out.

One of my coworkers was really pissy with me today, but I chose to keep it *separate* from my self-worth. And, it *worked*!

Severe anxiety woke me several times last night! I'm still freaked out about this higher weight. It doesn't matter what I tell myself, I'm still having panic attacks. I thought I was *done* being angry with Lyle, but I'm not! The anger is *still* there; still brewing! I was thinking about how I had told Lyle that I was getting used to the softness, or round-ness, of my curves. I thought he'd be pleased at this revelation, but instead he tells me to *gain 10 lbs?* I know it's been weeks since he said that, and I should be letting it go, but I can't!!! I am so pissed at him!!! It's as if we're in a *power struggle*. Can't we just agree to disagree? Maybe I'm *still* the child and this is my last attempt at independence. (While I'm still in the safety of the *nest*.)

I've thought about *lying* to Lyle about my weight. I could say that I've gained more than I have, but I can't lie to him. I just can't! And I *won't*, because of the trust we've developed. I can't risk losing it! It took so long to build. It's too valuable to me to squander. I've been pondering the so-called "unresolved anger towards my parents." Lyle's words, not mine. Let's say that Lyle is right; that I *do* have unresolved anger towards my parents. Then what?

My chiropractor commented about my higher weight being a good thing. I had been really embarrassed about it and had often wondered what he thought. I was surprised at his comment, both because he was talking about it, and because he thought I could gain *even more; that* it would be a *good* thing! Was he serious? Why would he lie? Thought provoking.

I finally gave in to Lyle's assignment and wrote the poem about my "anger." I honestly didn't know *how* I was going to write anything at all, since I wasn't angry. Imagine my surprise, once I got started, when the words just kind of *flowed*:

Childhood

Always wanting, always empty
Belittled and betrayed
My spirit was crushed again and again
How could they have hurt me that way

I was just a small child
Who deserved to be loved
If only for being alive
Instead, I felt worthless
The lost little girl
Who was slowly dying inside

Too many kids, I just didn't matter
Always one of the herd
I was terribly sad and very alone
Crying out, but nobody heard

My spirit was crushed again and again
And yet I kept climbing back up
I was so young, so little, so trusting
Hoping against hope…for love

But I just didn't matter
to the people I loved
The parents who gave me life
Betrayed and belittled,
ashamed and afraid
their rejection cut like a knife

INSTEAD HE SENT ME ANGELS...

So here I am now
An adult fully grown
Trying to face once again
The pain that they caused me
The hurt and the anger
All of it buried within

So why did they
My parents, I ask
Have kid after kid back then
None of us mattered
Not one little bit
No wonder I'm raging within

It was love that I wanted
For so many years
And love that I never got
They were my parents,
the people I trusted
And they held back
The love that I sought

They caused me great harm
And emotional pain
More than they'll ever know
They should never have had me
If they weren't going to love me
The scars will forever show

I don't know where exactly these words came from, because I really have forgiven my parents for any oversights on their part. After writing the poem, I sent it to Lyle along with the following letter:

Dear Lyle,

I finally wrote the poem about my parents. I felt the anger and the sadness. Now what? Can I stop being angry? Is it okay to forgive them? Can we lay this to rest? I'm so close to being well. To being whole. I want to get on with my life and not dwell on the past. If we can be done with this issue, and if we can agree to disagree about my weight, then what other hurdles are there? I trust you with all of my heart and I will continue to see you, until you say I'm well. I know that you truly want what's best for me and I can't help but love you for that. And even though you're too young, you've been like a father to me. Thank you.

Sincerely,
Terresa

It frustrates me that there seems to be no "rhyme or reason" when it comes to how quickly my meds kick in. I take them at night, because they make me sleepy, but I never know *when* they're going to take affect. It could be 20 minutes or 3 *hours*! I usually take them an hour before I *plan* to go to bed, but if they kick in earlier, I have to stop whatever I'm doing and go straight to bed. It's annoying. I could be in the middle of a conversation with my husband, when suddenly I have to excuse myself, because I can't keep my eyes open! On the other hand, I may postpone taking the meds until after I'm done with whatever it is I want to accomplish, and that's when they inevitably *don't* kick in! (Until long after bedtime.)

I'm more confident than I used to be. I'm no longer that person who was so damn eager to please! In fact, now when I see that particular behavior in other people, I cringe! In hindsight, I realize that I pushed some people away with my eagerness. Now that I'm more self-assured, I find that people are reaching out to *me*! I've learned to speak up for myself, without being defensive or *justifying* myself and my actions. When I'm sure about something, I'm able to speak without question or hesitation. As I've become more assertive at work, I find that I'm gaining respect and, surprisingly, it doesn't seem that I'm offending anyone! Of course, I still try to treat everyone equally *and* with kindness.

I am so burned out on socializing! Bill's "ON" 24/7! I'm not wired that way. I don't need, or want, constant social interaction. I've been trying to be a better wife, by joining Bill and his friends more often, but I don't enjoy their scene at all. Alcohol, loud music and crude behavior are *not* my idea of fun.

One of my coworkers quit without notice. She never said good-bye to me. I thought we were friends. In the past I probably would have reacted with self-injury, but this time, I just felt a little sad and then let it go. That's pretty big for me! There was a time, when my emotions were *never* "just a little." I *am* getting better.

I've been having trouble *winding down*. I've had to be "on" too much lately. I desperately need some quiet time. Bill hasn't been going to the gym in the mornings, so we've been visiting, which *should* be a good thing, but I'm not getting *any* alone time.

My eating is out of control! That's not entirely true. Yesterday, as I was constantly shoveling food into my mouth, I kept thinking, "I'm out of control." However, the *adult* in me countered back. "You *are* in control, even when you're overeating!" It's true! I *am* in control. No one is *forcing* me to eat. What I choose to eat... is just that: A *choice*! I need to stop blaming outside forces for *my* actions. It's time to take responsibility for *me*!

I can't go back to the unhealthy behavior of my *borderline* days! I know too much! I'm aware of *what* I'm doing, *when* I'd do it. No more excuses! The *borderline* no longer controls me! I *do*! It's up to *me* to make healthy choices. I've finally slipped from the grasp of *borderline* and I've landed firmly on my own two feet!

And those two feet are squarely in my mouth right now! Just when I think I'm well... Bill and I were cleaning out the spare bedroom, so that we could turn it into an office for me. I was excited and pleased that Bill was being supportive of my desire to have my own office. But, with one comment, he sent me reeling. It wasn't anything mean, but it was *crude*. Instantly, the *wall* went back up! I don't know why *vulgar* talk bothers me so much. Maybe I *am* a prude. I just know that when he talks dirty, I want nothing to do with him! I feel bad that I can't be the "loose" woman he wants. I've let him down in so many ways. It seems that as I'm trying to figure out who I am, and what I want, I end up pushing everyone away; but especially my husband. Why is this so hard for me? I adored my husband at one time. Where did those feelings go? I'm feeling a strong urge to cut because of the emotional pain, but I just can't bring myself to go down that road anymore! I feel so bad right now! I hate it when I let Bill down! God, I really, really want to cut myself! But where would I hide it? I am so tired of trying to be *normal*. Do I have *any* fight left?

Yesterday was the 10 yr anniversary of my step mom's death. I was missing her so much as I walked out the door to go to work. When I started up my car, the radio was playing *In My Daughter's Eyes*. I nearly burst into tears when I heard the words, "*When I'm gone, I hope you'll see, how happy she made me, for I'll be there...in my daughter's eyes.*" I hadn't heard that song for *years*, so it felt like maybe, just maybe, my Mom had a hand in it! And that perhaps, just maybe, she's still with me.

Bill wants me to be excited about the new 4-wheeler he bought, but I'm angry! We didn't *need* a new one! We already have two perfectly good 4-wheelers! He's always telling me that we're broke and then he goes and spends money on this? I'm pissed! I can't tell *him* though, so I did what I always do. I pasted a smile on my face and then later, when I was alone, I beat the hell out of myself.

It's still a struggle some days to take my meds every night, but I'm do-ing it. I've taken the correct dose for 144 days straight! So I guess I'm doing okay. I'm still pissed about my weight though.

Now that I no longer *need* to be accepted, I find myself speaking up when I feel I've been wronged. One of my coworkers has been *hot and cold* to me for as long as I've known her. I tolerated her verbal abuse over the years because I was so desperate for love and affection! Once in awhile she could be nice and occasionally she would even hug me for no apparent reason. However, most of the time, she was just plain *mean*! I realized, tonight, that I no longer need or *want* her friendship. It's time to *cut her loose*. At the very least, I will distance myself from her. Since we still work together, I'll continue to be pleasant, but I'm *done* being "friends" with people who are just plain rude!

I'm finding it to be very *empowering* to not care so much about what other people think! Dr. Stoune's words, "You're *not* that important," have come back to help me more times than I can say. It puts things into a proper and healthy perspective. Sometimes, when I feel that the weight of the world is on my shoulders, I'll think of that quote and it provides a measure of *peace*.

I'm excited about the prospect of *writing*! Bill's ordering a laptop computer for *me*! I remember when Lyle said that I need to spend money on myself once in awhile, but I didn't agree. At the time, I didn't feel worthy of anything; especially something expensive! Now I don't feel guilty at all because I know that I am worth it!

Today, I worked on accepting my curves. It's up to me to decide what my healthiest weight is. I know that I could ask 5 different people what weight would be best for me and I would get 5 different answers. So it really is up to me!

One of the most helpful things I've learned, through therapy, has been how to *not* take cranky people *personally*. It's much easier to help them if you're not angry at them because of their attitude. And, quite often, they'll cheer up if they get the chance to be *heard*.

I'm beginning to feel comfortable at this higher weight. I wore a bright coral-colored scrub top today, and I felt *good* in it! It wasn't too long ago that I was in tears when I tried wearing that color. I've been thinking that one of the reasons I liked being rail-thin, is that it made me feel *childlike*. Ten pounds ago, I had *no* curves and it felt safe! I found a sense of security in being as little as possible.

I was supposed to meet one of my friends for lunch, but she stood me up. I wasn't surprised, because she's done it before. The good news is that the urge to hurt myself never made its appearance! It just wasn't there! Lyle helped me to see how absurd it was to self-injure by saying to me, "So you were angry at _____, and to feel better, you hurt *yourself?*" Whenever I'm feeling the urge to strike out at myself, I just need to fill in the blank, and it works! (Most of the time.) I'm learning to calm the anxiety by choosing *helpful* thoughts! I'm no longer *feeding the anxiety*.

I'm skipping breakfast today. I've been eating like a pig and it's got to stop! I'm not angry at anyone except for myself! Sigh… the urge to cut is back, even with everything I've learned! I won't do it though. I know that I need to work *through* my uncomfortable feelings. I don't need to stuff them down with food or numb them with cutting. It's up to me to choose thoughts that can help me.

I get so many *mixed messages* from my husband! He's always pointing out women and commenting on their size. More often than not, the woman he defines as *chubby* looks *just right* to me! I know that what's most important here is what *I* think.

I'm getting more open with Bill when I'm angry at him for something. I'm not going to hold it in anymore. I try to be diplomatic of course, but he still gets defensive at times. I can understand why though, because he's not used to me being outspoken.

I did a stupid thing the other day and when Bill pointed it out, I got really angry with *myself!* He was very kind in his delivery, so I know that he was only trying to protect me from possible harm. As my thoughts gravitated towards self-injury, I *chose* to redirect them! I reminded myself that it's okay to make mistakes. We all screw up sometimes. So instead of hurting myself, I gave myself a break! I forgave myself and everyone else who has ever made a mistake! We're human after all and it's going to happen from time to time. No individual *knows* everything! In fact, that's a big reason for *why* we need each other! We are all part of a *team*; a *family*. Each of us has our own part to do. Maybe *that's* what makes us members of the Body of Christ.

I've been thinking about my *body image* problem. I don't think it's about the number on the scale anymore. Maybe it never was. It's about learning to accept *me!* All of me! Body, mind and soul! I wrote a poem, yesterday, about choosing *not* to cut:

Choices

Don't know who I am
Feeling lost inside
Pulling out the straight-edge
Can it make me feel alive

Wanting to be healthy
But clinging to the past
There's an emptiness without it
How can it be so vast

The battle rages on
Between the old and new
I know it's up to me
What I choose to do

Cutting brings me comfort
Like a treasured friend
But the cutting has to stop
It can't start up again

My mind is set on doing
What I know is right
So I'll put away the razor
I'm not giving up this fight

I've been taking my meds, as directed, for 5 months now! I'm winning this battle!

I wonder if I've been unfair to Bill, when it comes to how I *interrupt* what he says about women? Because of the *borderline,* my perception of *everything* has been distorted! I don't know how much of my life has been *colored* by the disorder.

I've wanted love and approval for as long as I can remember! I feel like I get that with Lyle. While he would never approve of *unhealthy* behavior, he's always made *me* feel valued as a human being. Lyle has become the parent figure for me; a loving father. He never tells me that I need to try *harder!* Instead, he encourages me to *just keep trying.* To me, there's a big difference between the two.

I'm so embarrassed about the 12 lbs I've gained since January! I've been such a glutton! I thought that I could accept 100 lbs as a good weight, if I just stayed there long enough, but it's not working! I find myself wanting to *hide* again. Lyle has added one more diagnosis to the battery: Obsessive Compulsive Disorder. He claims that it's the OCD that keeps me tied to the scale! I don't agree. But then again…

Lyle instructed me to say repeat the mantra, "It's not me! It's the OCD." He wants me to say it every time I'm tempted to weigh myself. Whether or not I actually *have* OCD, I can still benefit from repeating the phrase. Who knows, maybe it will help me to see the *constant* weighing as something separate from *me.*

Maybe Lyle's right about the OCD. I rejected it at first, but it got me thinking! I know it's *not* normal behavior to step on a scale 20 times a day! I'm embarrassed to admit this, but I *am* addicted to the stupid little metal box on my bathroom floor! How can I let this inanimate object control me? It really isn't about the weight at all. I know this, and yet I continue to step on the darn thing constantly! Lyle said that it's a compulsion, driven by anxiety and perhaps a need for control. He wasn't sure what the *control* was about, but he assured me that we'd figure it out. And to think that I thought I was nearly done with therapy!

It's amazing how our own perception *colors* everything! Good, bad or indifferent. Keeping the lines of communication wide open can help us to avoid misunderstandings. Everyone has their own *lens of perception.* If we can remember this, especially during disagreements, then maybe we can learn to live in harmony! Or maybe that's "Terresa Land" talking again.

I'm getting better at soothing myself when frustration hits. Having Lyle's voice in my head stops me now, before I can hurt myself. I think it's only a matter of time before the *voice* becomes my own! I'm beginning to see the disorder(s) as separate from myself. Viewing them this way, is enabling me to see them for what they are; *disorders.* They no longer define *me*! I know damn well that *I* am in control, even when I'm choosing unhealthy behaviors! With *awareness*, comes responsibility. It's time to embrace the *adult* in me!

A young man flirted with me! I was ok with being *looked* at! I don't have to be ashamed of my curves!

100 lbs is ok!

Later- Who am I trying to kid? I'm *not* ok with this pudgy body! It's gross and disgusting! I can't seem to get a handle on the *anxiety* I'm feeling about weighing this much. Everyone think I'm thin, but if they only knew! I'd be mortified if anyone saw what I look like *under* my clothes!

Lyle thinks that there will come a time when I will give up the scale, the tape measure *and* counting calories! He *doesn't* think it will be in the near future, but it *will* happen. Eventually. I'm doubtful.

I am so angry at myself for allowing this extra weight! I can't stand it! Finally, I had to strike out; first by punching my legs, and then pummeling my head. Now I'm bruised and hurting, but the wrath is gone. I've noticed that the fatter I get, the pickier about my hair I get! *Every* hair has to be in place before I can leave the house. For some reason, I can't stop pacing! I want to cut, but Bill will be looking for *signs!*

My sister sent me a book called, *90 Minutes in Heaven.* I was thumbing through it, and almost immediately came upon the following passage:

"There is no easy way through the recovery process, and they need to know that. Because I have been there, I can tell them (and they listen) that although it will take a long time, eventually they will get better."

Wow! I know that the author wasn't talking about mental illness, but the words truly spoke to me! It was exactly what I *needed* to hear.

❧

For every step forward, it *seems* like I take one step back; getting no-where. Today I desperately needed to get out of the house; away from the *blade* and the *scale* and the *mirror*! My mind was playing tricks on me and I couldn't see the big picture. I couldn't remember anything Lyle had taught me! I'm up to 101 lbs! I couldn't stay off the scale and now I'm freaking out!!!

❧

Maybe I should reduce my meds to give my metabolism a jumpstart. I can't focus on anything other than the damn number that I saw on the scale this morning! How can I be such a glutton? A depression is descending and I feel helpless to stop it.

❧

The binge eating is out of control! I don't want to do *anything* or go *anywhere*. I'm so embarrassed at how I've let myself go! I'm up to 102 lbs now. I don't feel suicidal. I just want to sleep. I definitely have *no* desire to *participate in life*. Not like this.

❧

My anger at Lyle has returned. Maybe it never went away. I wouldn't be this heavy if he had just left this *issue* alone! *Why* does his opinion matter so much? Isn't it *my* opinion that's supposed to matter?

❧

It's been 104 days since the last time I cut myself. The urge has been there a few times, but I've resisted! As I looked through my journals,

I saw that I'd been tempted to hurt myself on eight separate occasions in the past two months, and out of those eight, I refrained only twice! *But,* no cutting occurred! Does this mean I'm still getting better? Do I just need to, "Practice, practice, practice?"

105 lbs! I'm too disgusted with my chubby body to go out with my husband and some of our friends. I feel absolutely *huge!* I can't live like this! I'm too embarrassed to let anyone see me. At work, I've gone back to the big, baggy scrubs. I have to hide this fat!

Although I'm having problems with my body-image, I continue to improve in other areas, such as speaking up when I feel that I've been wronged. I'll also say something if I don't agree with someone, but only if it's important to me. I'm not going to disagree, just to argue.

It seems like Rachel disagrees with me just to push my buttons. Is she trying to make me look stupid? Lyle says that she's *competing* with me. It's part of the transition to adulthood. He said to try *not* to take it personally, but it still hurts! I find myself wanting to cut, to ease these painful feelings, but I'll resist! Am I ever going to be normal?

I told my husband, that if I had the chance to go back in time, I'd *choose him* again. After saying it, I realized that *he* probably wouldn't, if given the chance, choose *me* again. It makes me sad.

Why the fear of fat? Where does it come from exactly? My biological family is slender. Obesity does not run in my genes. So *what* am I afraid of? The anxiety of it all keeps building. I can't calm it with cutting, because I might get caught! I've taken to scratching my limbs with a fork; a nail; whatever.

I can't concentrate on anything since gaining all of this flab! I'm so flipping preoccupied with it! Bill continues to be kind and compassionate, as I continue to navigate this battlefield of body vs. mind.

The medics brought in an *overdose* patient today. I felt bad for his family and also for him. I thought about my own OD and how it must have affected *my* family.

I've shared some of my spiritual poems with a friend from work. She asked me if she could share them with her daughter. I said, "Of course." She told me that I need to share my story, to help others, but I don't know…

I've always had trouble with spatial perception and facial recognition. Lyle said that it's related to the *bipolar disorder;* something about *sensory overload.* I don't know if that's true or not, but I do remember reading about someone else's struggle with manic-depression, and how she had mentioned her problems with the very same thing! The more I learn, the more I come to know that I am *not* alone!

I know that I shouldn't, but I did. I reduced the meds a few days ago. I can already feel my energy returning! If I start to feel agitated, I'll increase them again. Maybe.

Lyle didn't mention my weight at our session this morning. I thought for certain he'd be happy that I'm *huge*, but he didn't say a flipping word about it! And I was ready to give him an *earful*. I had wanted him to know that I am *PISSED* at him! But he never brought it up and I lost my nerve.

What happened to the emerging desire to take care of myself? What happened to the insight, the tools, the *voice*? It seems that the monster of *borderline* is, once again, unleashed and I'm just too tired to fight it anymore. I can't keep trying. It's wearing me out. The borderline wins. I give up.

So much for my promise to continue taking meds! Of course my original promise was to take them properly until I saw Lyle again, so *technically* the promise was only good for a week or two! (I've seen him many times since then.) I've been at the decreased dose for about two weeks now. My weight is falling, but I can feel myself *escalating* again. Damn it! Why is it so hard to be *stable*? When I get into these agitated states, the self-injury is never far behind. I attempt, halfheartedly, to control my actions, but they seem to take on a life of their own!

My husband decided to go out with the boys last night and he didn't bother to call me. When I told him this morning that I was upset about it, he didn't have the decency to apologize. In fact he appeared completely indifferent! Maybe this is *his* way of "checking out" of our marriage. I know he's not happy with me. I don't think he ever was. By the time he left for work this morning, rage was boiling up inside of me! I held it in, until Bill was out the door, and then I exploded! I took all of the pent-up rage and frustration and directed it at myself! Within minutes, I had calmed myself down completely. I guess being *normal* still isn't in the cards for me.

I'm happy to report that I don't have any new cuts today; a few bruises yes, but no cuts! With that good news out of the way, I can now vent about Lyle! I'm so fricking mad at him for making me gain weight! I don't know if it was the *power of suggestion* that caused it or if he actually *convinced* me (albeit temporary) that a higher weight was better? All I know for sure is that it's *HIS FAULT*!!! I'm more consumed than ever with panic about my weight. This issue is invading my every waking moment! The obsession has got to stop! It's wasting so much of my time!!!

My energy continues to climb, as does my irritability! I got so angry at a nurse in the surgery department that I called her repeatedly and every time she answered, I purposely slammed the phone down in her ear! My behavior shocked my coworkers, leaving them speechless as they looked at me wide-eyed and with their mouths hanging open! I'm not at all proud of what I did.

I'm really needing some down time, but Bill keeps calling me into the other room! I wish that I could tell him that I need some alone time, but no matter *how* I word it, he just gets mad. So instead, I just suck it up and grow more annoyed. Even when he doesn't need my attention per se, he still commands it by how loud he talks when he's on the phone. He's always talking to someone. I just want a little peace and quiet! I feel bad for not being like other people, but I *need* alone time, just to *think*! And when I'm constantly interrupted, so are my thoughts! The very thoughts I *need,* in order to wind down, to become calm and centered.

It's hard to be productive when I'm constantly having to listen to someone. It's difficult for me to focus on both the task at hand *and* whatever the other person is saying. My husband says that it's *easy* to do both, but I disagree. Heck, most of the time when I talk to *him,* he starts looking around and thinking of other things to say or do. I get so angry when I'm trying to tell him something and he feels compelled to tell me something completely irrelevant. Is it too much to ask for the respect of simply *looking* at the person who is talking? He says that he can't help himself. Maybe it's true.

Tonight, when I tried to tell Bill about a funny incident at work, he showed no emotion at all! Earlier, I had relayed the story to several other people and they all laughed! A lot! Instead of laughing, Bill felt the need to tell me that I had handled the situation *wrong*! I don't understand *why* he insists on taking pleasure away from me; even with simple things, like laughing at a funny story. I know that he has a good sense of humor with other people, but when it comes to me, he seems to thrive on making me feel uncomfortable, awkward and boring. I'm constantly being knocked down a notch.

I was very animated tonight at dinner. I'd had a good day at work and was still on the *high* that comes from having a productive day, where everything seems to go right. And *then* I come home... As I was telling a story about one of my coworkers, Bill stopped me mid-sentence to say that I seemed high! It wasn't an innocent statement. It was delivered with condescendence and nothing short of contempt. Immediately the joy from my day evaporated, leaving me deflated. It isn't so much *what* he says, but *how* he says it. Even if I am a little high, a little manic, he doesn't have to be disrespectful about it.

One of the girls that I work with took me aside to ask me about my recent change in behavior. She'd noticed the increase in energy, the rapid speech, and the *boldness* of some of my statements. She's familiar with the symptoms of bipolar disorder and had apparently noticed an escalation in me. I told her I was fine! After being *called* on it, I realized that I really need to watch my behavior and increase the meds if I find it too difficult to control myself.

I still didn't increase the drugs. I'm waiting for my weight to go down first, but I'm getting really hungry! I've been munching on antacids to help keep the hunger at bay, but my stomach growls nonstop! I can tell that my family knows that I'm at *it* again, with the calorie counting. I can tell by their actions. My daughter keeps trying to force food on me. Sometimes it feels like she is the mom! It shouldn't be that way! I am so f--ked up!

It's a warm spring day and I can't go sleeveless because of the multiple bruises on my arms. I used to make up stories to account for my injuries, but Bill *knows* too much now. He's always on the lookout! I wish that I had never told him! I have no hiding places anymore!

Obsession with weight is straining my marriage. Bill's beginning to lose his patience with me and I can't blame him. He's been trying to help me feel good about my appearance. He even told me that I was the most attractive woman at a party we went to recently. But, even with his reassurance, I still feel like crying whenever we go out! I'm so embarrassed by all this weight! I'm *over* 100 lbs now! I can't relax! I'm paranoid that everyone is talking about how fat I have gotten! Bill reminded me, once again, of one of my favorite quotes: "You're not that important!" But I *still* couldn't relax. I just *knew* that everyone could see my "love handles." I feel really bad for Bill, because I whined and complained so much about myself the last time we went out. I was such a *downer* and incredibly self-centered! I kept comparing my weight *now* to what it was a few months ago. Bill finally got irritated enough to say, rather forcefully, "It's *just* a number!" He's right.

I was going to tell Bill about the OCD and how it factors in to this obsession with my weight, but I've burdened him enough, at least for now. I know this "weight *problem*" isn't really about the weight at all. It goes deeper than a number on the scale. Much deeper.

I kept seeing things at work today and the damn music was playing again. Not really of course; just part of the *escalation* process. Even after a full dose of meds, I'm still "in your face" with everyone! (Even with people I like!) I'm overreacting to stuff that normally wouldn't even annoy me. I'm still waiting for the meds to kick in, and hoping that I can "chill" enough until they do.

I've been back on the proper dose for a few days now and I'm starting to feel better. I was escalating and could no longer control my outbursts! I hate that I lack the self-control I need, but I know that it's not entirely about willpower. It's that damn disease! I came across a line in a book about someone who is bipolar and I just had to laugh, because I saw *myself!* It said, "When he's not manic, he just *thinks* people are stupid, but when he's manic, he actually *tells* them that they're stupid!" I can truly appreciate the humor in that statement, because I've lived it!

I absolutely, without a doubt, do *not* want to have to take meds!!!!!!!!!!!!! But each time I try to prove that I don't need them, I end up proving the opposite! It's a good thing that I got back on the correct dose. It was just in time because one of my supervisors really pissed me off! If it had been a few days earlier, I probably would have gotten myself into deep trouble! The Seroquel really does help with impulse control!

My obsession with my weight continues to cause me extreme anxiety, complete with full blown panic attacks! It's taken over my life! My every waking moment centers around thoughts of numbers! The number on the scale, the number on the tape measure, the number of calories consumed! It's so ridiculous. I almost called Lyle, but I know that I have the tools and insight to handle this. It's *not* up to Lyle to fix this. It's up to *me* now! I need to get inside my head, to redirect the thoughts that hurt me. Lyle has done all he can. The rest is up to me.

Weight isn't the real issue. I need to learn how to be comfortable in my *own* skin at *any* weight. I need to be comfortable with *me*! My body houses the very essence of me! My spirit, my soul. To live fully and joyfully, I need to honor this body. I need to remember who I really am! Thoughts are so powerful, so why not choose those that are helpful? And while I'm at it, I can *choose* to love and care for myself. Self-love will *not only* enhance *my* life, but also the lives of my family and friends. By loving *me*, by *starting* with me, I can learn to love others *without* condition.

The power of choice can free me from OCD *and* from borderline behavior. It's up to me. Lyle and I both worked hard to get me to this place. The least I can do is to honor him (and myself) by choosing my thoughts *and* my behavior wisely. It's time for this student, this child, to leave the nest! Maybe I'll just start with a field trip!

I gave my scale to Bill and asked him to get rid of it. He's right. It *is* just a number! But I'm still feeling panicky about this decision. It's a huge deal, parting with my scale, but I think I'm ready. After I handed the scale to Bill, I got into my car and headed to work. Instead of feeling victorious, I felt a deep sense of loss tinged with fear. My eyes filled up with tears, making it difficult to see the road in front of me; not only the road to work, but also the road to *wellness*. I wanted more than anything to turn back, to retrieve my beloved scale! It had been my friend, and constant companion, for over 30 years! But it was also my enemy. I couldn't turn back. I had come too far. Leaving it behind was a necessary death.

I did okay on the first day without my scale. I'm not sure *how* I feel exactly. Relieved maybe? I honestly don't know. It hasn't had time "to sink in" yet. I am feeling hopeful though. I still have my tape measure! (And *those* numbers point to a weight of 102 lbs.)

What the fuck was I thinking? I want my scale back! And why the hell did I allow myself to get so fucking fat? I can't stand it!!!!! I'm so embarrassed by all of this *blubber*! I've gained 13 or 14 fucking pounds! I'm so disgusted with myself! To help me to remember *not* to eat, I broke down and cut myself! I used the usual place so that I could hide it under the bandage that's always there, covering the old scars. The cutting seemed to help with the anxiety of not having my scale anymore. I pretended to be in a good mood for Bill. I can't let him know that I've regressed. He deserves a break from me *and* my problems.

Sometimes I'm so close to normal and then I blow it! It's as if I forget *everything* I've ever learned in therapy! I somehow disconnect from the past. All of it! Yesterday, last week, 20 years ago; it's all gone! I know it's up to me to connect the dots somehow; to make sense of what I'm feeling *when* I'm feeling it and to move through it, while at the same time keeping my *best interest* in mind. And that means *not* injuring myself physically or belittling myself with a negative internal dialogue. But *how* do I connect these dots? How do I make sense of seemingly random thoughts and memories? I don't have an answer.

I gave into temptation at work today and stepped on the scale. I weighed 102.5!!!! It freaked me out a little bit. Okay it freaked me out A LOT! I *had* been feeling really good, maybe even *attractive*, wearing my coral-colored scrub top and some figure-hugging black pants. But, as soon as I stepped on that scale, my good feelings dissolved into dismay and self-doubt. How could I have let myself go like this? I have to keep these feelings secret though. I can't let anyone know how unhappy I am about my weight. They wouldn't understand.

Bill wanted me to go out to go to lunch with him. My knee-jerk reaction was to say, "No." This time, it was because I didn't want to eat! I managed to stifle my first impulse and I told him that I'd like to go with him, but just to keep him company! (I told him that I'd already eaten.) How many times have I turned him down over the years? I'm ashamed of my self-centeredness! I'm amazed that he even tries anymore!

Without a scale at home, I'm definitely having problems with anxiety. To help quell it, I started trying on clothes from my closet. (Clothes in several sizes.) After *hours* of trying on everything I owned, I found myself surrounded by heaps of clothing. Before I could get any of it put away, Bill walked in! I had that "deer in the headlight look" because I *knew* that the piles of clothing were a dead give away. I was "at it" again. Since I was already *caught*, I decided to come clean with Bill about the OCD diagnosis. His reaction almost made me laugh! He had that "well duh!" look on his face. He said he's *always* known that about me. It seems I'm, once again, the *last* to know!

Bill and I talked about *learning disabilities* today. We were watching a program that was addressing the reason *behind* the problem of the "underachiever adult." (Which I have always been.) After watching the show, Bill realized that I didn't need to try *harder* like he was always telling me to do. He finally saw that what I *really* needed was to try *different*. Having my husband acknowledge this made me feel really good! It validated what I'd been trying to tell him for years; that I *don't* learn the same way that *he* does! And I'm *not* trying to be *defiant* when I do something different from the way he does it. What makes sense to him doesn't necessarily make sense to me.

I told my husband about a patient who's in the CCU. She had attempted suicide with an overdose and was unconscious. A vent was keeping her alive, along with an array of other machines and medications. I told Bill that it reminded me of how dark a place I'd been in, when I had made the same choice that this woman had. I knew, at the time of my overdose, that I *could* end up a "vegetable," but I was so miserable in my suicidal despair, that I thought it would be better to be dead, or in a coma, than to spend one more day with my tortured mind. What I hadn't thought of, was what it would have done to my loved ones! I told Bill that when a person is suicidal, they honestly think that *everyone* would be better off without them! What they forget, in their misery, is that they may linger in a vegetative state, which will hurt their families immensely; both financially and emotionally. Maybe, with my experience with suicidal depression, I can somehow reach out to help those who feel hopeless (*before* it's too late for them and their families.)

Wow! I spent 30 minutes with an RN who was taking care of another "overdose." Only this time, the patient was completely conscious, but in a body that no longer worked! Because of the drug she took, she's now in respiratory failure and is scheduled to be flown to Oregon Health Sciences University, where she can get the specialized care that she needs! I don't know whether, or not, her entire body was paralyzed, but it appeared that she couldn't move on her own. And she definitely couldn't breathe on her own. I couldn't stop thinking about how I'd overdosed to get *away* from my mind. I never realized that I could have been stuck with nothing *but* my mind!

ER was pissed at the lab and they gave me an earful when I got to work today. The amazing thing was that I didn't take it personally!

My appointment with Lyle this morning went really well. To help me with my obsessions, Lyle reminded me to say, "It's not me! It's the OCD." He also said that removing the scale from my house was a good *start*! Whenever the obsessing begins, I'm supposed to remove the object, or myself, from the situation. It's important to distract myself until the urge passes. He said it was okay to journal, as long as I *don't* write about weight.

I finally told Lyle about the anger I had, and still have, towards him about my recent weight gain. He had that *knowing* look as I rambled on about how pissed I had been at him; but that I wasn't *as* mad now. He'd known all along that I was angry with him. He was just waiting for me to own up to it. I admitted to Lyle, that I *know* that a part of this whole anger issue is about me growing up. This is my way of pulling on the apron strings. It's the natural order of things as a child grows into adulthood. (Even if that *child* is in her forties!)

Lyle and I talked about how this issue stems from a combination of disorders: Obsessive compulsive disorder, borderline personality disorder and also, to some degree, bipolar disorder. I confessed to him, that I knew I looked bad at 88 lbs. I admitted that although I had been embarrassed by my thinness, I didn't know how to stop! Lyle said that the OCD will *never* allow any number to be low enough. Even though the other disorders factor into this equation, I think it might be easier to tackle this problem from the standpoint of OCD. I can more readily look at the OCD as a separate entity from myself. I believe that by stating, "It's not me! It's the OCD," I may very well be able to end this battle! Choices! It's about choices! Choices can free me! I will no longer let *any* disorder control me! I can choose to *take back* my power!

Bill and I went shopping. He wanted me to buy attractive form-fitting *sweats* for wearing at *home*! I don't want form-fitting *anything* for lounging in my own home! I find it really annoying that he always wants me to dress sexy. What about *comfort*? I don't expect *him* to wear anything tight!

I opened up Rachel Reiland's book, *Get Me Out Of Here,* to read it again. As I leafed through her book, I ended up on page 314. It's where Rachel realizes, for the first time in her 31 years, that she believes in God. *Really* believes! I can identify with her! And just like Rachel, I too had dealt with anger at God, only to realize that He was there all along, rooting for *me*!

As I was thumbing through her book, I found an old bookmark of mine with the *Footprints* story on it. (Rachel had also written about *Footprints.*) It reminded me of how our Heavenly Father *never* leaves us; never forsakes us. No matter how downtrodden we become; how discouraged we are; how hopeless we feel, He's *always* there! Just like Rachel, many things have happened in my own life, at just the right moment, to bring me to where I am today. *Chance* meetings? Or *arranged* meetings?

The more I thought about it, the more emotional I became. Before I knew it, tears were streaming down my face; tears of gratitude to *God*. God who loves me *just as I am*! My heart was overflowing with love *from* the Father and *for* the Father. As I tried to wrap my mind around the enormity of it all, the words from one of my poems came to me, "Instead, He Sent Me Angels!" The words reminded me of *why* I'm still here! God, indeed, sent me Angels; *many* of them! Angels to show me *how* to be an instrument of His infinite love; *how* to do His will; *how* to let Him work *through* me! I believe that God sent me angels, so that I could be a *witness* to His love!

As I worked through the deluge of emotions, it was with a humbled heart that I thanked God from the very depth of my being; the very center of my soul.

I've decided to no longer record weight, measurements, or calories. That's part of the OCD. And if I can beat *borderline,* then OCD is a piece of cake! I'm feeling overwhelmed at the prospect of writing my story, and I'm still not sure about *sharing* such a personal journey! It would be embarrassing to say the least; but if it's meant to be, then God will show me the way. He sent me on this journey for a reason. I pray that He will give me strength, and the skill, to carry out His will.

Today, one of the surgery nurses was rude, as usual, but I didn't let her get to me at all. In fact, when she needed help with a patient, I immediately stepped up to the plate.

Bill and I went to another party. While we were there, he made a comment about a woman we all knew, who *wasn't* at the party. He said that she had gotten *huge!* A friend of ours spoke up right away, saying that she was *not* huge! I agreed! No wonder I'm so confused about what *I* look like!

It seems that oftentimes, when I need a lift, a song will play on the radio at just the right time! It's as if the words are speaking directly to me! Maybe it's one of those "Heavenly arrangements!"

✦✦✦

I surprised myself today when I spoke up to a man who was tying up the carwash! He was spending a *lot* of time *pre-washing* his truck and cars were starting to pile up behind him! He still took his sweet time, but at least I did it!

✦✦✦

Increasing energy. Seeing things. Faithful with meds. No scale at home now for 3 weeks. Good day at work. Better at taking things in stride. I told a co-worker that unless a patient is bleeding out, *not* breathing or his heart has stopped, then it is *not* a true *"STAT!"* (No matter what the Dr. thinks!) I'm sick of feeding their egos!

✦✦✦

Lyle was right about the OCD. There have been so many times when I've been practically *paralyzed* by OCD behavior. I can laugh about it now. Taking my power back, from *any* of the disorders, frees up a lot of time!

✦✦✦

As I've gone through my previous journals, in an attempt to form an outline for a possible book, I find myself emotionally *raw*! I suppose it's cathartic to see where I've been, and where I *am,* but it's still a painful process. I also find that my mind is a clutter-filled mess at this point! How can I possibly hope to organize *anything* enough to write a book? I'm trying not to lose sight of *why* I'm working on this project. If my story can help, even one person, then it must be told. I pray for the strength it will take to reach out to those who are hurting. I've been listening to Josh Groban's song, *Thankful,* with the hope that it will inspire me to reach outside of myself in order to be of service to others.

Bill and I had a good talk. I acknowledged how difficult it's been for him to live with someone like me. By talking, we discovered a recent misunderstanding. I had left a light on in my office that could be seen from the garage, as I worked at my computer. I turned it on so that when Bill got home from being out with the guys, he would know that I was upstairs. In my mind, the light was an invitation! I wanted to share with him, some of the work I'd done. But when *he* saw the light, he interpreted it as a sign that I was busy, so don't bother me! How many times has that happened in our marriage? It's amazing that we're together at all.

I typed a short essay about my healing and how I'm nearly ready to be done with therapy. It described my elation and sadness at moving forward. After writing it, I left it out for Bill to read. I wanted him to see how far I've come and to let him know that I'm very close to being well. When I came home from work, I waited for him to say something about what I had written. When it was obvious that he wasn't going to say *anything*, I asked him about it. His stoic response was hurtful. He asked me what it was that I wanted from him. I told him that I had just wanted to share with him, my excitement at being so close to wellness! I wanted him to be happy for me; for *us*! I wanted him to share in my joy and to empathize with my pain. His face remained devoid of all emotion. His *indifference* cut like a knife, deflating me. I was left feeling discouraged, confused and drained of joy. Why do I even try?

Lyle said that the OCD developed because of my "need" to be accepted by everyone. He warned me that the OCD *pathways* in my brain and those of the *borderline* will always be there, alongside the newer, healthier pathways. And there may be times, or in certain situations, where I might slip back into old habits and start down old pathways, *but* awareness can remind me of what's in *my* best interest! I can *choose* which path to take! It just takes...you guessed it, "Practice, practice, practice!"

I shared a journal entry with Lyle, but as he read it, he kept stopping to make comments about the noisy people in the office next door! As he was reading my heart felt words, he kept talking about other things; subjects that were irrelevant to what I was attempting to share with him! I tried to bury my disappointment, to hide it from Lyle, but I'm really hurt and angry about this! I'm used to getting Lyle's undivided attention! I feel like saying fuck you! Fuck everything. *Why* am I so upset by this?

"We, who we really are, can rise above the constraints of our human form." I read that line recently in a book called, *A New Earth*. After reading the book, I can now *see* that it was my "ego" that got me annoyed with Lyle the other day. His *not* paying attention was actually a lesson for me! My feathers were ruffled *because* things didn't go according to *my* plan. How the heck can anyone else *know* what my plan is if I don't tell them? They're not mind readers!

My reflection in the mirror is distorted again, but least I'm *aware* of it this time! The OCD is picking up speed. I've started picking at my scalp compulsively. I won't let up until it's raw and bleeding and even then, I don't always stop. Will I ever be well???

I'm learning that people are not going to behave according to the script that I have in *my* head! I'm beginning to let go of the *need* for everything to go as I've planned! I recently wanted a friend to listen to a song that I liked, but she was too hyper to sit still and pay attention. Instead of getting mad, or trying to *force* her to listen, I was able to *let it go.* And later, when I was trying to talk to my husband, he began to stare at the TV (even though he hadn't been watching it.) I stopped talking mid-sentence and walked away. He didn't notice and I chose to let that go also.

The song, "You Raise Me Up," made me realize that God has raised me up *through* other people. If God can work through people, to lift others, then He can work through *me*! *If* I will let Him. Can I be selfless enough to do that? I don't know. I guess I could *start* by being *fully present* with others; by *really* listening to them. And instead of isolating myself, I could reach out to help my neighbors. I'm excited at this prospect! Not for a reward, or a pat on the back, but because I truly want to make this world a better place. One person at a time. I want to share this love that I feel; this endless, infinite, all-encompassing love. I admit that there are days when I struggle to feel *anything*, let alone love! There are some days when I *don't* feel the joy or the peace, but always, in the depth of my heart, I *know* it's there, waiting to be awakened. No matter how cranky or worldly I get, it's *there*. The choice, of whether or not to tap into it, is exactly *that* … a *choice*.

I had a conversation, recently, in which a friend confided in me about her husband's behavior. He had promised on numerous occasions to *stop* his bad habit. I'm not stating what *his* habit was, because I want to protect his privacy. The habit could be any number of things. It could be alcohol, or drugs, or even self-injury! It doesn't matter what the habit was. What *matters* is what I told my friend. (Well, it matters to *me* anyway!) I told her, from my own experience, that there have been times when I've made promises to loved ones and, *at the time* of the promise, I truly *meant it!* But the addiction was stronger and I broke my promise over and over again! Every time I meant it and every time I broke it! I wasn't strong enough to keep it.

I wanted my friend to know that it's *possible* that her husband really believes that he *is* telling the truth; that he *will* keep his promise *this* time! At first, he's not *intentionally* lying. But eventually there comes a time, and I know this from my own experience, that the person making the promise realizes that he or she is *not* strong enough keep the promise, but makes it anyway. At this point, they *are* lying. I know, because I've done it! But once I made the decision to stop *lying*, I also made the decision to admit that I was powerless to stop the behavior; that I couldn't do it by myself. *That* was my turning point.

I dreamed that Bill put the scale back in our bathroom! I guess weight and calories are still on my mind. I felt way too curvy yesterday. My thighs and my boobs felt full and rounded. Pudgy? Or curvy? Either way, I don't like it.

Feeling blah. Down. Tired. So tired. Tired of *life*. Tired of living like this. Tired of depression that rolls in without warning or reason, bringing thoughts of suicide in its wake. Why can't I shake it off? Do I need a different medication? People keep asking me what's wrong. I wish they would just leave me *alone!* My husband is worried. I told him that I'm *not* going to hurt myself. I just feel *empty*. Blah. I know it will go away.

Eventually. I'll wait it out. What else can I do? I have no energy. Too blah to cry. Just want to sleep. I feel nothing. If I stay this way for too long, I'll tell Lyle. For now, I'll just wait.

Dragging myself through work. Napping before work and after. Very depressed. Avoiding people. Even Dr. Stoune whom I adore! (I ducked out of view when I saw him down the hall.) A coworker cornered me and asked me what was wrong. How do I explain it when I don't understand it myself?

Saw a news story about depression and realized that I've had bouts of it since my teens. And now, even with meds, I still have bouts. I don't remember any *rages* until about age 20. I guess the bipolar and/or the borderline started then.

Life is passing me by and I just sit here numb, unfeeling, uninterested. I told my husband, that even with the borderline cured, I will still have the *bipolar disorder* to deal with. It's not going away. It will always be there, lurking, waiting to pounce. What are the triggers? Which one started *this* episode? Depressed or elated, where is the mean?

No interest in taking care of me. Not exercising, not taking vitamins, not eating right. Nothing. Don't care about anyone or anything. Want to be alone. Bill's going camping for 4 days. Maybe I'll recharge in his absence. Maybe not.

Forced myself to keep my coffee date with Deb. I was quite agitated. Complained of noise pollution. First at home and now in her office! She quickly turned the scanner and the radio down. I apologized for my crankiness. I can't shake this black cloud. When I got to work, one of my coworkers checked on me first thing. She's been worried about me. I told her that I just don't have the energy to fake cheerfulness or even politeness. I apologized to her and she said it wasn't necessary, but it was. I shouldn't be rude to my friends. I owe apologies to lots of people. Don't care enough to do it though.

I'm not going to tell Lyle that I'm planning to lose this extra weight, because he won't understand. I've tried to accept my curves, I really have... Bill claims to like me at this weight, but I think he prefers me thinner. I believe this because he *praises* me when I get into my size 0 jeans. (Or even the children's sizes.) Intellectually, I know that I look okay at this weight, but....

Didn't talk much at my session with Lyle. He thinks that I may need to either increase my meds, add another drug, or maybe even change drugs altogether. Sigh. Bipolar is always going to be a part of me. Whether it's in the shadows or more blatant as in a depressed or a manic episode. I don't have it in me to fight right now. The spark is gone. Lyle moved our appointments to *every* week again. Is getting well possible? At the end of our session today, Lyle started to bring something up and then stopped, saying that he probably shouldn't. I said, "Go ahead," and he said that I'd probably get mad at him. He laughed when I said that it wouldn't be the *first* time. Lyle asked me to *increase* my meds, and to *stay* on that dose, until I see him again next week. I struggled with that, because of the possible weight gain, but finally I shrugged a wimpy yes. That was good enough for Lyle. He sent me on my merry little way.

Bill mentioned to me that he *knew* I was getting manic in the days leading up to my depression. He admitted that his first thought was, "Here we go again! But what can I do about it?" I told him that I was aware of how *abruptly* the "switch" flipped, but that I felt powerless to do anything about it. He said that he's seen this in me for as long as he's known me! We had a good talk about the rollercoaster ride of manic depression; a ride that no one, in their right mind, would want to be on.

Feeling very anxious about weight. *Thought* I had it under control. Now that I've let several people in, on the self-injury *and* the anorexia, it's harder to hide. I feel *trapped.*

Bill knows that the bipolar symptoms are acting up when I start sneaking out of bed at night. But it's too difficult to just lay there, when my body and my mind are screaming out with restlessness! It's hard to adequately describe the sensations. It's as if *every* nerve ending, or cell, or whatever, feels prickly, agitated and ready to explode! I'm not happy about having to increase my meds, but as Bill and I looked back over our 25 yrs together, we could see how we've *both* been *chained* to this disease. I can no longer hide the fact that I will *always* need medication. But I *still* don't want it.

The borderline is gone, but the bipolar disorder cannot be cured. All the therapy in the world won't make it go away. This is *not* a setback, having to increase my meds. It's just "treating a disease." I should be proud of myself for overcoming the borderline. I didn't drop out. I kept trying. As far as this bipolar thing goes, I need to remember what I said earlier, much earlier, "Compared to the borderline, *bipolar* a piece of cake!"

May '08 thru July '08

I've come a long way with therapy. The *borderline* is all but gone and I'm thankful for that, but I can't help but feel sad about having to increase my meds for the *bipolar disorder*. In looking back I can see clearly now that the therapy has cured me of *one* of the disorders, but all the therapy in the world can't cure me from the other. It's as though Lyle and I went in and cleaned house, eliminating the *borderline;* every last bit of it. But *now* as I stand back to admire the great job we did, I suddenly see, with a new clarity, how much is still left behind in the form of the bipolar disorder. I guess it's a good thing though; to be able to see that the two disorders are no longer mixed together, one feeding off the other, creating havoc and discord. Having the disorders separated, and knowing that I'm healed from *one* of them, is a blessing! I'm proud of myself for not giving up. And I'm grateful to Lyle for his guidance as we traversed the minefield of borderline. I know that *borderline personality disorder* can absolutely ruin lives; as can *untreated* bipolar disorder. Instead of being embarrassed at having to increase my meds, I'm *choosing* to be *grateful* that they *exist*!

Bill and our daughter decided to go out to dinner. Bill called me at work to ask me to join them after my shift. I don't like spur-of-the-moment activities and I wanted to say, "No," but I stopped myself and told him I'd be there. After hanging up, I felt really irritated because I didn't have a change of clothes *and* because I hate doing anything last minute. The old pathways of borderline are still in my brain and I really wanted to go down the path leading to self-injury, but I didn't! I was even able to enjoy myself once I got to the restaurant! "The power of choice *frees* me from life in the borderline zone!"

My daughter wanted me to join her, and some of her friends, on a mother-daughter outing. The mere thought of socializing with people I didn't know, filled me with anxiety, but I didn't tell her that. Instead, I said I'd be happy to go. I was able to overcome my nervousness and I even managed to have a nice time. I was a little burned out afterward, but not bad. I could have told her no when she first asked, but I knew it was important to her! I'm still new to this plan of mine, to think less about myself and more about others. It's *not* all about me! Not anymore.

The economy isn't doing very well right now and I found myself worrying about it. Almost immediately Lyle's voice popped into my head, challenging me. I realized that I have *no* control over the economy and since there is *nothing* that I can do about it, I need to stop with the worrying. All the "worry" in the world will *not* make the problem go away. Remembering Lyle's words of wisdom helped me to stay on the right path, the *healthy* path!

Lyle had to cancel our appointment. When he called, he asked me if I was still struggling with depression. I am, but I didn't want to cause any concern, so I told him that I was fine. He told me to call him if I needed to, but I won't. I don't feel like talking to anyone right now, not even him.

I know that I'm no longer controlled by the *borderline,* but this current depression is a constant reminder that the *bipolar* disorder will always be a part of me. My husband asked me, again, why I was depressed. My eyes kept filling up with tears as I told him that there really isn't a *reason.* It's just one of the poles of the disorder. He was confused because I had told him that the *borderline* was all but gone. But that doesn't mean that the bipolar will go away; not completely.

All day at work, I fought to keep the tears at bay. How much longer is this downswing going to last? It's taking every ounce of energy I have to get through the day. It feels like God has pulled back and I'm filled with doubt. Does He exist? Did I make Him up? No energy. Not even to eat. Wt down to 96.

Bill has been visiting websites on bipolar disorder. He's trying to understand *how* I can be depressed, when nothing is going wrong in my life. He thought that with the borderline gone, I wouldn't have anymore mood swings. I tried to explain the difference between the two disorders. The main point that I wanted to make, was that the *self-hate* and the desire to *hurt myself* are *gone!* (Even with depressive episodes.) As we talked, I had *no* emotion in my voice; none whatsoever. That's a far cry from my usual animated self! Usually Bill is the stoic one, but lately I can't muster up as much as a smile.

I told Bill that I've enjoyed seeing him interact with our female friends as *people,* not as sex objects! He's beginning to see them as equals! I told him that it does my heart good to hear him speak respectfully of women. He admitted that when he's around his male friends, he starts up with the vulgar talk. I told him that I'm ok with that, as long as he doesn't do it in *my* presence! If I'm with him, and his friends are present, he needs to be strong enough to resist their crude behavior. I know that he wants to join in, probably even *lead,* but I find that kind of talk repulsive and disrespectful. Wow! I'm setting boundaries!

The dark cloud of depression is beginning to lift. I told my husband that being able to talk more freely with him is helping. Knowing that I no longer have to "jump" because he (or anyone else) tells me to, is liberating! I have choices. If I don't want to cook, I can tell my family, "The kitchen's all yours." I no longer feel guilty when I'm not doing everything for everyone.

I was feeling fat and ugly, but I knew that I had a choice. I could sit and stew, and feel worse, *or* I could distract myself with something positive. Having the ability to choose my thoughts directly affects my behavior. I actually got myself *out* of a bad mood by choosing to do an activity I enjoy. Before I knew it, my bad mood was gone!

It usually makes me nervous to cook, while someone else is present, but today I did it quite easily! My husband and I visited, as I cooked, and I didn't stress at all. I even ate at the table with my family. I was a "normal" person for a whole day!

I slept 12 hours last night. What the heck? I thought I was getting better! Cried all day. Tired of life. Thinking about ending it, but I don't want to hurt my family. Achy. Want to be left alone. Slow at work. Can't get away from people who want to talk all the time. Questioning God's existence. Maybe He's made up, like Santa or the Easter bunny. So sad and empty. Self-hate is gone. Borderline is in remission, hopefully forever, but bipolar depression is worsening. Didn't know depression could hit so hard and so fast. Changed screen saver at work to, "Night falls fast." It's the title of a book about suicide. Erased message of love from a coworker. Feel like I'll never be up again. Feel bad for my family. They don't deserve this. Embarrassed about downswing. I was doing so well. Body hurts all over. Don't want to live like this. I'll just suck the life out of anyone I come into contact with. Will cancel appt with Lyle if depression lingers. What's the point if I don't want to talk?

Lyle thinks I'm grieving the old me. The borderline is dead and buried. It's a normal process, to grieve, when you lose someone. In my case, the "someone" was a *part* of *me*! And saying good-bye to that part of me, no matter how dysfunctional it was, is painful. But grieving is *healthy*. It's ok and it's necessary. It helps us to accept change so that we can move on. Embracing and continuing to build a *new* me is a *huge* change!

This recent depression is a reminder that bipolar depression can be *triggered* by both external *and* internal events. As I continue to say good-bye to the borderline, and its unhealthy behavior, I feel overwhelmingly *lost*. How can saying good-bye to something that was so obviously bad for me, be so hard? It's strange how we can miss something terribly, even when it played a negative role in our life! I imagine that's true for other situations as well. (Such as leaving an abusive partner or losing a loved one you also despised.)

Letting go of the borderline is hard!!!!!!!!

It does *not* seem like it should feel so devastating to say good-bye to a *disorder*! But the fact is that when it's been a part of your life for as long as the borderline's been a part of mine, it's difficult to leave it behind. Old dreams. Old regrets. Old thought processes. *All of it* was so much a part of *me*! My goal for 2007 was to embrace *wellness* and here I am, halfway through 2008, and *still* working on it! It's been a lot harder than I expected. Embracing the *good* should be easy, but the truth is, it's not that simple.

Lyle has been a Godsend and yet I continue to doubt God's presence. I know from counseling, that depression *colors* everything, even my longstanding beliefs. My perspective changes when I'm in the midst of a depression. My view of everything, including God, is muddied.

Borderline is like a comfy old shoe; one that I don't want to give it up! I felt angry at Lyle for telling me that this depression is grief-related. Why am I taking *more* meds, if it isn't bipolar-related? (In hindsight, I realized that *grief* was the *trigger* for this episode of bipolar depression.)

I'm *still* having trouble embracing wellness. It's not comfortable yet. Lyle has done so much for me. He's helped me in ways I can't even begin to list. It really is up to me from here on out. Lyle is fading more and more into the background. He's still a cheerleader of sorts, but the guidance counselor part of our relationship is becoming less and less a part of our sessions. He's given me the tools and the insight. The rest is up to me.

I'm a cheerleader of sorts, but the

My husband, and his buddy, just bought another *toy*! It's another 4-wheeler! This one cost over $11,000. I was angry the last time they upgraded, because there was *nothing* wrong with the *old* machines! My husband is *never* satisfied! He always wants *more*! It doesn't matter what it is; power, toys, size, money, sex! It's *never* enough! And it never will be. Sigh.

Bill said that when I'm *up*, there's no one else he'd rather be with. But when I'm *down*.... I don't blame him. He says that I've held him back over the years and it's true. It's just that we are *so different*. Opposites may attract, but I'm not sure that it's a good idea to try to spend a lifetime together; especially when you have absolutely *nothing* in common. In the early days, our differences weren't so obvious. He *partied* less and *we* spent more time with family and friends, just visiting and playing board games. I miss those days, but it bores him to spend a quiet evening with another couple or two.

At a recent relay, Bill looked very fit in his running attire. An attractive woman, another runner, was talking with him and I realized that he deserves a woman who *shares* his interest and isn't afraid to show off her figure. He needs a woman who *likes* to socialize all day, everyday. We're going out for the fourth night in a row, and I'm dreading it with every fiber of my being! Bill really does deserve a wife that *likes* going out all the time. I'm a homebody! Neither one of us is *wrong*. We're just mismatched!

Making conversation with anyone, for more than 2 min, feels exhausting! I'm just going through the motions and waiting to die. I feel lost right now. Without self-injury, or some other unhealthy coping mechanism, I don't know what to do with myself. I don't know how to *feel,* or conversely how *not* to feel, without self-injury. Whatever side of the coin I'm on, I can't use the old behavior. I'm too *aware* now, and that awareness keeps me from cutting or slipping back into borderline behavior. Even with the bipolar, I *know* that *I am* in charge of yours truly; *me* all by myself. I get to *choose* whether, or not, I take my meds. I get to choose whether, or not, I avoid certain triggers. I *know* what the right choices are. And *because* I know, *I am* responsible for any damage that ensues if I choose unwisely. If I don't take the meds, and then subsequently can't control my impulses, then it's *my* fault because I made the choice!

When I woke up this morning, the depression was nearly gone! As the day progressed, I could actually *feel* the depression lifting! After 6 weeks, the episode ended as abruptly as it had begun.

Work was fun today. I found myself laughing a lot! I felt playful and energetic and I really enjoyed my coworkers! And this morning, when I couldn't find my brush, I asked Rachel if she knew what had happened to it? She looked a bit sheepish when she confessed that she had left it in the *shower*! I laughed out loud! I would have *never* looked there! In the past I probably would've been furious but *now,* with the borderline behind me, I actually thought it was funny! Lyle told me once that stress is 85% perception. I don't know how accurate that number is and it doesn't matter. It's the *message* that counts! How we *perceive* something directly affects our reaction. I wish my new coworker could realize and utilize that concept. She gets stressed about things in which she has no control. (Just like I used to!) Hopefully she'll learn while she's still young. I don't want to see her suffer like I did. If I could protect her somehow, I would.

We had a potluck at work and I actually ate in front of people! I even ate two cookies, as I walked to my car after work, just like a normal person! I didn't *need* my little rituals. I didn't have to plan when, where and how, I was going to eat my food. For that matter, I didn't have to figure out *what* to eat or how many calories were in it. I was a *normal* person! For a whole day!

5,000 calorie binge Saturday night. (6,000 a few days ago.) Sigh. Butterscotch was my downfall. I feel puffy, bloated, and miserable, but

I'm not mad at myself. I just need to do better next time. I also need to be truthful with myself. I lied to myself when I promised that I'd only have one brownie. As it was, I ate the *entire pan* of fudge brownies with butterscotch chips mixed in. I know that with some foods, I can't seem to stop with one bite! It's like a shark that smells blood or an alcoholic who says he'll only have one drink! Once I get that sweet butterscotch taste in my mouth, the craving becomes unbearable and I don't stop until the addictive food is *gone*! The lesson learned: *Don't* have binge foods in the house or, at the very least, don't take that first bite!

I've done okay without having a scale in the house. Now I'm toying with the idea of getting rid of my tape measure. I *want* to be *normal.* Lyle said that people, *without* eating disorders, just eat less when their clothes get tight (and more when they get loose.) They're not *tied* to a scale or a tape measure or even calorie counting. I desperately want to be free from these obsessions! Is it possible?

Panic is gone about my weight. No hurry to lose. No need to starve myself. I've had a messed up view of food, and my relationship to it, for long enough! I am *not* a number on the scale *or* the tape measure! I thought I had to look and *be* a certain way in order to be accepted. I was so blind! As my inside heals, my outside will follow. I don't know where my weight will end up, but I *do* know that my identity is no longer tied up with a number!

Bill asked if the latest depressive episode was a menopause thing. Lyle thought it was grief. What the heck happened to being bipolar? I was thinking back to when I *thought* Lyle was taking away the diagnosis of bipolar and how it freaked me out! Without the bipolar, I was left with the monster of *borderline!* I couldn't deal with it and opted out of therapy for awhile. The whole thing ended up being a misunderstanding and I had totally overreacted. But, because of it, I realized just how *overwhelming* the borderline appeared to me at that time. It was terrifying and I was scared out of my wits! I didn't think I was strong enough to beat it. But I was! And I did.

My reactions of *overreacting* are disappearing. I no longer *re-act* when I feel out of my comfort zone. Instead… I've learned to manage my immediate feelings with no *visible* reaction, so that I can take a moment to think about the situation and then choose *how* to *act* on it. This puts *me* in control. (No more blind re-actions!)

I had a rather insightful dream last night: I was at someone's house and there was a toddler who had just done something wrong. The older brother was scolding her and pushing her away from whatever it was that she was trying to do. Although the older sibling wasn't *physically* hurting the younger child, she was still crying. At that moment, I reached down and picked her up and held her in my arms like a loving, caring parent would. The amazing thing, for me, is that I actually *felt* love for this little person. *Me!* I've *never* liked kids, not even when I *was* one! Later, in the same dream, the toddler opened the oven door. I firmly said, "No," and told her that it wasn't safe. When the child started to cry, I told her that I loved her and that I didn't want her to get hurt. I gave her a big hug and she stopped crying. It was as if I was making sure that the little girl knew it was the *behavior* that was unacceptable, and that *she* was completely lovable! I think this dream is about learning to love the child I was, and also about learning to love the *adult* that I am!

My coworkers have been commenting on my high energy level. I'm back to my usual hyper self. Hugs all around! One of the more stoic nurses said that someone needs to shoot me (to put me out of *his* misery!) He was teasing me. I find it interesting that, after working with this man for nearly 5 years, he has just *now* started talking to me and joking with me! Now that it's *not* important to me, to have everyone's "approval," it's like they *want* to interact with me!

When I'm up and I have energy, it's tempting to mess with my meds, but I won't! Not anymore! I finally value *myself* enough to make healthy choices. I'm also choosing to redirect my thoughts whenever they're getting too negative. Choosing to think, in more loving and helpful ways, makes complete sense now. I remember early in therapy when Lyle told me, that with lots of *practice*, I'd be able to get rid of that little voice in my head. The little voice that constantly berated me and belittled me, always telling me I was worthless... Well, Lyle was right! Again.

Lyle confirmed what I already knew about my last depression. It was just the bipolar cycling. He said that one of the *red flags* was how exhausting it was for me to stay in a conversation for even a minute. (*Two* was excruciating!) It didn't matter who I was talking with, I felt completely drained from the start. Lyle said that on the other hand, *grief* generally doesn't stop a person from talking. In fact, oftentimes, people who are grieving can benefit greatly by being *allowed* to talk about their grief. My difficulty in saying good-bye to the borderline *might* have been a trigger, but more than likely, it was just the good ole bipolar rearing its ugly head again. He went on to say that I *may* need to increase my meds in the future, but that eventually I will probably find a dose that I'll stay on for the rest of my life.

❧

I told Lyle that I know I'm responsible for doing what's in my best interest. I have the tools and the insight that I need. It was *because* of what I've learned that I knew, even in the midst of a full-blown depression, that I could weather the storm and I did! I can wait out unpleasant feelings and situations, without resorting to self-injury or other borderline behaviors. I also brought up the paradox that Lyle and I discussed early in therapy. He had said, "You are *not* responsible for what you did in the past, but you *are* responsible for what you do today!" It's still true! Awareness makes it so.

❧

Lyle and I laughed *a lot* today. We are both pleased with my progress. It's been a team effort from the start. Lyle was right when he told me that one day I'd be able to put down all of the masks *permanently*. His prediction came true. I don't have to *be* anyone but *me*! I'm so thankful to Lyle for staying with me on this journey. He promised, early on, that he'd never leave me and he didn't! He was also right when he said that a day would come when *I* would leave *him*. The day is fast approaching.

❧

I believe therapy is nearing completion. I'm ready to leave the nest. No longer will I *die* without Lyle. We're going a month between sessions this time. Lyle told me to call him if I need him, but we both think I won't. He's truly been my rock. I have so many memories of our time together! I need to grieve, not only the death of the borderline, but *also* the end of our patient/therapist relationship. I've got to stop thinking about this or I'll start crying! Of course, because of Lyle, I know that it's *okay* to cry! Tears are healing.

❧❧❧

It's time to be honest with myself about everything! My eating habits, my compulsions, my hang ups! All of it! From this day forward, I am a new woman!

❧❧❧

My husband seemed a little down this evening, so I asked him if he wanted to go for a ride on the new 4-wheeler and he perked right up! It's been about *me* for so long that I've neglected the very people I claim to love the most!

❧❧❧

I *resisted* the urge to weigh myself at work today. Yeah! You go girl! Good job!

❧❧❧

I'm getting better at *feeling* my emotions and not running from them! I don't need to snuff them out anymore. That's a good thing! Especially while Bill and I are trying to figure out whether or not to stay married. Neither one of us is pointing the finger at the other. We know that we're just different from each other. Maybe too different.

A few days ago, thoughts of suicide briefly crossed my mind. I recognized it for what it was and quickly changed my thoughts to something healthier! (I reminded myself that the borderline is *gone* and the bipolar is *controlled.)*

❧❧❧

I think I'm starting to accept my higher weight. I'm up to 105 lbs and

I'm not panicking. (I've gained 17 lbs in the past 6 months.)

Whenever I contemplate the end of therapy, I feel an *ache*, an actual *void*, a sense of *sadness*. I no longer *need* Lyle, but I'm having a hard time imagining my life without him! He's been such an important and integral part of who I've become, that to go on without him…

At times I entertain thoughts of regressing to a point where I can once again need him. Early in therapy, I *knew*, on a primal level, that Lyle was truly my lifeline. In the early weeks and months, he sustained my very existence. It was this seed of knowledge and ray of hope that kept me coming back week after week. Before therapy, and in the beginning, I honestly thought it wasn't a matter of "if" I killed myself, but "when." Somehow Lyle was able to get through to me, through all of the barriers I'd put up long before I'd ever met him. It wasn't that I'd never reached out before; it was just that no one had ever reached *back*. Until Lyle. He was willing to meet me exactly where I was, in all of its unpleasantness. He drew me out of the darkness and into the light. And for his patience and diligence, I'm incredibly grateful!

Lyle had faith in me long before I could even imagine having faith in myself. He saw something where I saw nothing! He was the one constant, as my turbulent mind tried to make sense of everything. Unlearn. Relearn. It all seemed so confusing. And then Lyle's voice would pop into my head, challenging my unhealthy ways of thinking, encouraging me to do whatever's in *my best interest.*

As the conclusion of therapy draws near, I'm trying my best to deal with this deep feeling of loss. How can I feel loss, when I've gained so much? (Heck, I've gained a whole personality!) Seriously though, I know that Lyle's *words* will be with me always, but I'm going to miss *him*. Damn, here come the tears…

15

July 2008 thru Sept 2008

Letting go...
  Of the Borderline,
    Of therapy,
      Of Lyle...

A friend of mine recently confided in me. She told me that her daughter was cutting herself. I hadn't shared my own story with this friend, so she didn't know that I too was a cutter. I told her that I knew, from *experience*, that she shouldn't take this lightly. I gave her Lyle's phone number and told her to try to keep the lines of communication open with her daughter. I advised, again from *my own* experience, that she should listen to her child *without* passing judgment. It's okay to be upset, horrified even, but *don't* let those emotions leak out when you're talking and *listening* to her. If she feels judged, or that you can't handle the truth, she may *never* open up about what's really going on inside.

I had a real heart-to-heart with my husband tonight *after* I let him vent about his renters. (They're *always* late with their payment.) I find that I'm getting better and better at listening *without* internalizing the speaker's *anger*. There was a time when I couldn't do that and my mind would overflow with unnecessary emotions. *Now* I can be fully present, as I listen, without the fear of losing myself. After we talked about the renters, the conversation turned to me and the end of therapy. I told my husband that I wanted to share my story. If it can help someone, then I need to get over my embarrassment and tell it. I'm not ashamed anymore, because I know I was doing the best that I could at the time. But, the thought of *exposing* the details, even if it's to *help* someone, is terrifying. I told Bill about Rachel Reiland's book, *Get Me Out Of Here*, and how it had helped me. I bought it when I was first diagnosed, and her story about her struggle with *borderline personality disorder* gave me *hope* throughout my *own* struggle. I choked up when I tried to tell Bill that I can see myself in Rachel's book, and how *I know* that I'm almost to the end of *her story*, in my *own* life, regarding therapy and healing. It took her 4 *years* to beat this devastating disorder, but she did it! And by sharing her story, she helped me and countless others to believe that recovery was possible.

I went to the CCU to draw a patient's blood. She's a member of my husband's extended family, so I was looking forward to seeing her, even if it wasn't under the best of circumstances. When I got there, I started my friendly banter, but she didn't recognize me. When I touched her arm, to feel for a vein, she tried to hit me! Her daughter tried to calm her down and her mother yelled at her. I felt tears welling up in my eyes! Normally I'm able to *separate* myself from the truth of the illness or the injury, in order to get the job done, but this time I couldn't. I quickly hugged the daughter and told her that I couldn't draw her mom's blood. I said I was sorry as I slipped out of the room. The nurse was in the hallway as I was leaving. She saw the tears in my eyes. I told her that I knew the patient and that I would get someone else to come draw the blood. The nurse gave me a hug before I headed back to the lab. When I got home this evening, I told my husband about what had happened and *his* eyes filled up with tears! It was *then* that I realized… my reaction was *normal*.

I've always had trouble with *spatial perception*. For years it's made me feel stupid, especially around my husband and my daughter. They don't share that *handicap* with me, so they're forever teasing me about it. But *now*, I can see the humor in my *goofs*! For instance, I decided to surprise Bill by hanging a wallpaper border around the top of our bedroom walls. It had, what appeared to me, a complex pattern in its design. I cut the border into manageable sizes and began to hang it. When my husband got home, he burst out laughing. Apparently, I'd hung several of the sections upside down! Another time, my daughter and I were watching a movie. I kept seeing the word "Russia" over and over throughout the show. I finally asked my daughter if she knew what the significance was. She laughed and gave me a hug, while saying, "Ah, my dyslexic mom!" The word wasn't *Russia*. In fact it wasn't even *English!* I don't recall what the word was, or what it meant, but I can truly see the humor in it now. I'm learning to *embrace* the differences between myself and others. It definitely makes for an interesting world.

Lyle has helped me to *relearn* so much. My thought processes have changed enormously for the better! I'm finally able to enjoy the people around me without fear. My daughter and I were making faces in the mirror the other day. It wasn't something I'd normally do, but I thought, "What the heck?" As we entertained ourselves, we got the giggles! We were laughing so hard and so loud, that I had to shut the bathroom door so we wouldn't wake my husband who'd already gone to bed!

I'm getting to be a pretty good *sounding board* for my family and friends. Now that I can do it, without being drawn into the emotion of the moment, I can offer that *service* more freely! I know that people just want to be *heard*. If I can be a good listener, then it will benefit others. And isn't that what it's all about; people helping people.

Bill called me at home, from boys' night, to tell me that one of *my* favorite singers was on the television singing the national anthem. It was a very thoughtful thing to do, especially with the guys giving him a hard time! (I could hear them in the background.) Despite our differences, he really is a good man.

Bill thinks I *still* have issues because I hate *interruptions,* especially in conversations. Personally I think it's rude when someone butts in and cuts another person off mid-sentence! It also annoys me, if I'm in the middle of something at home, when my husband walks in the door and immediately wants me to stop whatever I'm doing to do what *he* wants. I think this is more about good manners than "issues."

I was feeling guilty this morning because I have it so easy compared to so many other people throughout the world. Almost instantly, Lyle's analogy of the twin towers came back. I realized that I need to focus on what I *can* change! And with a healthy outlook, I can be a blessing instead of a burden.

One of my coworkers told me recently that she's proud of me and how outspoken I've become. We've worked together for a few years and she's seen me transform from a docile doormat into a confident, productive team player.

Bill wanted me to go 4-wheeling with him, and some of his friends, but I already had plans. I told him that if I had known about it ahead of time, I wouldn't have made the other plans. He prefers to be spontaneous; so more often than not, I don't join him. Perhaps it's a battle of the wills now that I'm being true to myself.

I don't feel the need to impress *anyone* anymore and I no longer feel *snubbed* when someone appears to be ignoring me. I've learned, over the years, that most people are lost in their own little worlds and half the time they probably don't even see you. It really *was* exhausting to wear all of those masks! For so long I tried to be what everyone *else* wanted me to be or, more accurately, what I *thought* they wanted me to be. I truly am on the right path now. It's time to give up my timeslot with Lyle. It's time to *let go* so that he can help someone else.

Occasionally I still feel the urge to self-injure. But that's all it is anymore, an urge. As I get stronger, the urge grows weaker. Calming myself, without injury, has become second nature. Measuring up to someone else's standards is no longer a goal; measuring up to my *own* healthy standards is. No longer do those of a higher status intimidate me. I am their equal in the way that counts. Embracing wellness is not only within my grasp, it's within my heart. By placing *Angels* along my path, God has led me "...*through* the valley of the shadow of death," and I have immerged a stronger person for having gone through it.

I'm looking forward to my visit with Lyle tomorrow. I haven't seen him in 4 weeks! That's the longest we've ever gone between visits. I'm excited, scared and sad. But I'm *not* freaking out about "leaving the nest." I know it's time. Time for this little birdie to fly!

I mailed some of my story to a dear friend of mine. After I didn't hear back from her, I began to feel the familiar stirrings of *borderline* rising up within me. I worried that I had shared *too* much! Not hearing from her left me doubting myself and the work I had begun. (In putting my story together.) I began to feel the abandonment, so typical of the borderline, when it suddenly hit me: *awareness*! I have a *choice* in what *thoughts* I will allow my brain to entertain. Awareness slammed on the brakes, stopping the *borderline* in its tracks! Awareness allowed me to remember that I am a *recovered* borderline.

Soon after this most recent epiphany, I heard from my friend. My fear of abandonment was unfounded. She had been moved deeply by my story and had just needed time to process what she'd read. (It was a lot to take in.) Over the years, I hid my demons so well that she never had a clue as to what was *really* going on behind the *mask*. Nobody did! My fear, that she would no longer love me, did not materialize. In fact, she said that by sharing my story, she couldn't help but love me *more*!

❧❧❧

Lyle truly saved me; if not from certain death, then from a life of hell. I get a knot in my gut whenever I think about leaving our upcoming session *without* an appointment for the next! It will be our final visit. I know I can do this, but a part of me wants desperately to hang on! Lyle has assured me that he's not kicking me out. The door will always be open. He agrees with me that I'm healthy enough to make this decision to end therapy. If I wasn't ready, he would tell me. But the fact is… I am ready. I'm able to bear distressing emotions like anxiety and anger, or even *no* feelings like numbness, without resorting to self-injury or any other unhealthy behavior. Occasionally I toy with the idea of starting up again, or cutting *one last time,* but I won't. I've come too far to ever go back.

❧❧❧

I threw out my tape measure a few days ago and thought I was doing okay. That is, until I realized that I had just spent *hours* trying on clothes, trying to reassure myself that I hadn't gained too much. Just one more pair of pants, just one more shirt, just one more dress… and then Lyle's words came to me, "It's not me, it's the OCD." But is it? Is this an OCD problem or is it *borderline*? I don't know and it doesn't matter. The problem right *now* is that I've held on to the tiny clothes from my *anorexic* days. Of course I'm going to appear *huge* when I try to squeeze into them! They're *child* sized! My healthy self has a good idea… get rid of them! If I'm truly choosing to be *well,* then the decision is made.

❧❧❧

I'm still trying to accept these *triple digits.* I've tried to stay off the scale at work, but the addiction is still too strong at times. Along with the triple digits, I'm also trying to embrace my *curves,* but it seems that I'm struggling with that as well; one day I like them and the next I curse them.

I want my tape measure back! How can cutting up a fricking tape measure cause all this turmoil? I managed okay without having a scale at home, but not having *something* to measure by is causing me extreme anxiety! I feel agitated and restless. I almost resorted to punching the frig, but I stopped myself. I didn't want *another* dent to hide! I started to think of cutting, but then I got choked up at the thought of *undoing* all the work that Lyle and I had accomplished! I just couldn't do it. I couldn't do it to me. I couldn't do it to Lyle. I need to *honor* what we were able to achieve. It wasn't easy, but he and I both stayed the course for one goal; to get me well.

I'm frustrated with the way my husband describes women by their weight and their beauty, or lack of it. I need to let it go. It's *his* problem. He's not going to change and neither am I. Many times I've told him how his comments hurt me, but he chooses to make them anyway. Well I'm choosing to let it go. It doesn't matter how *he* sees women or even how he sees *me*! I'm strong enough to *not* fall back into an unhealthy attachment with him or anyone else. I'm going to be true to myself, respectful of others, and I'll just see what happens. I'm letting go of the *need* to control.

I couldn't stand it anymore; not having a scale or a tape measure! I thought I was ready. I really did. But I wasn't! So I went out and bought *both*! I'm up to 103 lbs! I've gained 15 lbs!!!!!!! That's too much! I know that I'm not seeing myself clearly, but I feel helpless to change. Today

I realized just how ingrained my *fat* self-image is, when the dietician at work handed out BMI calculators. She said that I was *barely* in the green zone; the good one. I felt really panicked because my first thought was that I was bordering on *overweight*! (When, in fact, I was bordering on *underweight*!)

I hid the new scale from my family. I don't want them to know that I'm at it again. Bill was home all day, so I couldn't get my scale out of its hiding place. Without my *fix,* I felt like a junkie; restless, on edge! I *needed* my fix! I couldn't concentrate on anything! I paced and fidgeted and got absolutely nothing done today. All because I couldn't weigh myself! I *know* how this looks. I've got to get over this last hurdle! Only I can do this. No one else can make me better on this last issue. Lyle gave me the tools. It's up to me now.

Now that I'm not rail-thin, men seem to be noticing me. Having curves will do that I guess. I'm not sure if I like it or not, but I'm not feeling any panic about it. However, I am beginning to feel some stress about therapy ending. I'm afraid of life without Lyle. Heck, I freaked out without a scale! How the heck am I going to manage without Lyle? Seriously, I know that I still have a ways to go, but the rest of the journey is up to me. Lyle walked with me most of the way, but now it's time to stand on my own. It makes me think of a little kid who's learning to ride a bike. His dad holds onto the back of the bike while the child is learning; he goes part of the way and then the dad lets go! And sometimes the child doesn't even know that he's doing it on his own; not until his dad starts cheering him on! Lyle told me awhile back that I was *already* doing it on my own. Lyle let go and now it's my turn to let go.

I have the courage to move forward in spite of any lingering fears or hang ups I may have. It's okay to have feelings. They are neither right or wrong; they just *are*. The black and white thinking of the *borderline* has given way to color, allowing me to see myself (and my life) in a new way. I hid myself, and my demons, for so long. I lied to myself about everything. I hid behind the assorted masks. I hid behind the wall. *No one* knew who I *really* was, not even me! As each *mask* was discarded, I came closer to finding and knowing the *real* Terresa!

I'm seeing myself, and the world, with kinder eyes. Sometimes the only *control* we have over a certain situation is *how* we choose to look at it. It gets easier with, "Practice, practice, practice!" That same mantra helped me recently when the negative voice in my head tried to make a comeback. I recognized it for what it was and quickly silenced it. It's getting easier to *stop* when I start to go down the wrong path.

I'm still testing the waters as I try to figure out what it is that I like and don't like. Am I really as much of a *loner* as I think I am? Am I "just watching life go by" as my husband suggests? Bill recently accused me of being "content." I never thought that being *content* was a bad thing. I have to admit though, that I've accused Bill of *never* being content. We are definitely polar opposites! I'm feeling a little *lost* right now. How do I *not* fall back into unhealthy habits? I feel like I've made life miserable for my family. I was mentally unhealthy for so long. Can they ever forgive me? Can *I* forgive me? I'm trying to figure out *how* to be my *own* best friend. I'm feeling very disconnected from everything. Standing on my own two feet isn't very easy. Not yet.

I watched a movie recently. One of the characters states that "Love is an *ability*." I don't know whether or not I *have* that ability. If it weren't for the *visit* I received years ago, I wouldn't have believed that there was such a thing as *love*. We all go around professing our love, but do we ever really *feel* it? I'm not talking about lust or infatuation. I'm not even talking about the love a parent has for his child. I'm talking about the kind of love that's an *energy;* an energy that flows back and forth from one person to another. *Because* of that visit, I *know* that love is a real thing, but sometimes I can't tap into it! Perhaps, by *letting go* (of the need to control) and *letting God*, I'll be able to reconnect with the *source*.

I've been thinking a lot about my step mom lately. I miss her so much! When she died, I felt that I'd lost my best friend. And now I'm losing another best friend. I know *intellectually* that Lyle was just doing his job. But, for nearly two years, he's been my *surrogate* best friend, father figure, big brother, etc. It's time for me to stand on my own without slipping back into unhealthy behavior. I'm afraid though. I know I can do this… but I'm terrified! I can't imagine life without Lyle! Why is this so difficult? I know that I'm strong enough now, to do this without him, but it really, really hurts!

I can do this! I can stand on my own. It's time to dry my tears and move forward. It's my turn to *offer hope* to those who are just beginning the journey. This doesn't mean that I can't, or won't, ever ask for help. It's just time to implement what Lyle has taught me: To practice, to keep trying, to *not* give up!

I *am* getting better! I didn't stress at the usual triggers today. I was able to visit with Rachel *and* do chores at the same time. (For some reason, *multi-tasking* has always been difficult for me.) *Now* I can spend quality time with my daughter *while* I'm working on my to-do list. I've started listening to the radio again, which means that I no longer *have* to have silence in order to *quiet* the noise in my head. And when stressful thoughts *do* pop up, I'm able to change them into thoughts that are *helpful.* And in turn, I can stay *calm.* I'm also getting good at stopping the nagging little voice that's always telling me what I *should* be doing. By stopping that voice, I'm able to relax more and not feel like I have to be constantly productive.

What did I used to enjoy doing? Not just loner activities, but things with family and friends. I'm trying to remember. Before Rachel was born, Bill and I used to go to our parents' to play board games (which I always enjoyed.) But after Rachel was born, we somehow drifted away from that.

Bill's obsession with women, and their physical attributes, has been a *huge* hurdle for me. He's totally repulsed by fat! *Any* fat! I believe that a lot of my *distorted* body image was a direct result from the *conditioning* I received from him. He didn't hurt me intentionally of course, but it happened anyway. I was already the *fat* twin in my mind, so when Bill and I got together, I was already primed for developing any number of *disorders*! I'm healthy now, so it's up to *me* to change the unhealthy thought patterns. (The ones that keep the *borderline* alive.) Although I still struggle with the comments burned into my brain, it's up to me to *stop* fueling them. It's up to me to fully embrace *wellness*. There's no turning back. I know too much!

I'm not keeping the peace at all costs anymore. Whether I'm at home or at work, I'm speaking my mind. I'm holding people accountable for their actions, including myself!

My dad and his new wife visited. Dad said that he wishes that he could have had more time for us kids while we were growing up. But because of circumstances, he wasn't able to enjoy us like he would have liked. He was a struggling student with a rapidly growing family and before he knew it, we were grown and gone! His words made me realize that he really did the best he could. I know that he, and my first mom, never set out to hurt me. There were just too many kids! My twin sister and I are *not* identical; and because she *didn't* develop any mental disorders, it leads me to believe that physiology or *nature* might have played a bigger part (than *nurture)* in the development of my disorders.

When looking to my past, I'm choosing to see through the *lens of love*. None of us is perfect. It's part of the human condition. We all do the best we can with what we know. Awareness, however, brings a sense of responsibility to do better. For example, I *know* that the bingeing I do is an unhealthy form of self-medicating, or even self-abuse. I eat enormous amounts of junk food whenever I'm feeling anxious, or mis-understood, or for any other number of reasons. I'm aware now of what I'm doing, so it's my responsibility to hold myself accountable and to *choose* to do better. And on that same subject, whenever I *plan*

a crash diet to make up for my bingeing, I know that's unhealthy as well and definitely *not* in my best interest. If I am going to take care of myself and be the best that I can be, then I need to *own up* to my sins *while* looking at myself through the *lens of love.* Doing what's in my best interest *has* to come from a deep seated belief that I'm *worth* taking care of!

No matter how difficult "closure" is, I can do this! I'm *ready* to be healed; to be healthy mentally *and* physically. I need to take care of the *vessel* as well as the mind. I saw Dr. Stoune the other day as I entered the CCU to draw a patient. When he looked up and saw me, his face brightened and he exclaimed, "Now here's an angel!" His statement got me thinking. If I'm to do God's will, to be His *angel,* then I need to be as healthy as I can! No more anorexia or borderline behavior. It's also important to *avoid triggers* for the bipolar disorder, so that I can *remain* well.

Now that I'm listening to the radio again, I've heard several songs that have been very therapeutic for me; songs about hanging on to un-healthy behavior and *finding the will* to let go. I start each day with a prayer, that not only will God use me as an instrument of His love and grace, but that he would also help me to *let go* of my unhealthy coping mechanisms. He's been with me on this entire journey and I know that He wants me to be well and to do what's in my best interest.

As I have become healed, I've begun making the conscious decision to *love* others. I'm aware that some people are *not* very likable, but it doesn't mean that I can't *choose* to love them. I *don't* have to *like* them in order to *love* them. Another thing that I've become aware of... is how *one* person can affect the mood of an entire group. That person can either cause distress among the others *or* create a sense of calm. For example: When there's a *code blue* in the hospital, the doctor in charge of the code, sets the tone for the *entire* staff! I've seen it many times. If the doctor is *calm*, cool and collected, the staff follows his lead and the code is taken care of in an orderly, competent fashion. However, if the doctor is visibly *rattled,* and *not* calm, the staff will quickly become *stressed,* causing them to become less efficient. (Just thought it noteworthy.)

Bill just told me that his newest employee is chubby, like one of his other girls, but not as cute! *Why* does he do that? It really is *his* problem. (Or maybe I *am* "too sensitive" on this subject.) Another thing that bothers me about my husband is how he so freely spends money on *himself,* but he doesn't want me to spend money on our daughter! I told him that I wanted to take her shopping for some clothes before she starts up with college next month. He didn't think that we should help her like that, because no one helped *him* when *he* was her age! Well no one helped me either, but I *still* want to do this for her. She's been a good kid throughout her entire childhood and if I want to help her out, by buying her some new clothes, then I *will!* Regardless of what Bill wants! I bring home a decent paycheck, but he spends it faster than I *ever* would, so if I want to spend a couple hundred dollars on our daughter, then I *should!*

Rachel and I had a nice time shopping for school clothes. A couple of times she sounded like her father, and I felt my feathers ruffle a bit, but I changed my thoughts immediately to something positive and voila. The feathers *unruffled!* It's true that she's very outspoken and can be quite blunt in her delivery, but that doesn't make her wrong or bad. I tend to sugar coat things to avoid hurting people's feelings, but that isn't *her* way. It's *mine*! Neither way is right or wrong. They're just different.

No longer am I superficial. The masks are gone! It feels great to be free, to be *me*! There's a whole new world out there. I still have bouts of anxiety, now and again, but I've learned to put the brakes on it by changing the negative thoughts that feed the anxiety. Being *aware* is amazing!

When I got home from work last night, Bill wasn't home. I had been bursting with things I wanted to share with him. I wanted to tell him about how much therapy has helped me and how I could *see* that I'm truly getting better. I wanted him to know that I'm aware that this hasn't been an easy process for *him*. I wanted to let him know that I was grateful to him, and proud of him, for not giving up on me. I wanted to tell him how much I appreciated him! Since there wasn't a note, I sent him a text asking where he was. He was at the bar, but promised to be home soon.

Hours went by before he finally showed up and by then I was in bed, but not yet asleep. He crawled into bed and wanted to talk, but I wasn't very receptive. I no longer wanted to discuss *anything* with him! Apparently *he* felt the need, so he began to list everything that he *doesn't* like about me. He's angry at me for working on Sundays; his day off. I told him that I enjoy working at the lab on Sundays because the phone doesn't ring incessantly and I don't have to listen to, or participate in, small talk all flipping day! Plus, it's the only way I can secure a *set* schedule. Sunday *isn't* his *only* day off, so I don't see what the problem is. He went on to say that I need way too much *alone* time, which is probably true, but maybe it's *more* than that; more than just needing downtime or alone time. It might be that because I *never* feel comfortable around my husband, it feels safer *emotionally* to be alone. I've tried to be honest and *real* with him, but it's obvious he doesn't like *that* person. Of course he never seemed to like me before either. He then told me that I use too many OTC meds. He said that I shouldn't take allergy meds or aspirin; *he* never does! It goes back to him believing that *his* way is the *right* way for *everyone!* He told me that I need to improve my diet even if it meant *gaining* weight! I was so busy picking up my lower jaw after that comment that I couldn't focus on anything he said after that. I just know that he had quite the list and I felt completely blindsided!

Finally I'd had enough! I pushed away from Bill and jumped out of bed. He ordered me *not* to walk away from him, so I walked around in circles, trying to figure out what to do with the anger; especially if I couldn't leave the room! I wanted to punch the wall, or myself, but I couldn't do it with a *witness.* I stood by the door, rooted to the spot, rage building within me. With nowhere to go, and with the agitation growing, I began to shake uncontrollably. I *wanted* to scream at the top of my lungs, but I didn't dare!

Soon I could hear the soft snoring noises that indicated he'd fallen asleep, so I quietly left the room. I *needed* a fix bad! I *needed* a blade! As I gathered my *cutting* supplies, I realized that I *couldn't* do it! I couldn't even *touch* the blade to my skin! For three *decades*, I had used self-injury to *stop* painful emotions; feelings that hurt too much. *Now,* unsure of my next move, I curled up on the floor of the bathroom and sobbed.

Feeling unpleasant emotions is tough at best, but I know it's necessary if I'm going to learn how to deal with them *without* resorting to old behaviors. I've been thinking about what Bill said about me working

Sundays. He thinks I chose that particular schedule to avoid him, but that's not how I ended up with it. My boss thought it would help in keeping the bipolar symptoms at bay and he was right. But the truth is I *do* like working on Bill's day off. It's my way of avoiding his criticism, judgment and crude behavior. I don't have to deal with his demands for everything from fixing his meals, to finding something *he's* lost. I can never "just relax" when he's around.

I confessed to Bill that I had *wanted* to cut myself the other night, but that I *couldn't!* I thought this would be good news to him, but he freaked out over the fact that I had even *thought* about it! (And he wonders *why* I'm not more *open* with him!) After *that* reaction, I decided *not* to tell him about how I had *really* wanted to let out a bloodcurdling scream that night, and how it had taken *every* ounce of willpower I had, *not* to storm out of the bedroom in an anger-driven rage!

I think I'm beginning to get more comfortable with letting pain out (or perhaps it's too painful to keep it in.) I'm still working on retraining, or reconditioning, my brain. Putting *more* value on Bill's wants, than my own, does not make for a healthy relationship. On the other hand, many of my *reactions* to Bill are knee-jerk because of past conditioning. I've been trying *not* to say, "No" right off the bat when Bill requests something. I give myself a chance to think about it first and then sometimes I end up saying, "Yes." We really need to find some sort of *common* ground; something we can do together. It seems that we don't enjoy *any* of the same things. We need to find a balance without completely losing our individual selves.

I've wanted to call Lyle, but I've resisted! I know that *wellness* is up to me now. I'm aware of *what* I'm doing, *when* I'm doing it! Whether it's bingeing or isolating myself or falling into an unhealthy attachment to Bill, or anyone else for that matter, I *know* exactly what I'm doing. Awareness has removed the *blinders of borderline.*

August 26th, 2008

Today is *The Day;* my *last* scheduled visit with Lyle. Over 2 ½ years ago, I didn't think this day would ever come. I didn't think it was even *possible* for me to overcome my disordered ways of thinking. I held *no* hope for me at all. But, with Lyle's dedication and my will to get better…

Later—

My last session with Lyle was bittersweet. I gave him a framed copy of *Joyful Heart.* I put a sticker on the package that said, "For all that I am." Lyle seemed very touched. He gave me a hug and he told me that he had enjoyed working with me; that I was a talented and intelligent lady. I don't know *how* I kept from crying! When he said that he was going to display my poem to honor *me,* I said, "*No,* to honor *you!*"

Joyful Heart

My heart is overflowing
With the joy of being loved
At last the fog has lifted
There is light where darkness was

INSTEAD HE SENT ME ANGELS...

I saw the world in black and white
A choice I never knew
To see beyond the borderline
I didn't have a clue

My hate for me was more than strong
And love I pushed away
My will to live was all but gone
Until you came my way

At last I felt a glimpse of hope
For the first time in my life
Someone listened to my words
And saw the pain inside

Perhaps there was a chance for me
Perhaps I could be loved
But first it had to start with me
This foreign thing called love

And so with fear, the work began
The journey seemed too long
Without you holding steady
I believe I'd long be gone

But steadfast and true, you never wavered
Your guidance always there
My trust in you began to grow
I had someone to care

And step by step, I've come this far
To a place where I can see
That to truly love another
Begins with love for me

Because of all I've learned
And with the insight I have gained
My heart is truly bursting
With love instead of pain

My love for me is growing
Getting stronger day by day
I never thought it'd happen
But then you came my way

Now here I am with a joyful heart
Glad to be alive
Giving thanks to God and you
For standing by my side

When Lyle finished reading the poem, he got up from his chair and turned away from me to put the poem on his desk. While he had his back to me, it appeared that he was reading the poem again. He stood that way for several minutes, completely quiet. I wondered if maybe, he too, was feeling a sense of loss at the closing of our relationship. Perhaps he felt emotions well up in him, just as they had welled up in me. Our patient/therapist alliance was coming to an end. There would be no more sessions, no more conversations between us. We were preparing to say good-bye. His *child* was about to walk out the door, *forever*, leaving the *nest* behind.

I've been a little melancholy these last few days. Saying good-bye to Lyle and this painful, yet rewarding, chapter in my life has been difficult, but I *know* that I'm ready. I may *want* Lyle in my life, but I no longer *need* him in my life. Bill and I talked about the therapy that *we* endured these past two and a half years. I say *we*, because he's had to do some changing as well. Bill thinks that I was *always* doing it on my own, but I disagree! Before Lyle I was *trying* to do it on my own, but failing miserably! I was so immersed in the *borderline personality disorder* that healing was incredibly difficult. I could *not* have done this on my own. I'm sure that there are some people who are able to accomplish *recovery* with no more than a self-help book and a lot of determination, but *I* needed more. I *needed* a mentor. I *needed* someone with the wisdom, the education, the empathy, that would ultimately lead me to wellness. I was too full of *self-hate* to do it on my own. I needed *first* to accept that I was someone of worth. I needed Lyle to teach me that; to show me *how*. I needed someone, a parent figure perhaps, to *validate me*. Lyle was able to guide me to healthier perceptions. He was *never* judgmental against *me* as a person; his judgment was against the behavior(s). He had a way of making *me* feel valued and appreciated; even as he was telling me that my behavior was all wrong. He was like the parent who loves his child and wants what's best for his child, so he *guides* the child *without* attacking the child himself. In order to feel my innate sense of self, I needed Lyle to validate me and my feelings more than anything else. I had lost it somewhere along the way and it was Lyle who was most instrumental in bringing me back to *myself.*

I sat down to write the sequel to *Joyful Heart,* per Lyle's suggestion, but when I began to write, this poem immerged instead.

The "B" Word

You told me more than once
That one day I would find
The Beauty in myself
And I wouldn't have to hide

When at first you said the "B" word
It always made me cry
Beautiful was not okay
When me you did describe

I really thought you couldn't see
I even thought it cruel
That you would lie and say such things
As to call me Beautiful

I looked and looked into the mirror
But the reflection I did see
Was not at all what you described
And a tear slipped down my cheek

I'm not sure when it happened
But slowly I stopped crying
I let you say the "B" word
I no longer felt like dying

The days have come and gone
Turned into weeks and years
And when you say I'm Beautiful
No longer are there tears

The soul within has reached my heart
The wall I'd built is gone
And Beautiful is what I feel
You *knew* it all along!

After writing *The "B" Word,* I felt the need to share it with Lyle, so I made a copy of it and put it into a thank you card before mailing it to him. This latest poem speaks volumes for what Lyle was able to do for me! It reminds me of the early days of therapy when Lyle would try to convince me that I was a *beautiful* woman. The first time he used *that* word, I got very upset and started to cry. I told him to *never, ever* use that word when talking about me! He tried to use it a few more times, over the next few weeks, but I always got upset. I told him that I *hated it* when he used that word, so he finally referred to it as the "B" word.

Lyle told me that there would come a time when the "B" word would no longer upset me. He *promised* me that one day I would learn to see what *he* saw and when that day came... I would *know* that I was well. After writing *The "B" Word*, I knew without a doubt... that the day had finally come!

16

Post Therapy

"Therapy opens doors of opportunity,
and makes individuals strong enough
to walk through them."

Author unknown

Going through my journals has allowed me to see the tremendous growth in myself. My heart still tugs a little about not seeing Lyle anymore, but I'm realizing, probably for the first time, how *small* a role I actually played in *his* life. He was such a *huge* part of mine. Moving forward is bittersweet, but I'm ready!

I am no longer a child in my ability to see and think clearly. With therapy and hard work, I've been able to mature into the self-confident, capable, healthy, woman that I am today. I thought I'd stop journaling once the therapy was over, but since it's been very instrumental in my recovery, I thought it best to continue; at least for now. I've learned so much through the process of putting my thoughts down on paper. I've worked through countless issues by writing about them. I've learned that feelings aren't good or bad, in and of themselves. It's what we choose to *do* with them that matters. How we act, or re-act, in response to our unpleasant emotions is a learned behavior that can be *unlearned* by changing our thoughts. This is possible with, "Practice, practice, practice!"

Through much trial and error, the *borderline personality disorder* has been resolved and the *bipolar disorder* is controlled, for the most part, with medication and by avoiding triggers. I plan to *stay* healthy by taking care of myself. This includes *not* recording my weight, as this can exacerbate both anorexia and/or binge eating. (I'm choosing to let my body figure out, for itself, what weight is best.)

I was having a little trouble with wearing attractive clothing outside of work, when Lyle's voice popped into my head. I was reminded of a time, not so long ago, when I couldn't wear my new figure-flattering scrubs without extreme anxiety and oftentimes tears. It took courage to step out of my comfort zone again and again. I felt like a fish out of water. But *eventually,* with "Practice, practice, practice," I grew to love the cute designer scrubs. Now I don't think twice about putting them on each morning as I get ready for work. I need to remember that this is the *same issue* that I already overcame with my work clothes. Now it's time to do it for clothing outside of work. I can conquer this fear! Each new door or *path* will be scary at first, but a healthy person continues to move forward. Isn't that what courage is all about; moving *forward* in the face of fear.

Yesterday I went to a local pediatricians' office to draw blood on one of their patients. The staff warned me that the 8yr old boy was going to give me a lot of trouble. As I entered the crowded exam room, I saw that there were several adults in the room with us, including the doctor. They were all shouting out instructions to the boy without a thought to the chaos and turmoil they were creating! I ignored everyone *except* the little boy. I quietly and calmly talked to him. I reassured him and I let him know that it was okay to be afraid. I said that even if he was scared, he was still a *brave* boy! I told him that *courage* is being able to face your fear and do what has to be done. The child didn't give me any trouble at all and the next day, he and his mom came to the hospital just to say, "Hi!" I guess the point I wanted to make, is that I treated the little boy as a *real* person with *real* feelings and he responded favorably.

I'm still missing Lyle! I know as time goes by, I will miss him less and less. I have the skills now, and the insight, to depend on myself. I know how to work *through* painful feelings instead of avoiding them. I sure wish though, that I could fast forward to a time when it no longer hurts to think of Lyle! He truly saved my life!!!!! He also gave me the tools I needed to not only *stay* alive, but to also *want* life! I pray that I can somehow *pay it forward* by sharing my God given talents; whatever they might be.

I'm beginning to feel comfortable in my own skin. It's time for me to focus on helping others, to reassure and encourage those who are lost. My inner strength frees me to be the *strong one* now when it's needed. It's my turn to *give*! I'm not letting the *little* things get to me anymore. And as I continue to grow, I find that a lot of the *big* things weren't as big as I thought they were!

I sent a letter to Lyle to let him know how I'm doing. It read, in part:

Dear Lyle,

Hi! I feel like an excited little kid who can't wait to share his latest discovery! For 2 ½ years, you were the *parent* I so desperately needed. And even though I've left the nest, I still find myself wanting to share each milestone with you; in part, from sheer excitement and partly so *you* can be proud! Proud of me *and* proud of yourself! I'm absolutely bursting with the thrill of finally seeing what you saw! A beautiful woman, inside and out! I'm *not* hiding anymore; not in baggy clothing or behind any masks. I love who I am! I never need to hurt or hide myself again!

I watched an episode of *Law & Order* tonight and I immediately saw *myself!* The daughter of one of the main characters ends up being diagnosed with *bipolar disorder*. Before she's diagnosed, she's behaving strangely and that's when I saw *me*. Later in the program, the grandmother makes an appearance. She too has bipolar, but chooses to be un-medicated; a choice that has cost her dearly. The show reminded me of the fact that the *bipolar disorder* is *not* going to magically disappear. Near the end of the show, the grandmother is talking to her granddaughter about the consequences of *not* taking medication. She warns, "The higher you fly, the farther you fall." My eyes were full of tears for most of the episode. I thought back to some of the things I had done *before* I was medicated; things that *even* Lyle doesn't know about. I self-medicated the disorder before I even knew *what* bipolar was! I'm ashamed of some of the things I've done. We really do pay a high price when *bipolar disorder* is not recognized and treated. I saw myself so quickly tonight, both in the granddaughter *and* her grandmother. After watching the show, there is no doubt left in my mind about the need to stay on my meds.

Last night I had a weird dream that reinforced my knowledge that it *was up to me* to say "when" on ending therapy. Lyle would have stopped me if he didn't think I was ready, but we *both* knew I was. In the dream, I was attempting to hand over an electrical *cord* to a man who was waiting for it. As I tried to coil the cord, I kept dropping it. I told the man that I just wasn't myself today and as I looked up at him, I saw kindness in his eyes. By the time I finally got the cord wound up, I was crying. I knew, that by giving him the cord, I was saying good-bye to him. At first I thought the cord was a "means to the end" for this person. I thought he was unstable and wanted to kill himself, but then I realized that the dream meant the *death* of the borderline; not the death of the man! It also meant the *end* of the relationship that completely transformed my life! Near the end of the dream, I was calling the man Lyle and my tears were falling freely. By giving the cord to him, I was, in effect… *cutting the cord.* I was saying good-bye to the *borderline* and all of the disordered thought patterns it caused. I was saying good-bye to *Lyle.* I was saying good-bye to *me!* (The false me.) I knew that by cutting the *cord,* Lyle's role as my *lifeline* was over.

My self-worth is no longer tied up in another person. It's solely mine. Lyle taught me that it's *my* opinion that should matter most when it concerns my own self-worth. Being Lyle's patient was like being an only child. I got to be the center of attention for two and a half *years!* I finally got to be *heard* and *understood.* I flourished in the non-threatening environment that Lyle provided. Letting go of that environment, and letting go of Lyle, is heart wrenching but absolutely necessary. The wall I'd built is not only down, it's gone...completely. It's time to immerge from the protection and safety of the nest; the very nest that had also served as my cocoon, sheltering me through the dark days as my own wings were being formed. Lyle showed me the way. The rest is up to me.

Epilogue

My 2 ½ years of therapy ended in August of 2008. However, my journey, along with the growth that accompanies it, continues. January of 2010 brought with it great change, beginning with my divorce. I wasn't completely surprised when it happened, but I did regress a bit in the first few months after the separation. For the first time in nearly 27 years I was living alone and, although I was enjoying it to some extent, I found myself completely out of my element.

I was glad to be out of my loveless marriage, but it left me feeling more "disconnected" than ever! I couldn't figure out *why* I was so distraught. My job was going well. I had time to pursue my own interests, friends to hang out with, good health etc. It appeared that I had everything that I could want. I'd always been a loner at heart, so why was living alone so difficult?

One evening I found myself to be filled with a deep sense of sorrow. Suddenly I felt the overwhelming urge to cut myself! Where did *that* come from? I hadn't self-injured in over two years! Before I knew it, I was once again caught up in the grips of that old, but familiar, behavior!

As I began to slice open my skin, I felt bottled-up anger rising to the surface; anger at my ex-husband! Why couldn't he have loved me? Why? I found myself thinking that I would never trust a man again. Not as long as I lived! And to make sure that no man would *ever* want me, including my ex, I began to make cut after cut after cut. With no danger of ever being found out, I cut as deep as I wanted and *where* ever I wanted. I was out of control and I didn't care. Who would know? I sliced open my skin again and again, leaving deep lacerations all over my legs, from my calves to my thighs. I didn't stop to think that I would never be able to wear shorts or a skirt again, without having to explain away the numerous scars that would undoubtedly be left behind. My vision was limited to making sure that I would *never* be tempted to be physically intimate with my ex-husband again, or any other man for that matter!

When I woke up the next morning and saw what I had done to myself, I nearly passed out! This was by far the worst episode I'd ever had. I won't go into detail, but it was bad enough that I contacted Dr. Stoune and he asked me to come in immediately. As I sat huddled on a chair in the exam room, I wondered *why* I had slipped so easily back into this old behavior. I felt deflated, embarrassed and afraid. Then the door opened and Dr. Stoune walked in. Without saying a word, he held out his arms and I gladly fell into them.

After my visit with Dr. Stoune, I realized that I needed to see Lyle again. Dr. Stoune helped me to see that there was no reason to be embarrassed about my setback. I'd been through an enormous upheaval in my life, and it was only natural to fall back into old coping mechanisms; even unhealthy ones.

I called Lyle and we set up an appointment for the next day. I was embarrassed at my regression and of the fact that I once again needed his help! Lyle, of course, was gracious.

EPILOGUE

My appointment with Lyle helped me immensely. He pointed out that I had just gone through a huge change and even though, in the long run, it would be a change for the better, it was still a lot to deal with. First of all, I was now living alone for the first time in over a quarter of a century! Second, I was now living in *town* instead of out in the country. (Living in town felt like living in giant fishbowl with all eyes on me!) Third, I no longer knew where I "fit." Now that I was no longer the wife of Bill, where was my place in the social world? I'd been someone's wife for so long that I was feeling lost without the title. As Lyle pointed out each of these things to me, I realized that they were all true! I had been too close to the situation to see it clearly. Once I understood what was going on, I immediately felt relief. I wasn't going mad after all!

I told Lyle that I didn't think I needed a follow up appointment because I was already feeling so much better. Lyle, however, said that *he* would prefer that I come back at least once. (Just to make sure that I was okay.)

At our second visit, Lyle disagreed with me when I told him that I'm a loner at heart and that I *wanted* to spend the rest of my life without a partner. (I still believed that it was the *only* way for me to feel completely at ease.) Lyle said that humans are not meant to live alone, and he still believed that there was someone out there for me; someone who would want to *cherish* me.

Going back to Lyle, for a couple of sessions, was like a breath of fresh air. His guidance pulled me out of the dark and confusing place that I had landed in after my divorce. After talking with him, I felt ready to face the future and whatever it would bring.

It's now 2011 and I'm doing wonderfully. I'm happy to report that Lyle was right about my status as a self-proclaimed loner. When the right man came along, which he did, I discovered that not only is it possible to be completely at ease in the presence of another person, it's desirable! It turns out that I'm not the "loner" I once thought I was. Terry and I had worked together for a couple of years and had developed a workplace friendship. We both knew that neither one of us was "looking" for a mate. So imagine our surprise, when after my divorce, our friendship took on a life of its own and blossomed into something more beautiful than either one of us could ever have imagined! I could go on an on about what a wonderful man he is, but that would be another book entirely!

It's been over 5 years since that desperate day, when I tried to end my life. I am so grateful to be here, to be *well*. It's my plan to spend the rest of my life "paying it forward."

Oh, and one more thing... My self-worth has *nothing* to do with a "number" and *everything* to do with *me*!

Afterword 2011

In loving memory of my dear friend, Joan.

 I wrote the following story a few months after meeting Joan. The story is completely true and is a reminder to me that God is at work in my life. Joan and I were able to enjoy our friendship for 16 months before she passed away. A stroke took her quickly and quietly; the way she would want it.

Full Circle

In January of 2006, I attempted suicide. The final *push* for me, the one that sent me over the edge, came in the form of a needy, demanding patient named Paul. Because of his pushiness, something in me just *snapped.* I left work, swallowed a bottle of pills, and prayed to God to take me home. But God said, "No." (*I* may have been done with this life, but God wasn't.)

When I awoke in the CCU, I was told that I'd been rambling incessantly about someone named Paul. I have no memory of it, but apparently I was blaming *him*, a practical stranger, for my attempted suicide.

Now Fast-forward three and a half years:

After two and a half years of counseling, followed by months of honing my new skills, I woke up one morning and realized something amazing! *Wellness.* For the first time in my 46 years, I felt *normal!* Who knew? I'm still a person with bipolar disorder, and meds will always be a part of my life, but the other mental problems, including *borderline personality disorder*, have been resolved. Completely. My journey to wellness has reached its happy ending, but there's more…

Two days after this milestone "epiphany," and with wellness in the forefront of my mind, I met a wonderful lady named Joan. At 89 years old, she is still very vibrant and quite beautiful! As I drew her blood, we began to talk and I felt an immediate connection to her. During our visit, we discovered our mutual love of writing. (Both prose and poetry.) When she told me that she'd written a book about her son's schizophrenia, I opened up about my own struggles with mental illness. I found myself drawn to her, so much that it was difficult to leave. When I told her I was working on my own book, she urged me to get my story out there as soon as I could, because the only way to stop the stigma surrounding mental illness is to talk about it openly and honestly. By sharing our stories, we become educators.

The next morning I couldn't get Joan's words out of my head, so I sat down and wrote the following poem:

Broken

I was completely broken
An empty shell
And no one knew
Of my private hell

My thoughts were jumbled
And racing nowhere
My heart was heavy
And peace was rare

No sense of order
Inside my head
With inner anguish
I prayed for death

But God said no, I need you there
You have a job to do
I'll send you angels, one by one
To walk each step with you

I know you think you're broken
From the illness of your mind
But soon you'll see the blessing
And lasting peace you'll find

Insanity is not a sin
Or a measure of the soul
It's just another hand that's dealt
As the human life unfolds

I blessed you with this illness
To open up the door
To a path of understanding
To lift the stigma caught in lore

Tell the world your story
Take away the shame
Help educate the people
Erase the need to blame

Your struggle here, will one day pave
A road to greater health
For those who suffer silently
Thinking there's no help

So talk about your journey
As you walk this path in faith
Share the hope with others
And I will lead your way

The next day at work I saw that Joan was still a patient, so I hurried to her room to give her the poem. I told her she was an awesome lady with so much to offer. After a short visit, we exchanged phone numbers and addresses along with the promise to write. As I was leaving, she told me that she found our "chance meeting" to be very interesting. Before I could ask why, she told me that her longtime writer friend, Vi, had just passed away the day before. And now, within hours, God had blessed her with a *new* writer friend...Me!

There's still more...

Joan's daughter, Donna, committed suicide at the age of 47. (I'm 46.) This knowledge made me feel somehow connected to Donna, just as I'd felt connected to Joan. I told Joan that I'm sure God didn't punish Donna for taking her own life; because a person who does that is mentally ill. Joan told me that a priest told her the same thing.

Joan has become my mentor as well as my friend. It feels like I've been sent to her as much as she's been sent to me. In the five months that I've known her, I've come to love both she and her husband. Joan may be twice my age, but when she and I spend time together, it's as though we're a couple of teenagers! We have so much fun! Her husband told me recently that they both think of me as a daughter. Who knows... maybe their *own* daughter had a hand in bringing us together!

Now for the clincher...

Just days after meeting Joan, I had the chance to meet her husband in person. Imagine my surprise when her husband turned out to be... Paul, the pushy patient from 4 years ago!

Paul and I continue to be as close as father and daughter. I treasure his friendship.

CPSIA information can be obtained at www.ICGtesting.com
Printed in the USA
LVOW121832120112

263522LV00001B/271/P